Regional Perspectives
on
Learning by Doing

TRANSFORMATIONS IN HIGHER EDUCATION: THE SCHOLARSHIP OF ENGAGEMENT

EDITORIAL BOARD

SERIES EDITORS

Burton A. Bargerstock, *Michigan State University, United States*
Laurie A. Van Egeren, *Michigan State University, United States*
Hiram E. Fitzgerald, *Michigan State University, United States*

BOARD OF EDITORS

Jorge H. Atiles, *Oklahoma State University, United States*
Katy Campbell, *University of Alberta, Canada*
Jeri L. Childers, *University of Technology, Sydney, Australia*
Paul T. Crawford, *Public Scholar, United States*
Cristina Escrigas, *Global University Network for Innovation, Spain*
Pennie G. Foster-Fishman, *Michigan State University, United States*
Budd L. Hall, *University of Victoria, Canada*
Daniel Hall, *University of Louisville, United States*
Takoi K. Hamrita, *University of Georgia, United States*
Miguel Hoffmann, *Sociedad Argentina de Primera Infancia, Argentina*
Carol MA Hok Ka, *SIM University, Singapore*
Paul Manners, *National Co-ordinating Centre for Public Engagement, United Kingdom*
Lorraine McIlrath, *National University of Ireland, Galway, Ireland*
George L. Openjuru, *Gulu University, Uganda*
Michael Osborne, *University of Glasgow, Scotland*
Samory T. Pruitt, *University of Alabama, United States*
John Saltmarsh, *University of Massachusetts, Boston, United States*
Michelle C. Sarche, *University of Colorado, Denver, United States*
Linda Silka, *University of Maine, United States*
Louis Swanson, *Colorado State University, United States*

Regional Perspectives on Learning by Doing

Stories from Engaged Universities around the World

Edited by LORLENE HOYT

Michigan State University Press | East Lansing

Copyright © 2017 by Michigan State University

⊚ The paper used in this publication meets the minimum requirements
of ANSI/NISO Z39.48-1992 (R 1997) (Permanence of Paper).

Michigan State University Press
East Lansing, Michigan 48823-5245

Printed and bound in the United States of America.

26 25 24 23 22 21 20 19 18 17   1 2 3 4 5 6 7 8 9 10

LIBRARY OF CONGRESS CATALOGING-IN-PUBLICATION DATA IS AVAILABLE
978-1-61186-255-3 (paper)
978-1-60917-537-5 (PDF)
9781628953060 (epub)
9781628963069 (Kindle)

Book design by Charlie Sharp, Sharp Des!gns, East Lansing, MI
Cover design by Shaun Allshouse, www.shaunallshouse.com

Michigan State University Press is a member of the Green Press Initiative and
is committed to developing and encouraging ecologically responsible publishing
practices. For more information about the Green Press Initiative and the use
of recycled paper in book publishing, please visit *www.greenpressinitiative.org*.

Visit Michigan State University Press at *www.msupress.org*

*For Mitiku, Yeruksew,
Cynthia, Dad and Mom*

Transformations in Higher Education: Scholarship of Engagement

The Transformations in Higher Education: Scholarship of Engagement book series is designed to provide a forum where scholars can address the diverse issues provoked by community-campus partnerships that are directed toward creating innovative solutions to societal problems. Numerous social critics and key national commissions have drawn attention to the pervasive and burgeoning problems of individuals, families, communities, economies, health services, and education in American society. Such issues as child and youth development, economic competitiveness, environmental quality, and health and health care require creative research and the design, deployment, and evaluation of innovative public policies and intervention programs. Similar problems and initiatives have been articulated in many other countries, apart from the devastating consequences of poverty that burdens economic and social change. As a consequence, there has been increasing societal pressure on universities to partner with communities to design and deliver knowledge applications that address these issues, and to co-create novel approaches to effect system changes that can lead to sustainable and evidence-based solutions. Knowledge generation and knowledge application are critical parts of the engagement process, but so too are knowledge dissemination and preservation. The Transformations in Higher Education: Scholarship of Engagement series was designed to meet one aspect of the dissemination/preservation dyad.

This series is sponsored by the National Collaborative for the Study of University Engagement (NCSUE) and is published in partnership with the Michigan State University Press. An external board of editors supports the NCSUE editorial staff in order to insure that all volumes in the series are peer reviewed throughout the publication process. Manuscripts embracing campus- community partnerships are invited from authors regardless of discipline, geographic place, or type of transformational change accomplished. Similarly, the series embraces all methodological approaches from rigorous randomized trials to narrative and ethnographic studies. Analyses may span the qualitative to quantitative continuum, with particular emphasis on mixed-model approaches. However, all manuscripts must attend to detailing critical aspects of partnership development, community involvement, and evidence of program changes or impacts. Monographs and books provide ample space for authors to address all facets of engaged scholarship thereby building a compendium of praxis that will facilitate replication and generalization, two of the cornerstones of evidence-based programs, practices, and policies. We invite you to submit your work for publication review and to fully participate in our effort to assist higher education to renew its covenant with society through engaged scholarship.

>Hiram E. Fitzgerald
>Burton Bargerstock
>Laurie Van Egeren

Contents

ACKNOWLEDGMENTS · xi
FOREWORD, *Derek W. M. Barker* · xiii
PREFACE · xvii

INTRODUCTION · 1

Brigadas Comunitarias at Tecnológico de Monterrey in Querétaro, Mexico:
Some Values Are Universal, *by Ernesto Benavides Ornelas,
María Fernanda Pacheco Bravo, and Brianda Hernandez Cavalcanti* · · · · · · · · · · · · · · · · 21

The Activate Program in Glasgow, Scotland: A New Way of Thinking and Being
in the World, *by Margaret Fraser and Helen Martin* · 37

Amplifying Community Voices in South Africa: Nurturing Transformative Leaders
through Dialogic Action, *by Joseph Francis and Hlekani Muchazotida Kabiti* · · · · · · · · 57

The Refugee Action Support Program in Sydney, Australia: A Bridge between
Cultures, *by Loshini Naidoo and Eric Brace* · 81

The Kampung Tekir Project in Seremban, Malaysia: Worth All the Difficulties
That We Have Encountered Thus Far! *by Koh Kwee Choy and Wong Chin Hoong* · · · · · · · · · · · 103

Lazord Academy in Cairo, Egypt: Pedagogy for the Practice of Freedom,
by Nelly Corbel, Rana Gaber, and Amy Newcomb Rowe · 127

Living Democracy in Rural America: Engaging Students as Citizens,
by Mark Wilson and Marie Cirillo · 145

CONTRIBUTORS · 165
INDEX · 171

Acknowledgments

With profound respect and fondness, I acknowledge the chapter contributors who are leading the university civic engagement movement on the ground. Thank you all for walking the walk: Ernesto Benavides Ornelas, María Fernanda Pacheco Bravo, Brianda Hernandez Cavalcanti, Margaret Fraser, Helen Martin, Joseph Francis, Hlekani Muchazotida Kabiti, Loshini Naidoo, Eric Brace, Koh Kwee Choy, Wong Chin Hoong, Nelly Corbel, Rana Gaber, Amy Newcomb Rowe, Marie Cirillo, and Mark Wilson.

I thank too the university administrators, faculty, staff, students, and community partners who contributed significantly to our conversations along the way—Thabo Putu, Itumeleng Mafatshe, Wan-Amni Zulkifar, Silvia Arias, Juliet Millican, Magdelena Jara, Claudia Mora Motto, Alaa Ibrahim, Nyvea Silva Herrera, Saran Gill, Sergey Golubev, and Richard Hopper.

A very warm thank you to Derek Barker of the Kettering Foundation and also his colleagues, among them David Mathews, John Dedrick, Paloma Dallas, Alice Diebel, and Lane Wells. It was great fun and intellectually satisfying to work with Derek on this project for several years. Despite my best efforts, I have fallen short in convincing him to become a Red Sox fan.

I sincerely thank my colleagues at Tufts University. At the Tisch College of Civic Life, I offer my appreciation to Dean Alan D. Solomont and the staff, who deftly and persistently advance active citizenship on campus and beyond. And I am profoundly grateful for the camaraderie and support of the Talloires Network secretariat staff, including Brianda Hernandez Cavalcanti, Amy Newcomb Rowe, Matias Ramos, Rantimi Adetunji, Trang Vuong, Edwin Nelson, Gabriel Sub, Monique Ching, Rebecca Tumposky, Protiti Roy, Jacqueline DiMichele, Jennifer Catalano, and Maureen Keegan. This book would not have been possible without generous encouragement and support from Robert M. Hollister, founding executive director emeritus of the Talloires Network. Also, I would like to thank then Tufts University president Lawrence S. Bacow, who launched the Network at the Tufts European Center in Talloires, France, in 2005, as well as Tufts University President Anthony P. Monaco, who currently serves as Chair of the Talloires Network Steering Committee.

I also express my gratitude to the Network's most recent steering committee members, including vice-chair Cheryl de la Rey, Sara Ladrón de Guevara, María Nieves Tapia, Tim Tong, Ernest Aryeetey, Andrew Vann, Andrew Petter, Lorraine McIlrath, Muhammed Asghar, Haifa Jamal Al-Lail, Santa Ono, Adam Weinberg, Rajesh Tandon, Lisa Anderson, Olive Mugenda, Mark Gearan, Janice Reid, Scott Cowen, Sharifah Hapsah Shahabudin, Shamsh Kassim-Lakha, José María Sanz Martínez, Jerome Slamat, Rafael Velasco, and John Wood. In the Department of Urban and Environmental Policy and Planning, I thank my associates, including Mary Davis, Julian Agyeman, Penn Loh, Justin Hollander, Weiping Wu, Laurie Goldman, Shomon Shamsuddin, Barbara Parmenter, Jon Witten, Maria Nicolau, and Michael Flanary.

I am grateful to have had an opportunity to work with Burton Bargerstock and Julie Crowgey at Michigan State University and Julie Loehr and Kristine Blakeslee at Michigan State University Press. Their professionalism is unparalleled. And a sincere thank you to the series editors. A warm thanks to my amazing mom who reviewed the typeset page proofs.

Too many people to name here continue to nourish the growing university civic engagement movement. You know who you are. For the pioneers, the next generation leaders and those who will join us, I offer my relentless optimism. Let us strive together to redirect the generative utility of higher education for the purpose of re-creating systems that are more equitable. Onward.

Foreword

Derek W. M. Barker

Around the world, our political systems face numerous challenges, such as political polarization, weakening social capital, and distrust of experts and professions. While confidence in government in the United States continues to decline, the optimism for democratic change around the world provided by the Arab Spring movements has dissipated almost as quickly as it appeared. The fundamental insight of the Kettering Foundation is that these "problems of democracy" affect the ability of our political systems to address any particular problems within them, including education, poverty, social inequality, and environmental sustainability. Progress on these issues depends on developing the political will to deal with them, but that, in turn, requires addressing the dysfunctions of our political system. As a research organization, Kettering studies innovative efforts to address problems of democracy and make democracy work as it should.

Moreover, in studying democracy and democratic innovation, Kettering has come to a larger understanding of democracy than just the formal system of contested elections and government institutions. Democracy also includes the informal sphere of civic associations and community problem-solving described in Tocqueville's *Democracy in America*. Democracy so understood depends upon developing in young people the norms, habits, and skills needed to be active participants in their communities.

With the responsibilities of educating the next generation of citizens, and producing and applying academic knowledge to social issues, colleges and universities have an important role in maintaining the health of our political systems. Indeed, in recent years, higher education has developed a "movement" of leaders, faculty, and staff devoted to civic engagement. Due to this movement, one can now find volunteer activities as well as programs focused on "service-learning"—the use of volunteer community service activities for academic goals—on campuses throughout the United States and around the world.

From Kettering's point of view, however, neither volunteerism nor service-learning is enough to meet the challenges we face. Volunteerism is typically done as an individual, while politics involves diverse groups of people coming together. Service typically consists of benign activities, but political issues are divisive and conflictual. Moreover, service implies a separation between provider and client, while democratic politics requires communities to harness their civic capacities. While service-learning has successfully tied volunteerism to serious academic coursework and pedagogical outcomes, what seems to be missing from the conversations in higher education is a distinct concept of civic engagement that is more "public" than community service, but less adversarial than "politics as usual." Rather than reifying the traditional deficit model, we have developed experiments that teach students the skills to work *with* communities to address their own problems, and in so doing develop a new consciousness of the civic assets present in communities. Kettering has worked in collaboration with institutions and practitioners who seek to move beyond service-learning and work with us to develop, apply, and advance this democratic concept of civic engagement.

Beginning in 2012, we initiated a series of exchanges in collaboration with the Talloires Network to expose leaders and practitioners around the world to research informed by Kettering's understanding of democracy and civic engagement. Kettering's exchanges provide an opportunity for practitioners to reflect critically on their work with particular attention to questions related to democracy and civic engagement that our partners do not have an opportunity or incentive to address in typical professional contexts. We at Kettering do not see our role as simply supporting or cheerleading for success stories. Rather, we hope to create a space for critical questioning and openness to experimentation, and this requires an unusual degree of vulnerability and openness.

Working with Lorlene Hoyt, we began with an initial exchange in July 2012, in Dayton, Ohio, with an assortment of leaders and practitioners to explore the overlaps between Kettering's concerns and the mission of Talloires Network member institutions. This exchange helped us identify the area of civic engagement moving beyond service-learning as a key focus for both organizations, leading to the series of research exchanges that became the basis for this volume. Beginning with a meeting in Boston, Massachusetts, in December 2013, we then gathered together teams from a diverse set of campuses identified by Kettering and Talloires as having the potential to serve as exemplars for this type of civic engagement. We asked participating campuses to suggest representatives, including both faculty from the institution and community or student partners. The initial meeting allowed us to get to know the participants' work as well as their distinct concerns and challenges, while presenting Kettering's core concerns and distinctive understanding of civic engagement (several of the participants also encountered snow for the first time!). We reconvened in Dayton, Ohio, during the summer of 2014, for a detailed review of written drafts of the case studies. Finally, we made initial presentations of the resulting case studies at the Talloires Network Leaders Conference in Cape Town, South Africa, in December 2014, a gathering of key higher education leaders.

Throughout the process, the group was remarkably open to learning and reflection through Kettering's research lens. The participants were accustomed to describing their work in terms of academic outcomes or their particular areas of expertise (such as health, housing, and literacy). In the workshops, however, we asked them to focus on their success and struggles in educating students as active citizens. Rather than providing services or expert knowledge *to* communities, we asked how they were working *with* communities to strengthen their civic capacities. As a result of this process, the participants were able to distill and articulate new civic narratives for their work. We believe the result has enabled us to gather together a set of stories with the potential to transform how higher education understands civic engagement.

In the course of these exchanges, I have had the great pleasure of meeting dedicated leaders and practitioners from numerous countries (representing every continent except Antarctica!). We have shared stories of the civic capacities present in diverse places, from Appalachian coal country in the United States to rural tribal villages in Malaysia. With an enlarged perspective and a new hope for democracy and civic engagement as a result of these exchanges, this has truly been the single most rewarding experience in my work at Kettering. To the contributors and the Talloires Network: I am deeply humbled, honored, and grateful for the opportunity to participate in this work.

Preface

My experience working as an assistant and then associate professor at the Massachusetts Institute of Technology (MIT) has allowed me to develop my thoughts about higher education institutions and their societal purposes. An especially formative moment was cofounding and helping to lead the MIT@Lawrence Partnership. The Partnership began as a seven-week workshop in 2002 and evolved into an award-winning city-campus collaboration for guiding collective action among rooted institutions in the city of Lawrence, Massachusetts. Early successes, such as the approval of a zoning overlay district to permit housing in the city's historic mills, raised expectations among residents, civic leaders, students, and faculty, and gave us the confidence to do more. As the MIT@Lawrence Partnership developed a national reputation, the Kettering Foundation in 2008 invited me to join theorists and practitioners to participate in a series of colloquiums about other ways of knowing in a democracy. My collaborations with Derek Barker of the Kettering Foundation and others inspired me to make the case that universities have an obligation to function as catalysts not only in the discovery of new knowledge but also in its application—a fundamental premise of the scholarship of engagement.

With an interest in comparing the MIT@Lawrence Partnership to similar initiatives around the world, I accepted a position with the Talloires Network at Tufts University in October 2011. As luck would have it, Derek and I found ourselves at a reception at the Aspen Wye River Conference Center in Queenstown, Maryland, in early November 2011. We had been invited to participate in a National Civic Seminar entitled "Strengthening and Actualizing the Civic Mission of Higher Education." As incoming director of programs and research for the Talloires Network, I described my aspirations for the Network to Derek. Immediately, we understood that the Kettering Foundation and Talloires Network were natural allies. The Foundation actively partners with citizens, community groups, and institutions in more than eighty countries around the world. Its multinational focus is concerned primarily with what people can do collectively to address problems affecting their communities, with a focus on the role of higher education institutions. The Talloires Network—a global coalition of 363 engaged universities in seventy-seven countries—works to strengthen the civic roles and social responsibilities of higher education. Within minutes of our November meeting, Derek and I fermented the promise of starting a multiyear research collaboration between the Network and the Foundation. By raising and touching our beer bottles, we signaled a mutual interest in jointly exploring how universities around the world understand their democratic mission and engage their students to improve the civic life of their communities. The details and next steps, we agreed, would be sorted out in coming months.

Regional Perspectives on Learning by Doing

In early 2012, I tapped into the resources of the Talloires Network to identify "exemplars"—excellent examples of learning by doing from universities around the world. The process began with a letter of invitation to regional partners and steering committee members. The letter informed recipients of the nascent research collaboration, asking for guidance in generating a list of participant nominations. Leaders in the university civic engagement movement applied the following criteria to identify exemplars in their regions:

- The program has been sustained for several years
- Student ideas and contributions influence the program's design and implementation
- Community members contribute to the program as equal partners
- Community members have benefited in a variety of ways
- The university actively supports the program
- Program participants regularly assess their activities

Derek and I selected from the list of nominations an exemplar from each region of the world—North America, Asia/Pacific, Arab region, Europe, Oceania/Australia, Latin America, and sub-Saharan Africa (see figure). Though this group is representative, other university civic engagement exemplars exist, many using the same strategies, seeking to achieve similar objectives. The programs included in our group illustrate the experiences of a broader set of programs around the world.

To enhance the idea of gaining multiple perspectives on civic engagement practices, we invited an academic leader of the program to choose a community practitioner or a student to join the research collaboration. Six faculty, two staff, three students, and five community partners contributed to the collaborative research and writing exchange from 2012 through 2015. Derek and I co-organized and cofacilitated face-to-face workshops, bringing the group to a size of eighteen. The diverse and seasoned group talked and exchanged ideas by way of email and telephone. They cowrote papers and gave presentations. Workshops were held in Dayton, Ohio (July 2012 and July 2014); Boston, Massachusetts (December 2013); and Cape Town, South Africa (December 2014). Chapters in this collection draw on notes from these exchanges as well as personal interviews with university heads and program participants, award nominations, papers, and program descriptions.

Together we dug into the details—the history and activities of each learning-by-doing exemplar as well as the local and institutional cultures in which they are embedded. We focused our dialogue and exchange using such questions as these:

Figure. Regional Perspectives on University Civic Engagement

REGIONAL PERSPECTIVE, COUNTRY	NAME OF ENGAGED UNIVERSITY	NAME, YEAR STARTED
Latin America, Mexico	Tecnológico de Monterrey University	Community Brigades, 1997
Europe, Scotland	University of Glasgow	Activate, 2002
Sub-Saharan Africa, South Africa*	University of the Witwatersrand	Community Work Camps, 2004
Sub-Saharan Africa, South Africa	University of Venda	Amplifying Community Voices, 2006
Oceania/Australia Region, Australia	University of Western Sydney	Refugee Action Support, 2006
Asia/Pacific Region, Malaysia	International Medical University	Village Adoption, 2007
Arab Region, Egypt	American University in Cairo	Lazord Academy, 2007
North America, United States	Auburn University	Living Democracy, 2010

*A student and community partner associated with the University of the Witwatersrand, Community Work Camps participated in the research collaboration. Some of their many contributions are incorporated into the introductory chapter; however, they chose not to submit a chapter of their own to the collection.

- What practices are universities around the world using to better engage with communities?
- What difference have these practices made in the civic capacities of students and other participants?

Along the way, we discovered that university civic engagement leaders around the world are driven and shaped by regional values such as good citizenship, social responsibility, and social solidarity. They aim to address pervasive challenges to civic life, such as poverty, illiteracy, and disease, using an array of approaches including service-learning, volunteerism, extension, participatory action research, and applied research. Service-learning (a credit-bearing, curricular activity whereby students provide services to local communities) is the most common approach; it is practiced in all regions and many countries of the world—in all fields of study and university types (Hoyt 2014).

The book you are holding in your hands is at once a product of our engaged universities and our collaborative research and writing effort. In the end, we learned that too much attention is given to fitting learning-by-doing approaches into neat categories: service-learning, volunteerism, engaged scholarship, and so on. To create more equitable communities, praxis is what matters, not spending inordinate amounts of energy trying to perfectly classify all types of experience.

We discovered that universities around the world are using two vital practices to create more equitable communities, which, in turn, develop important civic capacities in student and other participants. These practices are (1) reinforcing multidirectional flows of knowledge, and (2) building inclusive systems of power.

We also found that engagement in these two distinct practices make a difference in the civic capabilities of participants. The learning process involves the following ingredients. Participants begin with action. They make mistakes. They call long-standing assumptions into question. They become disoriented. They learn to operate in frightening situations, and they develop the courage to act. They learn to recognize their weaknesses and limitations, and they develop humility.

Lastly, structured reflections give participants an opportunity to understand the impact of their actions on society as well as their own worldview, and they develop the ability to empathize. Learning-by-doing approaches that include these practices often awaken the desire to be an integral part of a group, to work in solidarity with others on issues of common cause. In this way they are democratic practices.

These capabilities—courage, humility, and empathy—are important because the world needs more people who are equipped to deal creatively with pressing societal challenges—to operate effectively in highly conflicted situations; to fashion bold approaches to combating poverty, promoting sustainability, and elevating public health; to organize coalitions for change that bridge social and economic divides; and to strengthen democratic decision-making in local communities and higher levels of governance. By developing these vital civic capabilities in people inside and outside the university, together we may create more equitable and prosperous communities around the world.

Introduction

> What we have to learn to do, we learn by doing.
> —Aristotle

What Is an Engaged University?

On a sunny summer day in early December 2014 and in the midst of our research collaboration, vice-chancellor of the University of Witwatersrand Adam Habib welcomed participants in the Talloires Network Global Leaders conference. He highlighted the efforts of universities to accelerate the demise of apartheid and encourage the emergence of democracy in South Africa:

> South Africa is such a fantastic social laboratory, particularly for the issue of civic engagement. It is an appropriate laboratory because these universities have both been an implicit part of the project to destroy a system and then they've been part of the project to re-create a system. The objective of re-creating that system was to create a system that is more human, more equitable, and more equal. So South African universities were active agents in the struggle for liberation and have been active agents in the struggle to reconstruct society.[1]

Habib's opening keynote was exactly the right spark to ignite three days of dialogue among conference participants gathered at the Spier Conference Center near Cape Town, South Africa. The audience consisted of university heads, faculty, staff, and students, as well as government officials, community activists, and philanthropic leaders. The diverse (and often conflicted) group was united by the belief that universities have a civic role, a special obligation to contribute to the public good and to empower those who are less privileged.[2]

Vice-Chancellor Habib is part of a growing global movement in higher education to expand beyond the "ivory tower." University presidents, vice-chancellors, and rectors on every continent have placed engagement at the center of their mission. These heads of engaged universities—with their faculty, staff, students, and community partners—are "reformers and revolutionists" coming together to "counterbalance the inertness and fossilism marking so large a part of human institutions" (Whitman 1871). From Malaysia to Mexico to South Africa, national governments, development agencies, and corporate and other foundations are investing in engaged universities. They champion unconventional research and teaching methods, including service-learning, volunteerism, extension, applied research, participatory action research, and engaged scholarship (Hoyt 2014). While there is significant variation with respect to goals, outcomes, and nomenclatures across and within regions of the world, the larger story is one of common vision and strategy (Hoyt and Hollister 2014a).

Engaged universities work in partnership with local communities and institutions, aiming to strengthen the society of which they are part. In contrast to the idea of the ivory tower, a term that connotes distance and invokes an image of a medieval castle, the engaged university actively confronts "wicked problems," such as climate change, xenophobia, poverty, and political disengagement. Wicked problems are complex, resulting from multiple factors and embedded in the moral, social, and economic dimensions of a community. Engaged universities encourage discussions and activities among people who are affected by wicked problems to reinforce productive relationships and a sense of common cause. These are vital steps in addressing wicked problems, which requires groups of people with different worldviews to change their mind-sets and behaviors (Rittel and Webber 1973; Mathews 2002). This is democracy, broadly defined. While engaged universities may serve as a refuge where one may contemplate problems of the world, they also practice democratic action—the mobilization of collective wisdom for the purpose of addressing problems with community leaders in their own backyards.

Many wicked problems are matters of human well-being and survival; they cannot be remedied by technical or rational approaches. Engaged universities overtly challenge the epistemology that dominates most academic cultures—technical rationality. Engaged universities blend conventional and unconventional research and teaching methods; they balance technical and rational approaches to research and teaching with approaches that are situational and relational (Saltmarsh and Hartley 2011). Engaged universities call into question the notion of expertise as a limited resource, encouraging interaction and learning among university faculty, staff, students, refugees, indigenous peoples, children, women, and the elderly. In turn, knowledge "is everywhere fed back, constantly enhanced" (Lynton 1994, 10).

Moving beyond the ivory tower to become an engaged university is not for the faint of heart. The design and use of unconventional research and teaching methods often begin with the courage of university faculty and staff who, at the very least, are willing to challenge the paradigm of technical rationality, and in some instances are willing to risk their health, safety, and livelihood. Institutional reform requires such leadership. Sometimes these experiments emerge and grow quietly on the margins of campus in small research centers while no one is watching. Sometimes the head of the university—a president, vice-chancellor, or rector—mandates an institutional shift, charts a new course, and offers incentives for faculty and staff to test new strategies. Most of the time, it is a combination of these forces as well as external pressures including student activism, community demonstrations, and governmental mandates.

Stories from Engaged Universities around the World

From Mexico to Scotland, South Africa, Australia, Malaysia, Egypt, and the United States, the faculty, staff, students, community partners, and funding partners who coauthored these stories are leading innovative learning-by-doing experiences at engaged universities in a variety of environments. Some environments are characterized by violent struggles for political power, others by multigenerational unemployment, out-migration, and exploitation by private industries. Some of the engaged universities leading these experiments are private, some are public. Some are large, others are small. One is old, constructed in medieval Europe, while another was recently created by a cadre of educators in Asia who decided to try something daring. One experiment began in the twentieth century; all have been sustained for at least five years. In some cases, students become part of the community, living and working with people in rain forests and on mountains for extended periods of time. In others, students engage with communities by tutoring young refugees and providing medical examinations. All university and community participants are striving to address pervasive challenges to civic life such as poverty, illiteracy, and disease.

Each learning-by-doing experiment challenges traditional flows of knowledge, from expert to student, engaging participants from different walks of life in collective decision-making and action. Each is a form of political engagement, striving to build inclusive systems of power. Each is an example of involving ordinary citizens in perennial problems in ways that challenge long-standing beliefs, and require participants to productively navigate conflict. By engaging with pressing problems and with one another, participants strengthen their own capabilities, generate a sense of individual self-worth and common possibility. The following brief descriptions will introduce you to each of the stories in this collection.

Community Brigades

Started in 1997, Brigadas Comunitarias (Community Brigades) at Campus Querétaro is the story of a flagship program at Tecnológico de Monterrey University (Tec), a large, private university in Mexico. With nearly half of the population living below the national poverty line, Mexico is one of a handful of countries in Latin America that have a mandatory service component for university students. In this chapter, director Ernesto Benavides Ornelas and María Fernanda Pacheco Bravo, a graduate student who became an employee of Tec, introduce Tec's Social and Citizenship Education Program and explain how the young institution tries to instil a "human sense" in its students, while also preparing them to compete internationally in their professional field. During summer and winter breaks, Tec students at Campus Querétaro strengthen personal ethical competencies while living in two nearby communities, San Ildefonso and Los Cues. One *brigadista* reports that through the program she realized that poverty is a collective mind-set more than it is "something physical, something you can see."

Activate Program

Launched in 2002, the Activate Program is a credit-bearing, community development degree program for working adults at the University of Glasgow, Scotland. A public university constructed in medieval Europe, today in Glasgow a "fourth generation of young people are unemployed," families are "on the bread line," and people have a lower life expectancy than in comparable cities (Barker et al. 2013; Layden and Martin 2014a). In this chapter Margaret Fraser, regeneration manager at North Glasgow Housing Association, and Helen Martin, who grew up in one of the city's largest housing developments and now teaches at the University, tell the story of Activate. Upon reflection, working adults who are recovering from addiction, seeking political asylum, and raising children on their own report "improved listening skills and an appreciation of diversity" (Layden and Martin 2014b). Many gain self-confidence. Activate has adopted a Freirean approach characterized by connecting people from different walks of life, challenging deeply held beliefs, and negotiating difficult conversations. As recent graduates, Margaret and Helen personify the program's mantra: "We grow our own."

Amplifying Community Voices

Amplifying Community Voices in South Africa is a story of collective deliberation and decision-making about water and sanitation, education, health, housing, and transportation. Discussions have included university faculty and students as well as youth, women, and the elderly in rural communities. It was created in 2006 at the University of Venda, a small but rapidly growing public institution located near Zimbabwe in the rural, northern tip of South Africa. Despite several legal frameworks in place to promote public participation and democracy-building after apartheid, many rural projects fail due to low literacy skills. According to Amplifying Community Voices' founder, Joseph Francis, who is director of the Institute for Rural Development, South Africa's homeland system created a "dependency syndrome" whereby ethnic groups "blame the government for their problems." Violent service delivery protests are common. Students from a variety of disciplines organize and lead "reflection circles" and collaborate with eighty-eight villages in the Vhembe District. The experience helps students "develop confidence, become aware of social differences and learn how to communicate more effectively," says graduate student Hlekani Kabiti, founder of the Amplifying Community Voices students association (Francis and Kabiti 2014a).

Refugee Action Support Program

Refugee Action Support in Sydney, Australia, functions as a bridge between cultures. Launched in 2006 by Loshini Naidoo, senior lecturer at Western Sydney University, Eric Brace of the Australian Literacy and Numeracy Foundation, and others, this multiuniversity initiative is embedded in their respective curricula. It prepares future teachers while assisting young refugees, especially unaccompanied minors from Iraq, Sudan, Afghanistan, and Sierra Leone. Education students from Western Sydney University—a young, public university—provide one-on-one and small-group language and literacy support on a weekly basis. These classes for students of refugee backgrounds take place at schools throughout the region. Through frequent one-on-one experiences, teachers in training move outside their comfort zones, becoming aware of their biases and prejudices and developing greater sensitivity toward diverse cultures. Simultaneously, young refugees dealing with considerable material, personal, and cultural loss have regular access to a mentor. Together they discuss and negotiate a range of knowledge and skills. Students' learning by doing deconstructs racism and xenophobia, while strengthening primary and high schools as stabilizing societal institutions.

Village Adoption Project

The Kampung Tekir project in Seremban, Malaysia, embodies the myriad challenges associated with learning by doing. It was initiated by The International Medical University, a young, small, private university in Kuala Lumpur, Malaysia, to realize the University's mission: to develop "competent, ethical, caring and inquiring citizens." In 2007, its Clinical School in Seremban adopted Kampung Tekir, a tiny, isolated village about ten miles from campus and home of the Temuan peoples. Since the village is engulfed by estates on which palm oil and rubber are produced, access to it is severely limited. Under the supervision of Dr. Koh Kwee Choy and others, students conduct diabetes and high blood pressure tests and eye examinations, and treat ailments such head lice, worms, and scabies. A student committee leads the project, scheduling home visits and obtaining approvals from a variety of governmental agencies, including Ministry of Health and the Department for the Welfare of Aborigines, as well as the private estates and village committees. A new lecturer, Wong Chin Hoong, is testing the extent to which the model may be replicated in a nearby village, Kampung Sebir.

Lazord Academy

Lazord Academy in Cairo, Egypt, is a shining example of how to engage with and develop a next generation of Arab leaders in a tumultuous civil society characterized by violent struggles for political power and high rates of youth unemployment. Commencing several years before young Egyptians led the January 25, 2011, uprising that ended President Hosni Mubarak's thirty-year reign, Lazord Academy is an ever-changing yet structured pedagogy. It is a yearlong learning journey and a practical response to the reality of the "youth bulge," the fact that one-half of the Egyptian population is below the age of twenty-five. In this program designed by Nelly Corbel and others at the American University in Cairo, a small, private, liberal arts university, students complete internships with partners, including Rana Gaber, director of programs at the Egyptian Youth Federation. Mentorship is the key ingredient of the pedagogy, which encourages "friendships based on mutual respect and understanding." The Academy's name originates from the Arabic word for the indigenous blue stone with gold touches that embellished the most valued jewelry of the royal courts in ancient Egypt, because Lazord participants are seen as a precious natural resource.

Living Democracy

"Living Democracy in Rural America" tells the story of an Appalachian classroom in the Clear Fork Valley. Built upon the lived experiences of people like Marie Cirillo who have called the mountains and hollows home for generations, the curriculum is a living-learning experience. Since 2010 students from Auburn University, an old, public university located seven hours from the valley, have come to live and work with residents for the summer. Together, and with guidance from Mark Wilson, director of Civic Learning Initiatives, they provide arts education classes for children and computer literacy classes for adults. Such seemingly small, local actions generate a sense of self-worth and possibility, and can be beginning points for a shift of consciousness. A form of political engagement, Living Democracy challenges the long-standing stereotypes of Appalachia as a region characterized by backwardness and lawlessness. It also counters the realities of multigenerational unemployment, out-migration, and exploitation by private industries of both the land and the people. The program prepares the next generation of leaders in lasting practices that undergird the kind of community development work where citizens are at the center.

Throughout our research collaboration, we did not attempt to measure the impact of these learning-by-doing experiments because there is no immediate or ultimate test of a solution to a wicked problem (Rittel and Webber 1973). They are "problems of greatest human concern," existing in the "swampy lowlands." They are "messy and confusing and incapable of technical solution" (Schön 1995, 28). Accurately measuring the magnitude of such problems or the impact of learning-by-doing experiments is, by definition, a daunting task. There are no solutions to wicked problems; therefore, seeking generalizable solutions is not an appropriate goal. Experiments in learning by doing are a response to wicked problems, an effort to understand and address them. Though our rational minds urge that we evaluate our intervention with some "standard of rigor," we may not know the full range of impacts on the people who participate in such experiments, nor the ripple effects of their participation on each other, their local communities, or beyond. We may not know, in a precise way, the consequences of these dynamic experiments because they are innumerable.

We did, however, formulate answers to our questions. In the end, we gained an understanding of the exemplary practices that universities around the world are using to engage students and others in creating more equitable communities. Unlike the exemplars in this collection, many learning-by-doing experiences are designed to emphasize service to clients. On the one hand, research shows that many learning-by-doing experiences influence students to become more responsible, caring, and culturally aware; increase student understanding and appreciation of diversity; and facilitate the development of skills such as communication, teamwork, the ability to stick to a task, and time-keeping (Birdwell, Scott, and Horley 2013; Grist and Cheetham 2011; Blouin and Perry 2009; Astin and Sax 1998; Densmore 2000; Eyler and Giles 1999; Kezar 2002; Markus, Howard, and King 1993). On the other hand, engaged scholars warn of a persistent disconnect between faculty and community partners, with collaborations being perceived by community partners as largely exploitative and disrespectful. Many such experiences create a distance between university people and community people, obfuscating sources of conflict and exacerbating power differentials. By engaging people in ways that reinforce multidirectional flows of knowledge and build inclusive systems of power, these exemplars demonstrate that students and others may develop vital civic capabilities *while* creating more equitable communities.

Moreover, each story in this collection reminds us that education is fundamentally a political act. It cannot be divorced from pedagogy; that is, what is taught cannot be separated from the act of teaching (Freire 1996). When participants reflect on their experience with reinforcing multi-directional flows of knowledge and building inclusive systems of power, they acknowledge the political dimensions of complex challenges and actively deconstruct oppressive systems of power. In many instances, reflection awakens a desire to be in solidarity—to be an integral part of a group. This desire may not be achieved by critically reflecting about the self in relation to one's political circumstance. It involves action and reflection (Freire 1985). Solidarity is a democratic ideal that requires consciousness—but not an awareness of oneself, the type of consciousness long understood by Western philosophers. It is consciousness as it was understood in the 1500s, the unification of two ideas: "con"—"together" and "scio"—"to know." This initial meaning reached far beyond individual understanding and reaction; it intended to convey ideas about "having common knowledge with another" and creating relationships of common knowing and cause (Lewis 1990).

Practices for Creating More Equitable Communities

These seven stories illuminate two vital practices engaged universities are using to create more equitable communities. The interrelated practices are reinforcing multidirectional flows of knowledge and building inclusive systems of power.

Reinforcing Multidirectional Flows of Knowledge

Knowledge does not move from the locus of research to the place of application, from scholar to practitioner, teacher to student, expert to client. It is everywhere fed back, constantly enhanced. We need to think of knowledge in an ecological fashion, recognizing the complex, multifaceted and multiply-connected system by means of which discovery, aggregation, synthesis, dissemination, and application are interconnected and interacting in a wide variety of ways.

—Ernest Lynton, *Knowledge and Scholarship*, 1994

Reinforcing multidirectional flows of knowledge often begins by challenging the classic idea of the classroom. According to Lisa Anderson, president of the American University in Cairo, Egypt, it is important for university leaders to create incentives for faculty and students "to think again about conventional practices in higher education and to experiment with new platforms and paradigms." In a decade or two, she predicts, "most student learning will be outside the classic classroom—an educational device, let us remember, that was designed to produce the workforce of industrial society, with its neat rows of desks, carefully timed study periods and disciplined hierarchies. In the digital world of the twenty-first century, learning will once again be recognized as happening everywhere and all the time." Teaching, she adds, will "increasingly be acknowledged to be guided learning-by-doing," learning to be "creative problem-solvers, effective colleagues and collaborators, and responsible citizens in many domains" (quoted in Hoyt and Newcomb Rowe 2015).

Across the stories from engaged universities, participants are calling into question the "logic of the present system." They are practicing freedom by refusing to conform to popular assumptions about the reality around them. Many have "learned to view curricular artifacts as instruments for—rather than barriers to—action." They are pushing the boundaries of space and time, experimenting with where they meet and deliberate and how frequently and continuously they engage (Hoyt 2010, 84; Hoyt 2013, 231). The University of Glasgow's community partner, Margaret Fraser, underscores President Anderson's reflection by emphasizing the relevance of geography. She states simply, "Place is hugely important" (Layden and Martin 2014b). The Activate learning experience is delivered in "settings such as community centers, church halls, and youth clubs" with students "coming from as many as fifteen community-based organizations." The experience challenges long-standing stereotypes and prejudices influenced by life circumstances and the popular media by creating a "common bond" among people from all walks of life—including refugees, asylum seekers, migrants. The experience exposes participants to different attitudes and perceptions, resulting in new perspectives. The story of Billy and his daughter, Abbie, is instructive. Billy is a thirty-one-year-old single parent living in the Springburn area of North Glasgow. Once a thriving community with an abundance of heavy industry employing many hundreds of local people, North Glasgow is now characterized by large areas of contaminated land, high unemployment, and other wicked problems. Reflecting on the difference the Activate experience made to him personally, Billy explains how the experience has impacted his perspective on life and relationships,

> It's changed the way I think and how I communicate. Previously I looked out for myself and didn't think much about others. I am more open-minded now and think more about what is happening in my community.... Now I think about why people are in situations and what can be done to support them.... Even the little things matter, showing someone that you care and will listen to them. Most importantly, the changes in my own life have had a positive impact on my daughter. She's always telling people that her dad is at college and that she is proud of me. She's in primary school now, and she laughs when I tell her I have homework because she says I'm too old for homework.... Never in a million years did I think I would ever be going to university—except maybe as a janitor. I'm excited about where my life is going and what I could achieve. I've never felt that before. I recently started volunteering with Inner Circle (a men's group), and we have made contact with another men's group in Maryhill, UNIS (United Nations in Scotland). We have worked together with a group of Syrian men on a book of short stories of our experience which was funded by Scottish Refugee Council and has been reported nationally through Sky News as an example of integration.

The practice of reinforcing multidirectional flows of knowledge arises from the assumption that everybody possesses expert knowledge and that new and relevant knowledge is developed in complex, dynamic, and diverse networks of collaboration (Hoyt 2013). As is the case with the Activate program and the Refugee Action Support program, participants bring their own very different worldviews to their collaboration, learning from each other as they grapple to find common ground and meet tangible goals. Similarly, medical, nursing, and dental students are able to learn about traditional medicines as well as native song and dance from villagers as they deliver health services. Additionally, Living Democracy (United States), Community Brigades (Mexico) and Community Work Camps[3] (South Africa) student participants live and work in communities far from their home and campus, becoming "part of" the community. In short, these eight engaged universities see local community members as collaborators rather than as recipients of services. Together, they define projects, goals, and indicators for success. There is a shared and explicit commitment to integrating community expertise and leadership. They also emphasize the importance of consultation and collective decision-making, which requires a long-term commitment. Such relationships take years to build and begin with the assumption that universities are gaining as much as they are giving in the partnership. The university functions as a convener, improving collaboration and coordination among civil society organizations (Barker et al. 2013).[4]

Building Inclusive Systems of Power

> Education either functions as an instrument which is used to facilitate integration of the younger generation into the logic of the present system and bring about conformity or it becomes the practice of freedom, the means by which men and women deal critically and creatively with reality and discover how to participate in the transformation of their world.
>
> —Paulo Freire, *Pedagogy of the Oppressed*

Building inclusive systems of power begins by taking action to reinforce multidirectional flows of knowledge, and necessarily involves reflection on those actions. Despite substantial differences in political and social conditions, these examples of learning by doing recognize the power and potential of people. They are ways of both practicing collective decision-making and collective action and, therefore, democracy.

It took more than two years of meeting, talking, and writing for the chapter contributors to discover they all had one thing in common—each learning-by-doing experiment delivers an unpredictable experience and relies on structured reflection to facilitate participant learning. Though described differently, using a variety of such phrases as taking students "out of their comfort zones," providing an "eye-opening" experience, and imparting a feeling of "culture shock," all of the experiments challenge student assumptions—how they see themselves as individuals and as citizens as well as what they are capable of enduring and accomplishing. These practical approaches to meeting the trials of civic life—what Freire called "the practice of freedom"—influence participants in a variety of ways, some known and others unknown. For certain, working hand in hand with people you do not know and who see the world very differently than you while coping with the messiness of wicked problems is a profound experience, especially the first time around. In short, discovering "how to participate in the transformation" of the world awakens a new way of seeing, a new way of knowing.

Within the boundaries of each learning-by-doing experiment exists unanticipated twists and turns, valleys and peaks, triumphs and failures. It is impossible to escape the reality that some people will benefit while others may be harmed. And though many universities have standard protocols for minimizing risks to humans involved in such experiments, the issues of harm and benefit are compounded experiences; they cannot be cleanly cut. More often than not, the valley where one experiences struggle, perhaps humiliation and agony, is at once the essential turning point. At a place of respite, after a slow escape from the "swampy lowlands," one is free to rigorously reflect on one's actions. This is where real learning occurs—where people develop vital civic capabilities.

María Fernanda Pacheco Bravo, a Tec graduate student who took part in Community Brigades, deftly reveals her expectations and frustrations through reflection. In addition, she describes what she came to understand about the world and about herself, including her newfound awareness of "wicked problems."

> The experience was not what I expected. People in the community didn't want to participate. Children joined our activities because we were using their play space, but they did not have a legitimate interest in the program even though we created it with some leaders in the community. At first I was really frustrated; I could not understand why the people of the community were so apathetic. And although nothing changed in the community, the experience transformed me. Over time, I have come to understand that poverty is not just something fiscal, something you can identify by what material thing people have or do not have. Poverty is much more than that. It has to do with culture, with years of hardship, with education, with the system. The people in the community where I lived didn't work to get ahead because they have already tried and lost so many times that they believe change is impossible.

Each in its own way, the learning-by-doing experiences illuminated here required student participants to reflect on the political dimensions of complex challenges after making an effort to build more inclusive systems of power. For example, reflection is core to the Lazord (Egypt) learning process. Through a variety of reflection exercises students analyze concepts, evaluate experiences, form opinions, and derive new meaning and knowledge. The exercises take many forms, including editorials, blog posts, one-on-one and small-group discussions, painting, sculpture, music, and dance.

Additionally, Living Democracy in the United States and Amplifying Community Voices in South Africa are vivid stories of taking action to build inclusive systems of power and reflecting on the political dimensions of those actions. In the Clear Fork Valley, students are learning by living and working with local citizens for the public good. The work takes place in a valley, where absentee companies own almost all of the land and an insidious, invisible power "serves to maintain prevailing order of inequality not only through institutional barriers but also through the shaping of beliefs about the order's legitimacy or immutability" (Gaventa 1982, 42). By digging gardens for spring planning and cleaning up the cemetery, students tackle seemingly technical problems as political problems, learning the issues must be "understood through history, culture, and the perspective of citizens." Their collective efforts reinvigorate hope in an area "experiencing the trauma associated with outmigration since nearly all the area's 30,000 residents moved north to find work" (Cirillo and Wilson 2014b).

Similarly, Amplifying Community Voices builds inclusive systems of power in dozens of villages in the Vhembe District near the university, where ethnic groups "blame the government for their problems" (Barker et al. 2013). University of Venda students from a variety of disciplines organize and lead reflection circles to build inclusive systems of power among children, elders, and university students. Many villagers are skeptical; there have been too many unfulfilled promises from various people and institutions. Often village leadership is arguably patriarchal and conservative.

Students learn to "think on their feet." As they facilitate reflection circles, students encourage intergenerational dialogue. According to Joseph Francis, students learn to "listen a lot, deeply process that which is heard, be very observant and talk when necessary" (Francis and Kabiti 2014b). They learn to ensure that all voices are heard, and no single voice dominates. By doing so, they learn about conflict, group dynamics, and how to recognize and handle power imbalances. Over the years, it has proven impossible for the students to be accepted in a village on their own. Community members do not trust that students can carry out meaningful activities without the hand of university staff and faculty. Despite the ongoing challenges, this learning-by-doing experience contributes to local knowledge about how government and community institutions work. It also reinforces multidirectional flows of knowledge. Participants have been elected to serve on ward committees and ward councillorships. Municipal officials and university students and staff use the development plans to address such issues as water and sanitation, education, health, housing, and transportation (Francis and Kabiti 2014b).

Developing Civic Capabilities: Humility, Courage, and Empathy

What difference have these practices (reinforcing multidirectional flows of knowledge and building inclusive systems of power) made in the civic capabilities of participants? A careful examination of reflections on these learning-by-doing experiences suggests they are building participants'

- Humility, the ability to see oneself as less than another, to understand one's own weaknesses and limitations, and at the same time to strive for bold visions for change
- Courage and confidence, a belief in oneself and ability to operate in frightening situations
- Empathy, an ability to understand people who have worldviews very different from one's own, and a desire to negotiate differences and work collaboratively

Humility

University of Glasgow's Activate is a "life changing" experience for participants. The course purposefully engages some of the most marginalized people living in Glasgow. Built on the tenet that everyone has something to contribute, the course creates the opportunity for people to come together across age, cultural, geographical, and social barriers to participate in meaningful dialogue for change. When prompted to reflect on her experience with Activate, Rosie, a single "mum," characterizes it as disorienting. She learned to understand and collaborate with people who had worldviews very different from her own. She also developed a sense of humility—the ability to consider her own shortcomings, to no longer see herself as better than someone else. In Rosie's words,

> It was good that we didn't always agree with each other's point of view; it made it more interesting and challenging hearing what others thought about asylum seekers, refugees, and poverty, for example. I changed my mind so many times I was dizzy!

She continues,

I began to value other things in life. My ambitions changed, and my love of people grew. I [saw] beyond the disability, the clothes people wore, the first impressions. I began to value everyday interactions, sharing and learning with people, small achievements more than I valued being able to buy the most recent fashion item. I measured success in a completely different way where I valued small changes as much as major ones and people over things.

Similarly, central to the Lazord experience is the opportunity to learn to identify and deal with internal conflict. The Lazord experience is unique in the Egyptian context because of its flexibility; participating students and community partners are continually shaping the curriculum. A dynamic pedagogy is vital in a country like Egypt where everything is changing quickly and students are seeking skills to assist with their immediate survival. According to Nelly Corbel (2014), "We cannot pretend our students are not dying on the streets protesting an autocratic rule. We must acknowledge this real experience and assist students with the life and death questions." Lazord's guided reflection exercises reinforce critical thinking as well as changes in attitudes and behaviors. One such exercise begins by students listing, from top to bottom, the following words: *practice*, *attitudes*, *skills*, *knowledge*, *values*. With a mentor, students articulate their personal values and the extent to which their espoused values align with their day-to-day practices. Mentors and students seek to identify internal contradictions. In the chapter on the Lazord program, Nelly Corbel explains,

A vivid example . . . would be a discussion I had one day with a student regarding homosexuality. The student expressed diversity and equal rights as a central set of her values. I therefore asked if, according to her, everyone should have equal rights and their differences accepted by the larger society and legal system, as long as they do not call for hatred or violence. She agreed without conditions. Subsequently, I told her that I therefore assumed she was for same-sex marriage, and she replied: Of course not! This is where reflection hits a nerve and becomes a true learning experience. We broke down her reaction and agreed that her attitude was in opposition to the value of diversity. As we further analyzed her feelings, we concluded that there were missing links between her stated values and her adopted attitudes. She did not know anyone openly homosexual and had limited exposure to this topic, mostly from opposing rhetoric. We consequently agreed that she had the right to be opposed, but her opinion had to be formulated on fact-based knowledge and exchange with the relevant community. We agreed that these conditions are required to formulate a solid argument as to why she is opposed to gay marriage, rather than merely perpetuating a cultural stigma.

Dealing with conflict—internal or external—in ways that help one develop the ability to see oneself differently requires skillful mentorship. "It is critical as an educator to not formulate any opinion on behalf of our students, but rather give them the tools to formulate their own opinions based on evidence and critical thinking around personally held core values," according to Corbel (Corbel 2014). Lazord's pedagogy breaks the hierarchal relationship between faculty and students. Instead it focuses on the development of friendships that span far beyond a student's university years. Corbel explains, "When you establish friendships based on mutual respect and understanding, you open the soul of the learner and each of us learns better. Students trust us, which opens their learning beyond the classroom" (Hoyt and Newcomb Rowe 2015, 32).

Community Work Camps in South Africa also aim to disorient student participants, many of whom come from working-class families. When university visitors arrive, they introduce themselves to the village chief. Next, villagers explain the community by-laws and the work to be done together. The operating assumption is that university visitors "don't know anything" and need "to be led" by, and learn from, the villagers (Mafatshe and Putu 2014). Students describe the experience of living and working with villagers as "eye-opening." Living without electricity or running water for nine to ten days while struggling to communicate in a foreign language exposes university students to the "realities" of South Africa and its neighboring countries.[5] Additionally, students encounter a variety of personal and group conflicts as they struggle to live in close quarters with strangers, cook their own meals, and sleep on makeshift beds on the floor far away from their homes (Putu 2014; Mafatshe and Putu 2014). During their stay in the village, students engage in discussions and debates among themselves and reflect by journaling at the end of each day to make sense of what they have seen and heard. The circumstances are challenging, and some students have difficulty coping. A student explains,

> The actual engagement with community members, children, and adults was difficult; the main frustration stemmed from an inability to communicate well because of the language barrier, and also from a sense of helplessness. Because of the intimate nature of the work camps, there was a point where I was a bit withdrawn because the reality was I would go back to South Africa to my township life, also with its many constraints, but at least in my head not as dire, and leave the community either inspired or unaffected by my presence. In this case, through conversations with the rest of the group, I was brought to the realization that the work camp is not intended to try and bring solutions to the challenges facing the community, but more to bring one to the understanding that you can make contributions to a community, and that these may not always be evident at the time, and also to make the community better in whatever ways that are possible and are within your reach (Putu 2014, 11).

Engagement with wicked problems is humbling. The frustrations associated with Community Work Camps are plentiful—lack of modern comforts, lack of personal space, and slow progress, to name a few. For example, it has proven difficult to effectively teach HIV/AIDS prevention, in part because some parents do not want university students to teach their children about condoms. With support from the village chief, students have conveyed the information to villagers in the form of theater performances. Itumeleng Mafatshe, a graduate student who has participated in Community Work Camps for several years, believes this effort is essential. At the same time, she perceives little progress with HIV/AIDS prevention in the village and questions the extent to which student engagement is impactful (Mafatshe and Putu 2014).

Courage

Courage, the ability to do something that frightens you, to believe in oneself and one's talents, is also cultivated by way of practice. Often one develops courage by taking a risk, coping with ambiguity, failing tremendously, reflecting on the experience, and doing something frightening again. It is reinforced by success, tangible results to which one may point, especially results that materialize against all odds—with scant resources, in settings replete with hopelessness and despair.

To begin, let us consider the story of Auburn University student Jelani Moore. In the town of Elba, Alabama, residents remember two devastating floods in the 1990s that decimated the town's infrastructure. In summer 2014, Jelani Moore arrived in Elba. A talented artist and media studies major with an interest in filmmaking, he discovered that a local business owner had begun plans for a wall mural on her downtown building. Jelani helped organize citizens for a weeklong Elba Renaissance Festival, which made the mural a reality. Other projects included creating a video entry for a successful matching grant for his partnering organization's newest project, a community garden, as well as designing a new flag for the city. After the summer, Jelani stated that he learned that he has skills in organizing people around common interests and goals. That's Living Democracy (Cirillo and Wilson 2014b).

Student leadership is a common feature across the learning-by-doing experiences. While they benefit from the support and guidance of university faculty and staff as well as community partners, students assume a lead role in organizing and implementing complex projects and activities. For example, Kampung Tekir is student-driven. Students are directly responsible for the planning events in the village. They organize themselves into committees and subcommittees, appoint student leaders, recruit student volunteers, delegate responsibilities, prepare and deliver health talks, conduct home-to-home visits, prescribe medications (under supervision of a specialist), and come up with creative ways to engage the community, especially the children. Wan (Pam) Amni Zulfikar, a student leader in the Kampung Tekir story, participated in the Kettering Foundation–Talloires Network collaborative research workshop in Boston in December 2012. She has since graduated and is working as a medical doctor in Sabah, Malaysia. Reflecting on her role as a project manager, Pam explains, in the chapter on Kampung Tekir,

> I have learned how to manage my time and improved my organizational skills best through this program. Each event took weeks of planning involving many meetings. I find joy in juggling work between hospital duties and event planning, as it was a welcomed change to the daily routine of a medical student.

In some instances, engaged universities institutionalize student leadership in the form of bona fide organizations. Learning by doing "gives students an appreciation of what they themselves can do with local communities," according to University of Venda's vice-chancellor, Peter Mbati (Hoyt and Newcomb Rowe 2015). In 2011, a student-led organization at the University of Venda emerged as a necessity for enhancing student participation in Amplifying Community Voices. The formulation of the organization was participatory, students playing a leading role in all the discussions and decisions. In the process, they learned to develop a constitution that outlined protocols for collective decision-making. During the same year the student organization was registered at the University of Venda with students from all university departments at different levels of study. The association is run by a democratically elected management committee with an equal number of men and women representatives who are responsible for implementing plans throughout the year. Hlekani Kabiti, chairperson of the Amplifying Community Voices student association, in her chapter reflects on her experience:

Serving as the chairperson of [the student association] for two years exposed me to immeasurable, life-changing experiences and skills. This position was a huge responsibility because it brought an extra load on my academic work. In addition to the skills which the other students usually gain, I learned to be more responsible and accountable even for things that were not of my own making. Serving in this position taught me to embrace failures and appreciate the efforts we made as we tried to succeed. The position made me realize that failure results from doing something.

Empathy

Refugee Action Support provides the next generation of Australian teachers an appreciation of other languages and cultures as well as an opportunity to develop skills in teaching the English language. Through practice, tutors gain firsthand experience with the realities faced by newly settled refugees, including the difficulty of learning a second language. Tutors readily acknowledge how the experience fosters cross-cultural understandings that help them become better teachers and members of the community. One who taught in 2008 notes in the chapter on Refugee Action Support,

> You get to grow in the way that you interact with students. You also get to experience their cultures in many ways, the way they view things, the experiences they go through. . . . Some of it is very beautiful. . . . At the end of Ramadan, [the students] cooked a massive feast and invited us [the tutors] to lunch. We sang. We danced. It was the most amazing experience I had at university.

As a result of these intensely personal exchanges, tutors develop a greater sensitivity toward recently settled refugees. The frequency of their interactions with one another requires tutors to cope with questions and assumptions they may have about people with life experiences very different from their own. Tutors thus become aware of their biases and prejudices, which may have developed in part in response to how refugees are portrayed in popular media. By experiencing, through personal interactions, the wicked problems in Iraq and other politically unstable societies, tutors call into question their standing in the world by standing in the shoes of another, albeit momentarily and figuratively.

Similarly, Mexico's Community Brigades, South Africa's Community Work Camps, and the United States' Living Democracy give students an opportunity to compare and contrast the culture they know with a different culture. Living and working hand in hand with strangers, often in challenging conditions and for more than a week, compels students to examine their own worldview. At first, students may observe how they are different from the people in the community with whom they are working. Over time, however, they find common ground, coming to understand "universal" human values. A summer 2009 *brigadista* quoted in the chapter on Mexico explains,

> Brigadas gave me the opportunity to be part of a different space in which I do not live commonly, and they let me see that some values are universal, independent of the place you are.

Another summer 2009 student describes the process of learning to understand and "love" a new and very different environment:

I believe that this experience leads you to the extreme. It pushes you because people in the community welcome you in their lives, making you part of their environment. So there is no place for you to be picky or question their culture. They offered you the best they have, and the things that were basic for you suddenly acquire a new meaning. You realize that you must respect the environment and culture that is welcoming you. You even learn to understand it and love it.

South African students working hand in hand with villagers in Maputo, Mozambique, by way of Community Work Camps uncover comparable insights. For example, they report feelings of frustration and anxiety associated with attempting to communicate in a different language to become part of village life. In short, the ability to understand another, to empathize, cannot be developed by reading a text or attending a classroom lecture; it evolves through a series of contentious internal struggles that only interacting with people who see the world differently can provoke.

The Generative Utility of Higher Education

Vice-Chancellor Habib embodies, in a way, the idea that higher education institutions have generative utility in developing civic capabilities. During his formative years, Adam Habib lived in and actively protested against apartheid policies at the University of the Witswatersrand, the engaged university he leads today. For decades, the University upheld its stand against apartheid despite cuts in government funding as well as the deportation and detention of students and staff. Did Habib develop the ability to collaborate with people who have very different worldviews than his own, to face danger without fear, and to understand his own shortcomings as he worked in solidarity with others, practicing the idea of justice? In what ways and to what extent did the environment in which he took action—the history, culture, politics, and economy of Johannesburg—affect his consciousness? Vice-Chancellor Habib himself says this period of his life explains in large part his commitment to university civic engagement. A highly accomplished and self-described "activist and academic," his capabilities are numerous. He and his counterparts have cultivated the types of civic capabilities essential for the creation of more equitable and prosperous communities. And the growing global network of engaged universities strengthens and grows as its offspring come of age, assume responsibility, and become "active agents in the struggle to reconstruct society."

Dozens of interviews with university leaders around the world reveal that they share common views about their own roles and the civic role of their institutions (Hoyt and Newcomb Rowe 2015). According to Mei Ling Young, provost and cofounder of the International Medical University in Malaysia, "Universities are the conscience of society. We will get lost if we have isolated ourselves from society in our ivory towers. We must serve our community" (Young 2013). Similarly, Rector David Noel Ramirez Padilla of Tecnológico de Monterrey in Mexico explained, "Universities need to be attentive to the surrounding needs in their communities, to eradicate poverty, and corruption. This type of awareness is contagious and is fundamental for any leader" (Ramirez-Padilla 2013).

Indeed, universities "are some of the few places left where a struggle for the commons, for public life" can be seen and heard through "collective voices and social movements" (Giroux 2013). University campuses in many countries around the world are spaces for debate and engines of knowledge generation. Additionally, institutions of higher education are multiplying, and the sector will continue to grow around the world for many years to come. The rate is staggering. For example, today global enrollment is approximately 200 million. At the start of the millennium it was 100 million. At the Talloires Network Global Leaders Conference in 2014, Reeta Roy, CEO of the MasterCard Foundation, characterized higher education as a monopoly on a very precious renewable resource:

> To my mind, unlike any other institution in society, you have an unparalleled access—I could even say a near monopoly—on a very precious renewable resource, and that is, you tap into the energy of young people. You tap into their energy and you tap into their desire to make a difference in the world. Young people enter higher education at a very formative time in their lives and you are there to provide an environment where they can discover their talents, understand their strengths and develop the skills that they need in order to make a difference.

Regional Perspectives on Learning by Doing is not about developing the capabilities of university students, though that may be how it appears at first blush. It advocates seeing and leveraging the global system of higher education as a project for destroying oppressive systems and re-creating systems that are more equitable. From this perspective, university students are people who, for a few years, become part of an institution that is actively engaged with wicked problems. During this time, they take on the wicked problems of the world while working in collaboration with colleagues inside and outside the university. In doing so, they develop the capabilities for their own evolution and survival and abilities to contribute significantly to societal betterment. By focusing on the people who are emerging as leaders around the world, this collection of stories is about community and societal change. Rana Gaber, a community organizer with the Egyptian Youth Federation, notes,

> It begins with civil society, where people see positive action, not just wasted words or slogans on the street, but action that changes lives and the course of history. (Hoyt and Newcomb Rowe 2015, 33)

Wicked problems threaten our well-being—disease, famine, economic inequality, climate change, political instability, and more. The good news is they are inextricably intertwined, each a symptom of another (Rittel and Webber 1973). Therefore, a change in education may cause new behaviors that cause other changes. In an interview Vice-Chancellor Habib questioned whether universities will function as a setting where "the new citizenship" gets constructed. He explained, "Universities are not mechanisms to create elites. What's important is to transform those elites and make sure they are socially conscience—that they care about what's happening in the world" (Habib 2014). South Africa's recent experiment points to a promising avenue for changing lives. As we have seen, equally "fantastic social laboratories" have experiments under way in Mexico, Scotland, Australia, Malaysia, Egypt, and the United States of America. There is a global movement of universities dedicated to civic engagement and social responsibility (Hoyt and Hollister 2014a). Its full potential has not yet been realized; however, it is being explored.

As individuals, what we do with our time and energy matters. In an increasingly interconnected and polarized world, the smallest of our deeds resound readily—they are quite literally seen, heard, and felt by people around the world in real time. Making a civil society work is work. It is the work of democracy, which is more than a system of government—it is a system of learning and doing that involves people from all walks of life in decision-making for their collective survival (Mathews 2014). As initially envisioned, our collaborative research project has led to this book—a collection of stories aspiring to inspire higher education reform around the world. For this small but mighty group of collaborators, it is a dream come true. And it is a dream not yet realized. The impact of our efforts will be determined by your future actions. Will you work to advance the idea of the engaged university? Will you leverage the potential of engaged universities to develop civic capabilities? Will you contribute to the creation of more equitable and prosperous communities? The future is in your hands.

NOTES

1. Adam Habib, Keynote Speech given at Talloires Network Leaders Conference 2014, https://www.youtube.com/watch?v=OwuWNWqWz9Y&feature=youtube.
2. Talloires Network Declaration, adopted September 17, 2005, http://talloiresnetwork.tufts.edu/who-we-ar/talloires-declaration/?c=7.
3. A student and community partner associated with the University of the Witwatersrand, Community Work Camps participated in the research collaboration. Some of their many contributions are incorporated in this chapter; however, they chose not to submit a chapter of their own to the collection.
4. It is important to note that all eight learning-by-doing exemplars fail to respond to the community rhythm and pace. Instead, each follows the university calendar, which is driven by semesters as well as summer and winter breaks (Hoyt 2010). This pattern silently communicates the university's presumed position of power over the community and reinforces the notion that the primary purpose of the partnership is to enhance student learning.
5. The Hokwe villagers speak Portuguese, as do many Mozambicans.

REFERENCES

Anderson, L. 2013. Interview by Lorlene Hoyt, Medford, Massachusetts, May.

Astin, A. W., and Sax, L. J. 1998. How undergraduates are affected by service participation. *Journal of College Student Development* 39: 251–263.

Barker, D., Brace, E., Bravo, M. F. P., Catalano, J., Cirillo, M., Corbel, N., Diebel, A., Francis, J. Gaber, R., Hoyt, L., Newcomb Rowe, A., Ornelas, E.-B., Kabiti, H., Keegan, M., Koh, J., Layden, M., Martin, H. M., Naidoo, L., Putu, T., Wilson, M., and Zulkifar, P. 2013. Group meeting, December 16–20.

Birdwell, J., Scott, R., and Horley, E. 2013. Active citizenship, education and service learning. *Education, Citizenship and Social Justice* 8(2): 185–199.

Blouin, D. D., and Perry, E. M. 2009. Whom does service learning really serve? Community-based organizations' perspectives on service learning. *Teaching Sociology* 37(2): 120–135.

Brace, E., and Naidoo, L. 2014a. Telephone interview by Lorlene Hoyt, Medford, Massachusetts, May 12.

———. 2014b. UWS Regional Perspectives on Civic Engagement. Unpublished paper, Sydney, Australia,

June 5.

Bravo, M. F. P., and Benavides Ornelas, E. 2014a. Telephone interview by Lorlene Hoyt, Medford, Massachusetts, April 22.

———. 2014b. Social and citizenship education program: Brigadas Comunitarias (Community Brigades). Unpublished paper, Monterrey, Mexico, June 16.

Cirillo, M., and Wilson, M. 2014a. Telephone interview by Lorlene Hoyt, Medford, Massachusetts, April 22.

———. 2014b. Untitled. Unpublished paper, June 9.

Corbel, N. 2014. Interview by Amy Newcomb Rowe, Medford, Massachusetts, January.

Corbel, N., and Gaber, R. 2014a. Telephone interview by Lorlene Hoyt, Medford, Massachusetts, June 10.

———. 2014b. Lazord academy—John D. Gerhart Center for Philanthropy and Civic Engagement. Unpublished paper, Cairo, Egypt, June 11.

Densmore, K. 2000. Service learning and multicultural education: Suspect or transformative? In C. R. O'Grady, ed., *Integrating service learning and multicultural education in colleges and universities*. New York: Routledge.

Dewey, J. 2008. Essays and how we think. In J. A. Boydston, ed., *The later works of John Dewey*, vol. 8, *1925–1953*. Carbondale: Southern Illinois University Press.

Eyler, J., and Giles, D. E., Jr. 1999. *Where's the learning in service-learning?* San Francisco: Jossey-Bass.

Francis, J., and Kabiti, H. 2014a. Telephone interview by Lorlene Hoyt, Medford, Massachusetts, April 24.

———. 2014b. Amplifying community voices for people-centered development in South Africa. Unpublished paper, Venda, South Africa, June 12.

Freire, P. 1985. The politics of education: culture, power, and liberation. South Hadley, Massachusetts: Bergin & Garvey.

Freire, P. 1996. *Pedagogy of the oppressed*. Trans. M. B. Ramos. Rev. ed. London: Penguin.

Gaber, R. 2014. Interview by Amy Newcomb Rowe, Medford, Massachusetts, January.

Gaventa, J. 1982. *Power and powerlessness: Quiescence and rebellion in an Appalachian Valley*. Urbana: University of Illinois Press.

Giroux, H. A. 2013. Angela Davis, freedom and the politics of higher education. Truthout. Http://www.truth-out.org/opinion/item/15595-angela-davis-freedom-and-the-politics-of-higher-education.

Grist, M., and Cheetham, P. Experience required. London: Demos, 2011.

Habib, A. 2014. Telephone interview by Lorlene Hoyt, Medford, Massachusetts, March 11.

hooks, b. 1994. *Teaching to transgress: Education as the practice of freedom*. New York: Routledge.

Hoyt, L. 2010. A city-campus engagement theory from, and for, practice. *Michigan Journal of Community Service-Learning* 17(1): 75–88.

———, ed. 2013. *Transforming cities and minds through the scholarship of engagement: Economy, equity and environment*. Nashville: Vanderbilt University Press.

———. 2014. University civic engagement: A global perspective. *Higher Education Exchange*. Dayton, OH: Kettering Foundation.

Hoyt, L., and Hollister, R. 2014a. Moving beyond the ivory tower: The expanding global movement of engaged universities. In B. Hall and R. Tandon, eds., *Knowledge, engagement and higher education: Rethinking social responsibility*. New York: Palgrave Macmillan.

———. 2014b. Strategies for advancing global trends in university civic engagement. *All Ireland Journal of Teaching and Learning in Higher Education* 6(1): 1691–1710.

Hoyt, L., and Newcomb Rowe, A. 2015. *Leaders in the civic engagement movement*. Http://talloiresnetwork.tufts.edu/wp-content/uploads/LCEM-Digital-Report-with-TOC-Feb-20151.pdf.

Kezar, A. 2002. Assessing community service learning: Are we identifying the right outcomes? *About Campus* 7(2): 14–20.

Koh, J., Ong, K., and Wong, C. H. 2014. Telephone interview by Lorlene Hoyt, Medford, Massachusetts, May 27.

Koh, J., and Wong, C. H. 2014. IMU Cares Kampung Angkat project, Kampung Tekir. Unpublished paper, Kuala Lumpur, Malaysia, June 9.

Layden, M., and Martin, H. 2014a. Telephone interview by Lorlene Hoyt, Medford, Massachusetts, April 23.

———. 2014b. Activate and ng homes. Unpublished paper, Glasgow, Scotland, June 13.

Lewis, C. S. 1990. Conscience and conscious. In C. S. Lewis, *Studies in words*. Cambridge: Cambridge University Press.

Lynton, E. A. 1994. Knowledge and scholarship. *Metropolitan Universities: An International Forum* 5(1): 9–17.

Mafatshe, I., and Putu, T. 2014. Telephone interview by Lorlene Hoyt, Medford, Massachusetts May 20.

Markus, G. B., Howard, J. P. F., and King, D. C. 1993. Notes: Integrating community service and classroom instruction enhances learning. Results from an experiment. *Educational Evaluation and Policy Analysis* 15(4): 410–419.

Mathews, D. 2002. *For communities to work*. Dayton, OH: Kettering Foundation.

———. 2014. *The ecology of democracy: Finding ways to have a stronger hand in shaping our future*. Dayton, OH: Kettering Foundation.

Nyerere, J. 1978. Development is for man, by man, and of man: The declaration of Dar es Salaam. In Budd L. Hall, ed., *Adult learning: A design for action*. Oxford: Pergamon.

Putu, T. 2014. Community work camps. Unpublished paper, Johannesburg, South Africa, June 18.

Ramirez-Padilla, D. N. 2013. Interview by B. Hernandez and A. Newcomb Rowe, Medford, Massachusetts, November.

Reeta, R. 2014. Plenary speech. Talloires Network Global Leaders Conference. Cape Town, South Africa. December 3. Https://www.youtube.com/watch?v=9A6VCMssrJo.

Rittel, H. W. J. and Webber, M. M. 1973. Dilemmas in a general theory of planning. *Policy Sciences* 4, 155–169.

Saltmarsh, J., and Hartley, M. 2011. To serve a larger purpose. In J. Saltmarsh and M. Hartley, eds., *"To serve a larger purpose": Engagement for democracy and the transformation of higher education*. Philadelphia: Temple University Press.

Schön, D. A. 1995. Knowing-in-action: The new scholarship requires a new epistemology. *Change* 27(6): 26–34.

Whitman, Walt. *Democratic vistas*. 1871.

Young, M. L. 2013. Interview by Lorlene Hoyt, Medford, Massachusetts, December.

Brigadas Comunitarias at Tecnológico de Monterrey in Querétaro, Mexico: Some Values Are Universal

Ernesto Benavides Ornelas, María Fernanda Pacheco Bravo, and Brianda Hernandez Cavalcanti

When I approached my fourth semester of my bachelor's in communications, I started to worry about satisfying my social service requirement. As a person that intends to graduate from a university in Mexico, I knew I had to accomplish 480 hours of social service before my graduation day. So I started to research the options my university offered. I knew I wanted something that would allow me to make a difference. After all, since I had to do it, it would be best if my service would have an impact on others too.

I was already working as volunteer in an NGO named Un Techo para mi país (known as "Techo"). Techo is dedicated to eradicating poverty by mobilizing youth volunteers to construct transitional housing and implement social inclusion programs.

Because of this background, I decided to participate in Brigadas Comunitarias. This service program would require me to stay in the community for a period of one month, which sounded exciting. And, I thought to myself at the time, it can't be so different than the time I spent in the slums with Techo. I signed up for Brigadas Comunitarias and went through a carefully designed selection process, including an interview. Finally I was accepted. I was excited to work on a development plan for the community, then work with the community for a month to implement the plan. I didn't realize at the time the experience was going to change me forever.

The experience was not what I expected. People in the community didn't want to participate. Children joined our activities because we were using their play space, but they did not have a legitimate interest in the program even though we created it with some leaders in the community.

At first I was really frustrated; I could not understand why the people of the community were so apathetic. And although nothing changed in the community, the experience transformed me. Over time, I have come to understand that poverty is not just something fiscal, something you can identify by what material thing people have or do not have. Poverty is much more than that. It has to do with culture, with years of hardship, with education, with the system. The people in the community where I lived didn't work to get ahead because they have already tried and lost so many times that they believe change is impossible.

I used to imagine myself as a savior, as the good one that shares what she has. The truth is that they saved me, they changed me and made me a better person; they showed me that change and mobility are hard and that sometimes they have a lot more to worry about than creating a development plan.

Today I understand that change takes time, lots of time, as much time perhaps as it has taken for people to call themselves outsiders, to lose hope and believe they don't have a choice. I understand now that real social change needs more than money, food, and houses. It should be grounded in education, focused on possibilities and giving every human the right and capacity to choose their future.

Brigadas Comunitarias changed my life because as a participant I had the opportunity to understand the complexity of social problems, and how they do not come alone. I came to understand how everything is related, how causes and consequences intertwine, resulting in society as we know it today.

—María Fernanda Pacheco

The History and Mission of Brigadas Comunitarias

Tecnológico de Monterrey University's Brigadas Comunitarias (Community Brigades) program seeks to develop and strengthen students' personal ethical competencies and link those competencies to their civic aspirations. It also aims to facilitate the development of Mexican communities. In turn, students are expected to realize that their rights and obligations go beyond their own personal interests. This commitment to work with others extends into the practice of their profession. In this way, Brigadas Comunitarias aims to help develop students' personal and professional competencies, while working with communities to overcome social problems.

With thirty-one campuses across Mexico, Tecnológico de Monterrey University (Tec) is a large, private institution.[1] Its mission is to "form persons with integrity, ethical standards and a humanistic outlook." Brigadas Comunitarias is a flagship program at Campus Querétaro, located about 220 kilometers northwest of Mexico City. During summer and winter breaks the program has engaged students with more than thirty different communities in Mexico, two of them since 2008: San Ildefonso and Los Cues.

San Ildefonso and Los Cues

San Ildefonso is a small community of more than two thousand inhabitants, a majority of indigenous origin. The Otomi people live two hours from the Querétaro campus. The Otomi people are an indigenous ethnic group inhabiting the Central Altiplano. The two most populous groups are the Highland and the Sierra Otomi, who live in the mountains of La Huasteca, and the Mezquital Otomi, who live in the Mezquital Valley in the eastern part of the state of Hidalgo and in the state of Querétaro. In the Mezquital Valley lies the Amealco municipality, where the small community of San Ildefonso is located.

Their main activities and form of income comes from farming and raising livestock. Their staple crops are corn (maize), beans, and squash. The fields are cleared by slash-and-burn methods, and planting is done with a *coa*, a tool that is a combination of a hoe and digging stick. Women are an important part of the familial economy; they practice crafts including weaving, pottery, basketry, and rope and cloth making, both for home use and for sale.

Though they speak indigenous languages, their manners of dress vary from traditional to completely modern. A common outfit in conservative areas consists of a white cotton shirt and pants, sandals, and hat for men and a long tubular skirt, embroidered cotton blouse, and shawl or cape for women. Since the conquest of Hernán Cortés, a colloquial term for this phenomenon is *malinchismo*. It refers to indigenous peoples taking on the mannerisms and culture of their colonial conquerors instead of living in accordance with more traditional patterns and modes of life.

A religious association named Las Obras de Catalina that works to address issues in these indigenous communities includes the various ministries of charity of the Poor Handmaids of Jesus Christ in Mexico. They use indigenous tradition in religious ceremonies and practices, and include indigenous peoples as employees and benefactors.

They are dedicated to working with marginalized people, especially the poor, the sick, and children. In San Ildefonso Tultepec, Amealco, in the state of Querétaro, they provide opportunities for low-income rural and indigenous people. It is with the help of comprehensive, somewhat formal, education that they are able to face life with dignity.

The partnership with this organization and with Sister Mary—the organization director in San Ildefonso—occurred because she approached the University searching for volunteers who wanted to complete their social service hours. After talking with Sister Mary and getting to know the two main projects she works on in the community Tec decided that the best approach to contributing to community well-being was through the Brigadas Comunitarias program.

One of the two main projects Sister Mary directs is Mujeres de Esperanza (Women of Hope), where Otomi single mothers, widows, or separated wives are trained as seamstresses and receive economic, spiritual, medical, and personal care. Women of Hope helps generate income for the women and community. The women make quilting and patchwork products that are sold in Mexico and the United States with help from the students.

Centro Nazaret del Aprendizaje (Nazareth Learning Center) is the second main project Sister Mary directs. The program benefits more than sixty children at a time by strengthening their formal education and helping them acquire educational skills from kindergarten to sixth grade. This program is only available to children in kindergarten and primary school. The activities and resources available to them include:

- Tutoring help with homework assignments
- Feedback depending on the topics and issues they are facing in school
- Participation in various types of sports, hiking, and special community events
- Talks about health and hygiene to implement in their daily lives
- Daily snacks
- Experiences that allow them to approach the Christian faith, such as talks, moments of praise, reading books, and playing games that promote human values

During the eight years that Tec and Las Obras de Catalina have worked together, more than sixteen different groups of students have fulfilled their social service in the community through *brigadas* with the support of the religious association. In partnership with Las Obras de Catalina, students have worked to provide food and schooling and to incubate small businesses. They support existing programs, develop marketing and business strategies for the products made by the women, lecture Nazareth Learning Center students, cooperate with the development of the Learning Center installations, teach new crafts, and involve the community with the projects and activities that the association provides.

Located in an industrial zone, Los Cues is a community of 1,622 inhabitants, where 3 percent are of indigenous background (INEGI 2010). Los Cues is a community with little water supply where people rarely finish more than their basic education. There are 122 illiterate people aged fifteen or older and 120 people in that age range who have never received formal education. Of the entire community, 467 have never completed schooling, 258 are in primary school, and 52 have middle school or high school education (SEDESOL 2013).

To address these literacy challenges in Los Cues, the University works in partnership with the secretary of social development. This partnership began in 1995, when Tec's mission changed to forming professionals committed to social and personal well-being. At the time, the secretary of social development had experience working with the community to provide Internet and computer access to children and adults, which Tec did not. The Learning Center in Los Cues is one of forty-three in Querétaro.[2] Under the professor's guidance, students take part in a transfer of knowledge by providing online assistance and tutoring to microenterprises in areas such as health and housing. Learning centers create a space for students to interact with community members. In this space, students and community partners are equals, exploring and learning new skills together.

Such programs require university support. Brigadas Comunitarias is well aligned with Tec's mission and is recognized as an important program in the Social and Civic Engagement Department.

The Emergence of the Social and Citizenship Education Program

In Mexico, where 53.2 percent of the population lives below the national poverty line (CONEVAL 2014), the higher education system plays a key role in promoting change by educating professionals who can improve economic and social conditions. Many institutions of higher education share a common mission and purpose: to contribute to the public good by educating socially responsible citizens. Mexico is one of the few countries that have a mandatory service component for students enrolled in higher education; Article V in its constitution requires that students complete 480 hours of "social service" to obtain a bachelor's degree.[3]

"Social service" is interpreted broadly and may include community engagement on issues of health, education, housing, infrastructure, or promoting democracy. Some students work with nonprofit organizations, while others partner with government programs. There are numerous options for students. The requirement is intended to result in direct benefits to marginalized sectors of society while raising students' awareness and deepening their sense of social responsibility. Tec's social service is understood as the public work done by students to address ethical controversies linked to social needs. Moreover, students are expected to contribute in the cocreation of solutions to those challenges and to build citizen capacity in the community.

The national mandate does not drive the University's focus or goals. Tec is committed to creating "the new cosmopolitan citizen." Programs such as Brigadas Comunitarias are crucial because they provide opportunities for students to develop critical thinking and other professional skills. For Tec, these skills are not only a matter of employability; they are central to the notion of university social responsibility. Students, in effect, develop professional skills and citizenship skills simultaneously. In short, Tec wants students to become excellent professionals who will contribute substantially to the betterment of the country and the world. Before students become professionals; however, they must develop as citizens with a desire to contribute to important societal improvements.

At Tec, three imperatives create the foundation for the Social and Citizenship Education Program. The first is the society's aspiration to have a better quality of life and the urgent need to positively transform the immediate environment—the city, state, and country. Second, the school's mission is to develop citizen professionals who are aware of the magnitude of social inequality and its consequences, and who possess the agency to produce useful solutions to social problems, students capable of responding ethically to moral misunderstandings and indifference. Last, there is the University's obligation to give meaning to vocation, to apply meaning and ethics to all professions.

Tec's mission is compatible with postulate of Daniel Coit Gilman, president of Johns Hopkins University (1876), who saw the University's task as to "make for less misery among poor, less ignorance in the schools less suffering in the hospital, less fraud in business, [and] less folly in politics" (Le Roy Long 1992, 184). In its effort to operationalize such a vision, Tec recognizes that there are various arguments to be considered with respect to the fundamental purpose of higher education. Is it intended to contribute to the development of human capital? Is its aim to generate economic wealth for society? The idea that resonates most with Tec is that the university's obligation is to form upstanding citizens who contribute different areas of knowledge to the solution of major societal problems (Aristizábal, Lozano, and Walker 2010). To do so, universities must ask and answer such questions as "What does a good citizen need to know in our day?" (Martha Nussbaum, cited in Aristizábal, Lozano, and Walker 2010).

In 1996, Tec articulated this vision by committing to prepare students who are contributing to social, economic, and political development and "improvement of their communities," and are "internationally competitive in their field of knowledge" (ITESM 2015). In 1997, Tec selected five campuses to pilot its Social and Citizenship Education Program, Querétaro among them. This marked the beginning of the Brigadas Comunitarias program. The pilot initiative included the design and delivery of training programs for Tec staff in areas of social service. One of the most important decisions made during this period was the addition of the word "community" to the social service programs that students are required to complete.

This was not just a matter of a name: the idea was that the students' work, for which they first needed to develop some basic competencies, should have a definite impact on the development of communities. In this way, social service was transformed from a noncommunity, vaguely controlled requirement into an essential component of an integrated social education plan to which a diverse set of academic criteria would be applied.

In 2005, Tec's mission was revised to emphasize the relationship between ethics, citizenship, and an individual's professional obligation to society at large:

Tecnológico de Monterrey's mission is to prepare upright, ethical people with a humanistic vision who are internationally competitive in their professional field and are citizens committed to the economic, political, social, and cultural development of their communities and the sustainable use of resources.

The substance of this mission has shaped the development of Tec's Social and Citizenship Education Program.[4] This program serves as a framework and supports all of the activities oriented toward educating students as citizens who are committed to the development of their communities.

Tec is part of the civic engagement movement in American higher education, aligning its mission with the Wingspread Declaration on the Civic Responsibilities of Research Universities (Boyte and Hollander 1999) as well as a seminal report by the Kellogg Commission entitled "Returning to Our Roots" (1999). In short, Tec believes in, and has taken action on, the idea that universities ought to "reclaim their public purposes" (Saltmarsh and Hartley 2011, 16).

Student Preparation

Brigadas Comunitarias introduces students to community life. The expectation is that students will work hand in hand with community members to identify and find solutions to development-related problems. The preparation of students consists of several distinct stages. It aims to achieve the following competencies: modify their ethical and civic behavior in a positive manner, build their ethical and civic knowledge, develop attitudes and skills that reflect respect for and sensitivity toward the social reality of their environment, and demonstrate a commitment to themselves and to society. First, students who want to participate in Brigadas Comunitarias undergo a thorough screening process that includes an evaluation of their academic performance and a skills assessment. Selected students are expected to demonstrate such skills as leadership, adaptability, teamwork, planning, and organization.

In the second stage, the planning stage, a team of six to eight students is assigned to a community. They make visits to the community, learning enough to generate an inclusive and legitimate development plan. Concurrently, students take preparatory courses. Their plan proposal is reviewed numerous times. The next stage is the experience itself. During winter and summer breaks, students spend a period of two to four weeks living and working in the assigned community. During this period of immersion, students implement their development plans in collaboration with the community. Students and community partners may make changes to the plan if needed. After the immersion period, each team reports the results of its work. The final presentation includes making recommendations to the community as well as the next group of students who have been assigned to work with the community. During the reporting stage, students also share their reflections and learnings.

Brigadas Comunitarias gives students an opportunity to understand the complexity of social problems that exist beyond the campus by letting them experience life in a nearby community. Students are taught by the "tree methodology," which requires them to explore root problems of society such as education, health care, and work. Next, they are asked to talk with the leaders of the community they were assigned to and identify the five major problems of the community. Their task is to work with community members to solve one or more of those problems. But it is not until they experiment with the implementation of their solution with the community that they really understand how social problems are interconnected and how an intervention in one area may aggravate conditions in another area.

Through Brigadas Comunitarias, Tec aims to transform participating students into agents of change committed to social development and respectful of human dignity. The program's methodology is based on the planning, implementation, and evaluation of initiatives that address the social needs of a community and that are organized with the participation of the beneficiaries. The involvement of the community is emphasized as a strength. It therefore facilitates the development of problem-solving skills in underprivileged conditions as well as the ability to apply professional skills through interdisciplinary collaboration, thus contributing to student self-awareness and community well-being.

Furthermore, the methodology of the program promotes the involvement of different stakeholders: government bodies, educational institutions, civil society, and the community. Thus a comprehensive view of the target social problem is generated, and strategies for change emerge from the collective knowledge of participants. For example, during one immersion period (in summer 2009) a group of seven students created what they later called *Fábrica Ecológica*, or "Ecological Factory." This is a business model that promotes the development of vulnerable groups through education and training for the production of different goods from waste materials. This model creates jobs, thereby changing the social reality of people by producing wealth and other direct impacts on the environment.

Development of Civic Capacities, Skills, and Knowledge

Student participation in the Brigadas Comunitarias program enhances their ability to learn about, and become sensitive to, the social, economic, and political reality of the community in which they are involved. Data culled from student field diaries, life histories, and Reporte de Experiencias Ciudadanas RECs, or Citizenship Experiences Report shows what students have learned and captures the experience in their own words.

At a very basic level, the immersion experience may prompt students to challenge the very notion of poverty. Students may question, for example, whether poverty is a condition of being without money or if it is more than that. A summer 2009 program participant reflected that she found poverty to be a collective mind-set, a "cultural sickness" whereby people are lacking power and the feeling that change is possible.

> Before Brigadas I used to think poverty was something physical, something you can see, and separate between the ones that have and the ones that have not. After spending a month in the community, knowing the people and their way of life, I understood that poverty is much more. It is like a cultural sickness; it has to do with empowerment and possibilities much more that it has to do with having or not.

Brigadas Comunitarias gives students an opportunity to participate in activities that complement their academic and professional training. In turn, the experience helps students develop an awareness and understanding of a new environment. The program takes students out of their "comfort zone." It also requires students to learn to communicate and work as part of a larger team. A winter 2010 student reflects:

> As a *brigadista* you have to take different preparation courses, and that gives you a plus, but I think that the time you spend in the community really takes you out of your comfort zone, and that makes you develop different skills that in another context would not be necessary. Living with your team makes communication and teamwork really acquire a new meaning, and learning how you can affect the ones around you gives you a different dimension of responsibility.

The immersion experience challenges student assumptions. It exposes students, many of whom are middle class, to the political and social reality of Mexico. By working with a community to solve pressing local problems, students come face-to-face with the questions of citizenship and democracy. In the words of a summer 2009 *brigadista*:

> Before Brigades, I used to think I knew about the political and social reality of Mexico; after my experience in the community, I got to really understand it. I wish it could be easier to explain, but, before being a *brigadista*, I knew things were hard and was aware of the problems that democracy faces in Mexico, but nothing was remotely near what I used to believe. Experimenting and living as an insider gave me a deeper comprehension of problems and their circumstances. Now I can see they have different dimensions and lots of complexity. It is not just a matter of voting or not.

Students' exposure to a new community develops their sensitivity toward others, allowing them to further develop their personal and professional knowledge. At first, students observe how they are different from the people in the community with whom they are working. Over time, however, they come to understand "universal" human values. A summer 2009 student notes:

> Brigadas gave me the opportunity to be part of a different space in which I do not live commonly, and they let me see that some values are universal, independent of the place you are. Dignity is a word that has different interpretations, but this experience helped me understand that its meaning has to come from people and their intrinsic value without regard to the place they came from.

Students demonstrate the knowledge, skills, and attitudes needed to respect people and their environment. They come to understand the value of realities different from the one they experience daily by getting out of their comfort zone and looking at social problems from the perspective of those who are most affected. A 2009 summer student notes:

> I believe that this experience leads you to the extreme. It pushes you because people in the community welcome you in their lives, making you part of their environment. So there is no place for you to be picky or question their culture. They offered you the best they have, and the things that were basic for you suddenly acquire a new meaning. You realize that you must respect the environment and culture that is welcoming you. You even learn to understand it and love it.

Students understand that their work, and every social work, requires continuity to be successful. If individuals use their knowledge to solve some of the community's problems but do not teach others how to fix the problems, if the problem surfaces again, the community will not be able to solve it themselves. A 2011 summer student powerfully highlights the relationship between professional development and citizenship:

> I remember that during my time in the community we discovered that the computers of the high school were misused and people did not know how to arrange them. The computers had different problems, some simple, some complicated, but me and another member of my team worked on it, and it took us three days to make them work. It was unbelievable when we had the opportunity to give computer classes to the students. I used my knowledge as a computer-engineering student, but I also understand that it was important to teach someone to maintain the computers, so we taught some students and teachers. Suddenly what I was studying in school had great impact and possibilities in the community.

Students participated in activities that promote the development of their civic responsibilities defined in Tec's mission. They understand that social development requires daily work and that it has to be done by sharing knowledge and working with people. A 2009 summer student said:

> I believe that as a student Brigadas changed me, though I never noticed until I graduated. This experience showed me that the ultimate purpose of knowledge is to share it with others. I know that every decision I make could have a good or bad impact. I know that I can make a difference. I just have to be conscious of my environment and the people around me and share what I love.

Students prove their capacity to plan, implement, and participate in coordinated actions in solidarity to solve some problems with the help of the community (related to the areas of impact of projects that have already been identified). This evolution occurs when they stop looking at social problems as statistics or numbers, seeing actual faces, names, and people. While they experience time in the community and live among the people, sharing ideas and searching for solutions, they get to understand local families and the culture. This leads them to ask important questions: Am I proposing the best solution? What if I am generating new needs instead of proposing a solution? Is my culture better than theirs? Why or why not? Am I supposed to change them or change my ideas to mimic those of the community?

Success and Challenges

The need to educate the citizens of the future is increasingly urgent. Brigadas Comunitarias aligns well with this overall idea, and the successes of the program in doing this could be replicable in different ways.

One way of assessing the program is by looking at the social mobility that communities have achieved by having students come and work alongside them. Communities acquire economic and financial skills, develop new solutions for their local programs, and become empowered to continue solving the problems they face on a day-to-day basis.

The second way of assessing the program is by looking at students' RECs where they write about their experiences and how their attitudes and conceptions of the world are transformed when they come face-to-face with their country's social conditions. Many are faced with a reality they were not aware existed, since the majority of Tec students come from the top of the social pyramid (middle- to high-income households) and are not in contact with poverty. (This is also mentioned in students' RECs.) Thanks to the program, they have the opportunity to understand and solve problems they did not realize needed addressing.

Students also gain a better understanding of the complexity of social problems and come to challenge stereotypes of the poor that circulate throughout society, such as "The poor are poor because they want to be." They also experience how empowerment can change a community and how history has marginalized some groups to such an extent that they do not have a voice any more. These learnings help students develop citizenship skills that grow from understanding a reality different from their own. Over time, the program cultivates a sense of civic professionalism; this attitude is the culmination of a set of objectives and skills that instill a passion for creating knowledge that serves the public good through influencing political structures, products, and texts in the service of the community (Boyte and Fretz 2010).

To assemble evidence of the civic competencies students gain, we began to measure and assess students' competency in the summer of 2009. What we measured the first year was citizen competency; 34 percent of the students scored medium to high competency. We then measured the same competency in summer 2014, and 70 percent of the students achieved medium or high levels of citizen competency. The doubling of this percentage in just six years speaks to the success of the program in a tangible way. One downside to these types of evaluations, however, is the high cost. The challenge to sustain the budget in order to continue doing these important evaluations continues year after year.

Another competency identified in the evaluation sessions each year is the concept of global citizen. According to Tec, a global citizen is "one who appreciates the importance of learning about the interconnected world [while] simultaneously seek[ing] to improve local conditions" (Battistoni, Longo, and Jayanandhan 2009). A global citizen is one who is prepared to understand, live successfully, and lead in an extremely diverse and complex world (Wilson, cited by Jacoby and Brown 2009). Brigadas Comunitarias, as one of Tec's social service programs, helps form students as global citizens by integrating a curriculum and service program that emphasizes the interconnectedness of the wicked problems plaguing so many communities around the globe.

Nowadays, it is not enough to simply acquire experience working in the community or doing social development work. It is also not sufficient to be sensitive and informed to acquire a social consciousness. Through Brigadas the student experiences a pedagogical process that includes completing social and political trainings, developing a sense of civic and personal responsibility, and fostering a zest for citizen participation and an eagerness to promote democracy and justice.

The biggest challenge for the program in the coming five years is to create student service opportunities in all fields of study. We want all students to experience and learn the values and habits associated with active citizenship:

- Direct citizen participation in the political system and the public realm
- Appreciation of socioeconomic equity and the common good

- Understanding and appreciation of democracy as a way of life and system of government
- Understanding of and respect for the law and a sense of justice
- Understanding the importance of local, as well as individual, action in the political realm for the creation of new and better public policy

However, the biggest challenge for Brigadas Comunitarias has to do with the continuity of the program and ensuring that the communities themselves are properly empowered by the experience. This issue is most pressing for the communities because students stay for only a short period of time. After their stay is finished, the community is without the Tec students for five months until they receive the new cohort. Sometimes the projects implemented during the summer continue for two extra months, but students usually do not return for another five months, besides maybe a few visits. This means that the projects tend to disappear and the new group of students has to reimplement them.

The continuity problem does not affect students' learning. The experience of living in the community remains with the student long after the program ends. For example, some students are interviewed years after their graduation and asked to explain how Brigadas changed their life, and to demonstrate it with some of the activities they do on a day-to-day basis. All of the interviewed graduated students declared that they want their professional work and collaborations to make Mexico and the world a better place.

At the end of their Brigadas experience, the students are asked to turn in various deliverables, including a field journal, a biography or life story of someone from the community, impact indicators of their Brigadas activities from their point of view, and a final report of their experience. The field journal provides a detailed account of the student's day-to-day activities. Some students use the journal to write down their feelings. In addition to the journal, the students are asked to choose one person in the community with whom they identify and write a biography on that person—his or her life history, problems, and dreams and aspirations. This activity helps students realize that people in the community are not that different from themselves.

The impact indicators are important because they help Tec understand what needs to be improved or changed from the students' point of view. For this deliverable, students are asked to evaluate every activity they took part in in the community and answer questions: How many people were impacted directly by their work? How many microprojects did they implement? How did the community react to the students, the projects, and the University?

As a final deliverable, the students are required to turn in a report on their overall experience. The report consists of essays about their Brigadas term where the students reflect on their own personal transformation, learnings, and the social experiences they encountered. The students also identify, in their own way, the systemic problems in the country and reflect on how their work has helped, or failed, to address the issue.

Looking Ahead

The creation of the social service program represents the establishment and use of innovative spaces for teaching and learning processes in favor of civic education. These spaces help students develop personality traits that are linked to social responsibility and are later put into practice throughout their personal and professional lives. In the context of their social service, the students build their own idea of citizenship, and assume the role of citizens who consider their actions in relation to others and the environment.

Some graduates have gone on to create their own social enterprises, such as EmpreDiem. EmpreDiem is an initiative that trains the community through the lens of social innovation to address the lack of access to tools for entrepreneurship and innovation.

Graduates also participate in social entrepreneurship activities and take on roles at various NGOs and other nonprofit organizations that seek to generate positive social impacts globally by finding and supporting sustainable early-stage enterprises. An example is SenseCube, an accelerator program for social start-ups. SenseCube supports innovative entrepreneurs, using digital technologies to mobilize communities and solve social and environmental issues. Students who do not actively participate with an NGO, civil organization, or social venture get involved by way of donations or promoting humanistic values and social thinking in their workplace.

Brigadas graduates students with critical thinking skills who are aware of social realities and possess a base of philosophical thought regarding public practice. Most importantly, Brigadas graduates are advocates of active citizenship, democracy, solidarity, freedom, the common good, justice, sustainability, and equality.

Brigadas Comunitarias has gone through a series of improvements. For example, it has incorporated the use of dialogue and deliberation in the program to improve the capacity of teachers, students, and community members who are working together to create solutions to social and economic problems. Deliberation and dialogue consist of genuine discussion that aims to create a space where participants can hear different points of view and analyze the advantages, disadvantages, and costs of one or more of the discussion points. Deliberative practices have been introduced to the program, as they are an excellent resource for developing citizenship skills in our students, while encouraging them to use critical thinking to form a base of mutual understanding between those participating (Wright 2009; Levine 2011; McCoy and Scully 2002).

This is an effort that includes many of the points mentioned above. We are working hard within academic departments to create a greater commitment to programs that seek to improve public life. Understanding the implications of being "professional citizens" has moved those of us working in these social service programs to be active at an institutional level and within academic departments.

After analyzing the results of the citizenship competencies evaluation in 2012, we have more clarity than ever in our purpose to form civic professionals. Working from the results of the evaluations, we have implemented structural changes. We stopped focusing exclusively on nurturing the civic engagement of students and have begun the daunting task of instilling civic engagement within the culture of academic departments.

To do this we have mobilized all available resources to generate public value from the University. Our efforts to promote the cocreation of social capital via a pedagogy that educates through service to the community cannot succeed without institutional help. If the professors, directors, and staff remain indifferent to the challenges that plague us within the program and those living in the communities we work with, our efforts will have only token value.

The task of forming civic professionals who are engaged in solving societal issues is shared by everyone. It is not only the task of older professors who have worked endlessly doing community work with students. We are hopefully entering a stage where departments themselves are engaged. We are moving from the individual faculty level to the collaborative and engaged department level. All of this feeds into our vision for a new kind of pedagogical model.

The institutional focus that we are developing helps integrate what we have achieved so far into the basic processes of the university, like student trainings, as well as enrollment and graduation requirements. This is the future of our program.

We believe that at Tecnológico de Monterrey, students and graduates are receiving a truly integral humanistic education, which is confirmed by the evidence contained in their classwork. It comes out in the reports on their community social service experiences (all students must turn in a report of their experience when they conclude their service, which is then graded against a rubric to determine the development of their citizenship competencies); in the results of the reflection workshops, which are presented in writing; in the graduate follow-up surveys administered periodically; in the social impact works undertaken by alumni who send us their news; in the social services they provide to communities through their own start-ups and companies; and in their work as civil servants, leading companies in their field, as active members of civil-society organizations, and as volunteers in many social causes. Within the academy, students, faculty, administrators, researchers, and directors must all accept this responsibility to act on behalf of the community as well as for themselves.

• • •

Mexico, like every country in the world, faces major political, economic, and social challenges. Solutions to these challenges cannot come from the same formulas that caused the problem. The university owes itself to society. It was born to provide a scientific and humanist approach to social development. Academic departments, colleges, staff, students, and professors are all actors in the process of society's social transformation. Brigadas Comunitarias is one of the efforts of the Tec citizenship program that provides a citizenship perspective to the University's educational model. What are the implications of providing a citizenship perspective to a university educational model? It provides the opportunity to continue to innovate citizenship training programs, to become a private university that generates public value for society through social service that helps solve Mexico's social problems. Brigadas Comunitarias supports teaching, learning, and knowledge generation to build a healthy and equitable society, with a social fabric strengthened through the practice of professions. Brigadas gives meaning and social relevance to the vision of Tec and to the curriculum. Brigadas removes indifference from those who only have a utilitarian purpose to their profession and life—individualists and [those] unmindful of the common good, democracy, and citizen participation. To us, it is very important to count on institutional support for this program. Having institutional support does not mean the task is over; it rather allows the program to form the citizens of today while simultaneously decreasing the vulnerability of those who suffer from inequalities and lack of opportunities for professional, social, and personal development. This program inspires us to carry on because it represents hope to those who envision a day when higher education fulfills its most important mission: Education to positively transform society.

—*Ernesto Benavides Ornelas*

NOTES

1. Tec has more than 100,000 students enrolled in high school, undergraduate, and graduate programs; 8,700 students studying abroad each year; and more than 8,000 faculty members.
2. Community Learning Centers are supported by the government, through the Secretaria de Desarrollo Social, or SEDESOL, and a nonprofit organization called Congregación de Carmelitas Descalzas.
3. According to Mexico's Ministry of Public Education, approximately 780,000 higher education students complete more than 374.4 million hours of service every year.
4. Today, Tec's mission statement is shorter, yet remains unchanged in terms of substance and intent. It is "to prepare people with an entrepreneurship spirit, human sense, and to be internationally competitive in their professional field."

REFERENCES

Aristizábal Boni, A., Lozano Águilar, J. F., and Walker M. 2010. Educación superior desde el enfoque de capacidades: Una propuesta para el debate. *Revista Electrónica Interuniversitaria de Formación del Profesorado* 13(3): 123–131.

Battistoni, R. M., Longo, N. V., and Jayanandhan, S. 2009. Acting locally in a flat world: Global citizenship and the democratic practice of service-learning. *Journal of Higher Education Outreach and Engagement* 13(2): 89–109.

Boyte H., and Fretz, E. 2010. *Civic professionalism*. Https://www6.miami.edu/cce/Resources/Civic_professionalism.pdf.

Boyte, H., and E. Hollander, 1999. "Wingspread Declaration on Renewing the Civic Mission of the American Research University." Http://compact.org/wingspread-declaration-on-the-civic-responsibilities-of-research-universities.

Cherwitz, R. A., Sullivan, C. A., and Stewart, T. 2002. Intellectual entrepreneurship and outreach: Uniting expertise and passion. *Journal of Higher Education Outreach and Engagement* 7(3): 123–133.

CONEVAL. 2014. Medición de la pobreza en México y en las Entidades Federativas 2014. Consejo Nacional de Evaluación de la Política de Desarrollo Social. Http://www.coneval.org.mx/Medicion/Documents/Pobreza%202014_CONEVAL_web.pdf.

Conroy, N. 2012. *Applying the entrepreneurial model of experiential learning in political science courses to encourage civic engagement.* Http://papers.ssrn.com/s013/papers.cfm?abstract_id=2002689.

INEGI. 2010. Censo de Población y Vivienda 2010. Instituto Nacional de Estadística, Geografía e Investigación. Http://www.inegi.org.mx/est/contenidos/proyectos/ccpv/cpv2010/.

ITESM. 2015. Filosofia, Misión hacia el 2005. Http://www.itesm.mx/wps/wcm/connect/Campus/CVA/Cuernavaca/Acerca+del+campus/Filosofia+Institucional/Misiones+anteriores/Mision+hacia+el+2005//.

Jacoby, B., and Brown, N. C. 2009. Preparing students for global civic engagement. In B. Jacoby, ed., *Civic engagement in higher education: Concepts and practices*. San Francisco: Jossey-Bass.

Le Roy Long, E. Jr. 1992. *Higher Education as a Moral Enterprise*. Washington, DC: Georgetown University Press.

Levine, P. 2011. Teaching and learning civility. *New Directions for Higher Education* 2010 (152): 11–17.

McCoy, M. L., and Scully, P. L. 2002. Deliberative dialogue to expand civic engagement: What kind of talk does democracy need? *National Civic Review* 19(2): 117-126.

National Conference on Citizenship. 2011. Civic health and unemployment: Can engagement strengthen the economy? Issue brief, September 16.

National Task Force on Civic Learning and Democratic Engagement. 2012. A crucible moment: College learning and democracy's future. Http://www.aacu.org/civic_learning/crucible/index.cfm.

Parada Barrera, C. S. 2009. Hacia un nuevo concepto de ciudadanía global. *Revisto via Iuris* 7: 98-111.

Saltmarsh, J., and Hartley, M. 2011. To serve a larger purpose. In J. Saltmarsh and M. Hartley, eds., *Engagement for democracy and the transformation of higher education*. Philadelphia: Temple University Press.

SEDESOL. 2013. Unidades Micro Regionales Reporte 2013. Http://www.microrregiones.gob.mx/zap/rezago.aspx?entra=pdzp&ent=22&mun=00.

Steinberg, K. S., Hatcher, J. A., and Bringle, R. G. 2011. Civic-minded graduate: A north star. *Michigan Journal of Community Service Learning* 18(1): 19-33.

Wright, W. 2009. Deer, dissension, and dialogue: A university-community collaboration in public deliberation. *Journal of Higher Education Outreach and Engagement* 13(2): 17-44.

The Activate Program in Glasgow, Scotland: A New Way of Thinking and Being in the World

Margaret Fraser and Helen Martin

Rosie is a single mum who worked part-time in a low-paid administrative job in her local Glasgow community. She was also a member of a local action group offering activities to children, helping them stay safe. Content with her life, although struggling financially, she "just got on with it," moving forward, surviving day to day. One day, she got the opportunity to attend an Activate course being delivered in her community. She had heard about the program before, and it ticked necessary boxes for her: it provided care for her young son while she studied; and her pals from local organizations, PEEPS (Parents of East End Primary Schools) and FAB (For All Bridgeton) in the East End of Glasgow, would be coming along with her. When later prompted to reflect on her Activate experience, Rosie explained,

> It changed my life. I never once thought that I would be clever enough to do this. I really enjoyed the weekly sessions with my group and learning new things and making sense of my own stuff in my community. It was good that we didn't always agree with each other's point of view; it made it more interesting and challenging hearing what others thought about asylum seekers, refugees, and poverty, for example. I changed my mind so many times I was dizzy! It was great that our children had the play workers to watch over them when we were studying. When we met up at break time, they always wanted to know what we were doing, so they became involved also. They started to voice their own thoughts on the issues we spoke about and wanted to know why the world was like this.

Rosie, who "never dared dream" she "would or could go to university," gained confidence and learned new skills by way of Activate. Her experience in the Activate course, which is an element of the Community Development Programme, empowered her to question her life, her decisions, and her values. Reflecting on her new way of thinking and being in the world, Rosie said,

> I began to value other things in life. My ambitions changed, and my love of people grew. I [saw] beyond the disability, the clothes people wore, the first impressions. I began to value everyday interactions,

sharing and learning with people . . . more than I valued being able to buy the most recent fashion item. I measured success in a completely different way where I valued small changes as much as major ones and people over things.

Rosie graduated from the University of Glasgow with a bachelor of arts in community development in 2010. She is now the project manager of a local community and heritage center not far from where she lives. According to Rosie,

> None of this would have been a possibility if I had not joined the Activate course. My life has come full circle, as I am now an Activate tutor—can you believe it! My passion and commitment for the course and the people like myself who take up the opportunity is huge. It changed my life, and to think I might have some part to play in doing that for others is fantastic. I love it—I just love it! I am currently being mentored by the University and the more experienced tutors on the program. I think I have sent a really powerful message out to my son and other family members that education is for the likes of us also.

The University of Glasgow

Rosie's story is possible because an "ivory tower," which John Fallon describes as "a world of academic superiority, even snobbery . . . disconnected from day-to-day realities, a closed environment in which knowledge and intellect is the preserve of the self-selecting, privileged few" (2011), broke that trend. The University of Glasgow is home to the Activate course, which is part of the BA Community Development Programme. The course brings people working in the field of community development, in a paid or unpaid capacity, together to learn from each other by reflecting on local community practices.

Founded in 1451, the University of Glasgow is the fourth oldest university in the English-speaking world. Its impressive history includes breaking new ground in medicine, science, and industry across the world, as well as top positioning in the QS World University Rankings, and membership in the Russell Group of leading UK research universities. Today it enrolls more than 28,000 undergraduate and postgraduate students from around the world. Its mission "to undertake world leading research and to provide an intellectually stimulating learning environment that benefits culture, society and the economy," aligns with Glasgow 2020, a global strategy document produced in October 2010.

The Activate course exemplifies the University's mission to provide a learning environment that benefits society. The idea for Activate, in a way, began in 1997 when the West of Scotland Accreditation and Training group was established, primarily made up of community practitioners and academics. Its purpose was to provide learning opportunities for communities in greatest need. In response, the Community Development team—those charged with overseeing the bachelor of arts Community Development Programme at the University—designed and delivered the Community Work Skills foundational course. After five years of teaching the course, the Community Development team and tutors met to review it based on feedback provided by previous students and tutors. This process quickly revealed the tutors' commitment and drive, over and above the normal duties required of academic staff, to bring Activate to local communities. Their enthusiasm to create and deliver a course that offers new opportunities for those engaged in community action explains, in large part, why the Activate program emerged and continues to grow.

Located in the College of Social Science's School of Education, the Activate course engages some of the most marginalized communities in Glasgow and the surrounding regions in Scotland. It focuses especially on those who are working to bring about change in their local communities. These community activists and volunteers have campaigned tirelessly to put an end to top-down initiatives. Additionally, they are forced to put up with a "make do and mend" attitude from those in positions of power, as they advocate for a shift in moving beyond "treating symptoms" to collective community action. Activate students may be viewed as "nontraditional" learners, in the sense that they are all adults who come from and live in so-called disadvantaged areas. This background means they are likely to have experienced a range of personal, social, economic, and educational disadvantages related to their circumstances. Because they are also adults who have decided to try to bring about changes in their communities, they are learners who are highly self-motivated in everyday life, though they may not necessarily be academically astute. Many require more support than traditional learners, but they also know how to make demands on providers and educators to ensure that the learning is relevant to them and has wider social purpose; their savvy and know-how allow them to create opportunities for their own self-development. This combination of practical courage and intellectual uncertainty calls for a dynamic pedagogy that is continuously negotiated between learners, tutors, and university- and community-based partners.

The approach is Freirean (based on the work of Paulo Freire), in the sense that the relationship between student teacher is reciprocal and the values are congruent with the National Occupational Standards for Community Development. This ensures that Activate takes the lived experience of those participating in the course as its starting point for discussion and discovery. The course begins and is built on the tenet that everyone has something to contribute. This way of working is congruent with the Asset Based Community Development (ABCD) approach defined by John McKnight and Jody Kretzmann (1993), who challenge the traditional approach of solving urban problems by focusing on the needs and deficiencies of neighborhoods. Instead, they take the view that communities have an abundance of assets and are able to steer the development process themselves by identifying, using, and leveraging community strengths. They see this as building on the skills of local residents, the power of local associations, and the supportive functions of local institutions; all of this is made possible with the development of relationships and a sense of community, similar to the notion of social capital defined by Robert Putnam (2000). He describes this as building, bridging, and bonding capital. Activate is a strong example of this in action, as it creates the opportunity for people to come together across age, cultural, geographic, and social barriers to participate in meaningful dialogue for change and growth. It creates the opportunity for people to "share a space" in a society that is becoming increasingly insular and enclosed. It fights against the concept of individualization and, conversely, promotes local networks and reciprocity that continue far beyond the course. Students regularly refer to their participation as being "life changing."

Activate is a way of developing community capacity by giving the students an opportunity to reflect on their practice in light of basic community work values and principles. It builds on the experience of those who work in the community, in either a paid or unpaid capacity. Although the

Figure. Areas Covered in a Typical Activate Course

Key concepts:
- What is community?
- Values and principles of community development
- Power and participation
- Social analysis
- Local and global issues

Practice approaches:
- Learning for change
- Popular education
- Group work/identifying needs
- Community conflict
- Evaluation

---

teaching and learning is informal and participative, it challenges students to think more deeply and critically about their community. Some of the areas covered in a typical Activate course are listed in the figure. In each course students will undertake a number of tasks that include a short essay exploring discrimination, a community investigation, and a presentation on group work practice. In short, Activate opens the doors of the ivory tower to local community organizations and their members. It provides an opportunity for community workers (paid or unpaid) to work together to change their way of thinking and to take action on issues affecting them and the wider community.

Since 1995, the BA Community Development Programme has had many guises, but in every configuration it has held firm in its belief in the values and principles that underpin community development processes. These values include working and learning together, equality and anti-discrimination, community empowerment, and social justice, to name a few. These values inform and strengthen our commitment to an approach that ensures we raise awareness of the systems and institutions that maintain the status quo. Activate reinforces the view that education should be transformative. Accordingly, Margaret Ledwith (2007) maintains that for work to be considered transformative it needs to get to the root causes of societal ills, not simply perpetuate the hegemonic nature of society as it is. Activate attempts to do this.

City of Glasgow, Scotland

The University of Glasgow's main campus is located in the West End of the city. Its tower is a beacon in the Glasgow skyline, visible from many parts of the city and one of Glasgow's main landmarks. The West End houses numerous upscale hotels and restaurants frequented by tourists. The area includes the largest museum and art gallery in the city and is surrounded by Kelvingrove Park, which offers a variety of leisure activities and plenty of public space for all ages. The West End is known to be one of the most vibrant parts of the city and is rich in cultural diversity, hosting its own annual festival attracting thousands of people each year. House prices within this area are among the highest in the city and would be out of reach for ordinary working-class people. This area stands in stark contrast to the North and East End areas of Glasgow, Scotland's largest city. In these communities, people have poorer health and lower life expectancy. Once sites of heavy industry and full employment, they have declined significantly over the decades, mainly due to Westminster national policies and the denationalizing of public services and industries. As a result, unemployment, food insecurity, and chronic illness are high (e.g., workless households, 70 percent; food insecurity, 45 percent; and chronic illness, 38 percent).

Ng Homes, Community Partner

North Glasgow Housing Association (ng homes) is the largest community-based housing association in Glasgow. It is also one of the University's main community partners through its continued support in bringing Activate to the north of the city. Ng homes manages and maintains approximately seven thousand properties in the north of Glasgow, an area also characterized by unused and derelict land, low educational attainment, and lack of hope. The vision for ng homes is for a new North Glasgow, one that is "a great place to live, learn, work, visit and invest in." Ng homes closely adheres to the Scottish government's Regeneration Strategy, which looks to encourage innovative strategies to reform the way in which mainstream resources are used to support vulnerable communities. A key element of the strategy is a stronger focus on community-led regeneration. It is also aligned with the recommendations of the Christie Commission, which aims to support and empower individuals and communities by involving them in the design and delivery of public services.

As a social housing landlord, ng homes' remit is to be "more than bricks and mortar." It is expected to provide a "wider role" in society through direct community involvement. The governance of ng homes is tenant-led by way of a voluntary management committee that includes elected local residents, a member from the city council, and academics. Additionally, there are high levels of community involvement through a number of resident committees, focus groups, and projects consisting of participants representative of all age groups and cultural backgrounds. Impressively, ng homes has charitable status, and its profits are directed back into the community. It has established a subsidiary company, ng2, which over the past four years has created employment opportunities for more than seventy-five people, including young people and long-term unemployed.

Ng homes has a dedicated regeneration team using an ABCD approach to working alongside people in communities to identify, and contribute to, solutions. All activities are designed to strengthen the bonds within multicultural neighborhoods: reaching out across ages, cultures, and faiths to build stronger and safer communities. Programs include sporting and football activities across all age groups; environmental activities linked to recycling, fuel poverty, and food growing; and cultural activities for older people and various cultural groups. The Build, Bridge, Bond program brings an emphasis on volunteering and food insecurity, community engagement activities, and learning programs, including the Activate program in partnership with Glasgow University. Funding to support community regeneration programs is accessed from a variety of sources such as the Scottish government, the Big Lottery Fund, and the Glasgow City Council, in addition to ng homes' own contribution.

As noted earlier, the area in which ng homes operates is challenged by a number of "wicked issues" such as high unemployment, crime, alcohol and substance abuse, poverty, and the cascading effects of these. Therefore, partnerships and coproduction are vital in providing effective solutions. Dzur (2013, 6) notes that "wicked issues have no one dimensional response." He goes on to say that "a strategic advantage trench democracy, performed by practitioners at the local or institutional level, can improve lives immediately because it does not depend on the lengthy grinding of legal or political machinery." Ng homes concurs with the idea that partnerships/networks with communities across sectors are key to creating sustainable and resilient communities with local people at the center. Their involvement with the University of Glasgow through Activate has been a key way to promote active citizenship that empowers individuals to become more confident in coming together to solve common problems. They have also worked closely to connect people with other networks and have been proactive in providing accessible space for groups to come together. This links into the notion of coproduction. We are reminded of this central issue raised by Mathews (2012) who speaks about community action and creating democratic systems of development that empower citizens to leverage support from local institutions.

The strategic impetus of ng homes' commitment to regeneration and to the partnership with University of Glasgow to develop Activate was driven by key individuals: Chief Executive Robert Tamburrini and Director of Regeneration John Devine, together with the Voluntary Board. They have been instrumental in developing a number of partnerships and could be described as the "democratic professionals" outlined by Dzur. He notes

> the alterations democratic professionals are making to their organisations; they take their public responsibilities seriously and listen carefully to those outside their walls and those at all levels of their internal hierarchy in order to foster physical proximity between formerly separated individuals, encourage co-ownership of problems previously sees as beyond lay people's ability or realm of responsibility, and seek out opportunities for collaborative work between lay people and professionals (2013, 6).

The Regeneration Manager at ng homes, Margaret Fraser, has played a pivotal role in opening up the "ivory tower" to the wider Glasgow community. Margaret was born and brought up in one of the poorer areas of Glasgow, and her expectations, and indeed those of her family, were that her destiny would include working in a low-skill job. The opportunity and choice to even think about being educated at university was not one that would have been considered. It was only in her forties, working in a community-controlled housing organization, that she had the opportunity to attend university to undertake a housing degree. It was this experience that awakened the notion in her that the "ivory tower" could be breached and its powers used to benefit local, marginalized communities. What became evident to her was that people did not lack ambition, but rather that they lacked the opportunity and the tools to act on that ambition. Margaret directed her focus to the people of ng homes and North and East Glasgow who were volunteering and taking an active part in their communities.

She first heard about Activate when a leaflet was popped through her door. It caught her interest as it focused on community development, an area she was involved in as a volunteer in a youth and community group. She was unable to take part in Activate at the time because she was working full-time and the course was being delivered during the day. A few years later, however, she was employed at Playbusters, a collaborative program with housing associations and social inclusion partnerships to address the lack of quality play areas for children in the East End. Her role at Playbusters was to drive forward the organization to become community-led, "to bring people together from a variety of areas and work to increase service provision." As Playbusters developed, the confidence of those involved grew. Margaret recalls,

I reached a point where I stood back and watched in amazement the amount of time that parents and others were giving to their communities. It was clear that people were highly motivated and wanted to see both physical and social improvements. A number of those involved were unemployed, stay-at-home mums and dads and young people. I could see their skills and their ability to make a difference. It occurred to me that many of them were natural community workers. I was keen to ensure that local people got the chance to explore and widen their skills and knowledge, so I contacted the University in early 2005 to discuss the possibility of Activate coming to the East End.

Margaret began scheduling initial meetings and information sessions with community and university members to discuss the program and offer community members the chance to ask questions. Margaret and Helen, a lecturer at the University of Glasgow, invited a former Activate participant from another district to participate in one of the meetings. Vivienne was a single mum of three young children. She shared with the group how participating in the course had opened up new opportunities and challenges for her following the sudden death of her partner. She told the audience that she was now in her first year at the University of Glasgow, studying to earn a bachelor of arts in community development; something she said she never thought possible for "someone like her." Similarly to Margaret, she came from a poor, working-class environment that held little or no expectation that anyone from the area would amount to much, let alone think of pursuing higher education. Her testimony was moving and likely motivated many community members in attendance to enroll in Activate. Margaret's determination and commitment to bring Activate to the East End of Glasgow delivered fast results. In the first six months, three Activate courses were delivered with more than forty community members successfully completing their course. As part of their participation, students were invited to participate in a first-year Community Development class at the university. We believe this feature of the course was an important aspect of dismantling the "ivory tower" concept and for challenging the popular mantra "The University is not for the likes of me."

In that first year when Activate was introduced to Glasgow's East End, sixteen students secured a place at the University. Thirteen of them completed their bachelor of arts in community development, and the other three earned a national qualification in community development. Moreover, the local community's culture began to change, in Margaret's eyes. She felt that community members began expressing their views more freely and that their enthusiasm soared as they were better equipped to deal with problems strategically. According to Margaret,

> The culture change impressed me so much that I decided to go back to Glasgow University to study for my BA in community development. Although I was managing a community organization, I did not have a formal qualification in this field of work. I graduated with my BA in community development in 2011.

In 2012, Margaret moved into her current post with ng homes. As regeneration manager, part of her role was to build up community capacity and to work with internal and external partners to develop a community regeneration strategy. At an Activate awards ceremony, the chief executive and director of regeneration from ng homes were invited to attend and hear the personal stories of those who had participated. The ceremony was so moving that since then ng homes has secured funding for, and developed new partnerships with, Activate and the wider university community.

Ng homes and Activate are natural allies with common values. Both rely on an asset-based approach to regeneration, which emphasizes connecting people from different backgrounds, those recovering from substance abuse, and representatives of public agencies such as the police. Through ng homes and Activate, people who would not normally have the opportunity to "share space together" now study community development and explore community matters from a diverse range of perspectives. Through its partnership with ng homes, Activate has engaged over 90 people across fifteen local organizations. Three of these participants will soon earn a bachelor of arts in community development at the University of Glasgow. Others are studying at Glasgow Kelvin College for the national qualification in community development, while some have increased their volunteering role within the community. The university views the role of ng homes as being crucial to the success and growth of Activate in North Glasgow. This has been reciprocated with an invitation to Helen Martin to join one of the strategic management boards of ng homes.

The Activate and Ng Homes Partnership

Since its official launch in 2002, Activate has seen a variety of different partnerships develop, some on an ad hoc basis, and others more sustained (as is the case with ng homes). The process begins, crudely speaking, when local organizations approach the university to "buy in" to Activate. In some cases the organization will directly meet the costs of participation, and, in other cases, costs are met by Scottish government sources or charities.

Successful partnerships are built on shared values such as respect, trust, and reciprocity (Putnam 2000). When partners operate out of a set of shared values, both sides have common ground upon which to exchange ideas, experiences, and resources. Being "on the same page" is crucial to the development and sustainability of the partnership. A common sense of purpose enables people to journey without fear of "otherness," to see each other as part of a greater whole. Furthermore, strong partnerships foster growth and expansion by attracting new partners to come on board.

In the early days of Activate, the only educational pathway from Activate was for students to move directly into full-time study with the BA Community Development Programme at the University of Glasgow. However, this leap was considered by some as being too big, partly due to a lack of self confidence in their academic ability as well as other factors such as dependent care responsibilities. As a result of these concerns a partnership was developed with the local Further Education College (Glasgow Kelvin College) to provide less-intensive options for participants to continue their education. Today, Activate and ng homes work very closely with the College, which has campuses in both the North and East End of Glasgow. They have provided an alternative route for Activate students to continue their studies by providing national qualification (NC) or higher national qualification (HNC) courses in community development. This gradual approach has been fundamental to providing means for Activate students to build their confidence in their academic ability and empowers them to join the university community. Additionally, NC and HNC qualifications enable students to apply for direct entry into the second year of the bachelor of arts in community development degree program at the University of Glasgow.

From an ng homes perspective, Activate provides added value to the development of new partnerships. With students from as many as fifteen community-based organizations participating together on an Activate course, new partnerships and networks have emerged. These include the Bridges program, which is Scotland's specialist agency: supporting the social, educational, and economic integration of refugees, asylum seekers, migrants, and anyone for whom English is a second language living in Glasgow. Furthermore, there is a huge improvement in communication among staff representing the various organizations because of the common bond—Activate. The community development scene is not only expanding, there is a sense that there is a culture shift within local organizations. Previously community organizations at times acted in a very parochial and insular manner, fearful of other organizations stealing ideas, as they all compete locally for ever declining funding streams. Today, there are clear examples of improved relationships being developed; these include improved working relationships between organizations and between organizations and individuals.

Community volunteers from the Activate courses now work with a number of local groups. An example of this is a local mum who helps out at a youth activity program with ng homes. After undertaking the Activate course and participating in her "community investigation" task, mapping services for people with disabilities, she now volunteers two days a week at a local disability center. This is a further example of the "bridging and bonding" power of social capital, as this work takes her out of her own geographical area to support the development of herself and others around her. There are examples of people making changes to their own attitudes and perceptions after being exposed to different ideas and ways of looking at things through Activate. This partly comes about because of the rich diversity of the students found in any one course; this in itself challenges the stereotypical attitude and prejudices that a number of students may carry into the course, often as a result of being influenced by life circumstances and, in most cases, the media.

Students: Unlocking the Ivory Tower

The students who participate in the Activate program buck the trend for the traditional university student. Most of the students will not have engaged in formal education for many years, and in many cases will have had negative experiences of education. Therefore, there is a real need to break down barriers to learning; this is why the starting point is crucial as a means of gently reintroducing them to academic activity.

The students, in the main, will have viewed studying at the University of Glasgow as something other people do. Quite often we would hear the university is "not for the likes of me!" or "They wouldn't let the likes of me in there." Many people living in Glasgow view attending the University as an unreachable goal. They do not see it as a place that would value their local knowledge, knowledge from experience that is both relational and contextual (Hoyt 2013). However, now that we are seeing a shift in culture in these communities, people are beginning to think education *is* within their grasp, given the right set of circumstances. These include breaking down barriers people face, such as child and dependent care responsibilities, transportation, and cost. One strategy for dealing with the issue of childcare is to negotiate with potential students—to figure out a suitable time and place within the community for people to meet and to also provide a crèche (play school) if needed. Margaret explains,

> Place is hugely important. Although students are studying with University of Glasgow, the fact that the program is delivered within the local community is important, as there are many barriers to attending university, including affordability of transport, childcare, and confidence in entering the physical building that many see as an ivory tower, particularly for those who have had a negative learning or educational experience. Therefore, Activate continues to be delivered in community settings, such as community centers, church halls, youth clubs, and other appropriate community space. Students are provided with study bags, with [a] university logo as symbolic, reinforcing the message that they are studying with the University.

Taking the Activate course to the "heart of the community" has gone a long way in supporting this cultural shift in terms of making a statement that the "ivory tower" is accessible to the "likes of us." The symbol of the "study bag" itself has shifted somewhat: previously, people would have been reluctant to use it, as it would indicate they were stepping out of an area that was expected of them, or "getting above their station in life." It is now viewed by participants with a sense of pride and belonging. This has led to what we would term the "ripple effect," as neighbors, families, and volunteers are affected positively by the change they see in others to the extent that they want to participate themselves. This was the case with Billy, as demonstrated in his story.

Billy and His Daughter, Abbie

Billy is a thirty-one-year-old lone parent living with his young daughter Abbie, aged five, in the Springburn area of North Glasgow. The area was once a thriving community with an abundance of heavy industry employing many hundreds of local people. As in many other formerly industrialized areas in the UK and beyond, these businesses have either closed or moved their operations. In their wake they have left large areas of neglected, polluted, and disused land; high unemployment; and a number of social problems that are recognized as "wicked issues." Billy had previously worked in the building trade before getting laid off. He first started volunteering with a local charity and also helped out at his daughter's nursery in its gardening program. This gave him a different focus and he quickly realized that he enjoyed being involved in community activities. Having heard about the Activate course from others in the community who had participated in previous courses, he could see for himself how it had affected them and became interested in finding out more. He later attended an information event where he got to meet the Activate coordinator and tutors from the University of Glasgow and hear firsthand from other people who had completed Activate. When asked what he thought about the program, Billy said:

> It gave me a lot to think about. It opened me up to different views, and I worked with people from different areas and backgrounds. It made me want to do more in my community, and I started to get involved

even more. I started volunteering and helped to form a group called Row for Shore, a boat-building project for the local community. I recently started volunteering with Inner Circle (a men's group) and we have made contact with another men's group in Maryhill, UNIS (United Nations in Scotland). We have worked together with a group of Syrian men on a book of short stories of our experience which was funded by Scottish Refugee Council and has been reported nationally through Sky News as an example of integration.

Reflecting on the difference Activate made to him personally, Billy explains how the program has transformed his perspective on life and his relationships:

> It's changed the way I think and how I communicate. Previously I looked out for myself and didn't think much about others. I am more open-minded now and think more about what is happening in my community. I have made new friends and volunteer across a number of projects, including ng homes' Link Up program.[1] If you had said to me five years ago that I would be volunteering in the community, I wouldn't have believed it. But I have discovered that community work really motivates me. Now I think about why people are in situations and what can be done to support them. It's made me look at my own life, and I don't want to go back to working on building sites. I've realized I get a buzz out of supporting people. Even the little things matter—showing someone that you care and will listen to them. Most importantly, the changes in my own life have had a positive impact on my daughter. She's always telling people that her dad is at college and that she is proud of me. She's in primary school now, and she laughs when I tell her I have homework because she says I'm too old for homework. So now, here I am studying at college, and the feedback from my tutors has been great. I've passed all of my assessments so far. When I am finished my HNC I want to go on to university. Never in a million years did I think I would ever be going to university—except maybe as a janitor. I'm excited about where my life is going and what I could achieve. I've never felt that before.

In many ways, Billy's story is not unique. One of the most poignant stories from the Activate program comes from single working mum, Marie. When asked what impact she felt Activate had on her, she replied that the biggest impact was experienced by someone who wasn't even in the classroom. She explained that when she went home at night after class, often to complete a reflective diary entry, her son would ask questions about what she was doing and why. Before long he began talking about his ambition to one day go to the University to study like his mum. For her this was a conversation that she believed would never have taken place if not for her participation in Activate. Freire (1972) refers to this as breaking through a culture of silence. Here we have an example of shaking off the myth that "education is not for the likes of us," which is often perpetuated by institutional snobbery and elitism, as previously defined by Fallon (2011). Evidence of this can be witnessed in the story of Willie and Sylvia.

Willie and Sylvia

Willie and Sylvia are born and bred Eastenders, married and parents of seven children, with five grandchildren. In an attempt at keeping the children safe, Willie set up local football sessions, often at his own expense, regularly taking kids away from their environment and therefore away from potential trouble. He volunteered in the local youth project that some of his own attended. He worked part-time as a porter for a local mental health hospital. Sylvia was a stay-at-home mum.

Willie heard about Activate through Playbusters, where he carried out some youth work, and joined a local course. He admitted he was near scared to death about returning to education, as he had not had a good educational experience in his earlier life. He flourished in the course and managed to secure some paid sessional and part-time hours with some local youth projects. Upon completing Activate, he said, there was a fire in his belly and he didn't want to stop learning. Not convinced he could manage university study just yet, he secured a place at college to continue to study community development, with the intention of joining university at a later date. In the meantime, with some of their children growing up and leaving home, he convinced Sylvia to join the Activate course that was about to start in their area. She came along and after a while began to actively participate in the discussions, finding a voice inside her and realizing that her opinions mattered.

In December 2014, Sylvia graduated from the University of Glasgow with a BA in community development (with distinction). She has secured paid employment with the local youth project as well as work with the Glasgow Disability Alliance. She volunteers as a board member in a local women's project, Say Women, which supports young women affected by sexual abuse. Willie is in his final year of study at the University and has continued to work with young people in a paid capacity on a sessional basis along with some volunteering hours. He continues to work part-time as a porter in a local hospital, and volunteers with a local faith group supporting asylum seekers and other groups. His goal is to work full-time in the community development field when he graduates in 2015. Their story is a source of local pride, hope, and inspiration to many people in the community and especially to their own children, two of whom are now studying: one at Glasgow Kelvin College and the other at West of Scotland University. In a recent conversation, Sylvia said,

> If I hadn't done the Activate course none of this would have happened. It opened my eyes to what is going on around me as well as presenting many new opportunities and challenges. It has given us some financial security—we've never had that.

Willie added,

> Activate changed my whole life and that of my family; it challenged my way of thinking and being in the world. I recommend Activate to everyone I meet in my community and beyond. I just want them to have this experience. I just need to convince them to take the chance—it's worth the risk. It was magic.

Tutors: The Key

There is no doubt that an essential component to the success of Activate lies in the hands of its tutors. All have many years of experience in community development practice and are therefore firm believers in the values and principles that underpin community development work. They are advocates of local people being able to define and decide for themselves issues, concerns, and solutions in their own communities. All of the tutors started out in circumstances very similar to those of the students they now work alongside. They all share the belief that people living in conditions of deprivation and poverty don't lack ambition or ability, but opportunity. Tutors therefore see Activate as a stepping stone in the right direction for those who take the opportunity to engage in the course.

Tutors take on a vital role by encouraging critical thinking in the group. Their involvement creates a course that leads to individual, collective, and social opportunities for transformation, as demonstrated in the personal stories. As mentioned earlier in this chapter, the approach lends itself to the Freirean education process that is based upon the development of colearners. In this framework, the teacher is a student and vice versa. Participants are not simply passive learners being told what they "should know," and this is epitomized by the exploration of generative themes: learning that comes out of the students' own experiences through critical reflection and action. This is carried on through the democratization of learning and by valuing the student's knowledge in addition to academic thought. These attitudes, compounded with the notion of learning for change, learning that enables action, in turn transform the lived experience of learners and their communities (Beck and Martin 2005). The aforementioned concepts are the key principles that tutors operate with and embrace in their delivery.

The relationship between student and tutor is crucial: for many of the students this will be a huge step back into education after many years away and, quite often, after being written off by the education system. Therefore, as mentioned previously, the process used to engage a student is of great importance. Starting from where the students are at in terms of their own lived experience demonstrates a commitment to a Freirean approach to education (1972), which underpins the learning from a university perspective.

Relationships are crucial in such a process, and students commented on this on numerous occasions. A feeling of "We are all in this together" was evident in the support and encouragement students gave and received. This is the community development way, an appreciation of what people bring in terms of their own stories as a basis for transformative change, the telling of untold stories that Freire (1976) refers to as the beginning of emancipatory practice. These stories can only be told if there is a deep respect and trust present in the room and is reciprocated, tutor included. This would also be an example of community development values in action.

Tutors also work closely with the community organizations that are providing the courses in order to ensure they are equipped to offer students additional support outside of the learning environment. They have commented on a noticeable change of culture within the community. People are actively discussing Activate principles and practices. Conversations often include new friends, theorists such as Freire, Saul Alinsky, and John McKnight.

In order for the tutors to carry out their roles effectively there is a need to create an environment whereby they feel supported and valued. This is done in various ways; regular nourishment times together, providing the opportunity to explore what drives and energizes us to be the best, have helped maintain the motivation and commitment of tutors. The sharing of time and resources between tutors has helped create a very strong bond. Furthermore, creating a space that encourages both personal and group reflection has been very beneficial. In the last year the pool of tutors has increased with arrival of two new tutors, both of whom are graduates of the BACD program and started out by attending an Activate course in their own community four or five years previous.

Challenges

Activate is a relatively small program, albeit with a big impact on communities. However, a consideration we have is this: to what extent is this course viewed as an important function within the institution in comparison to the traditional programs of the University? For example, how does it stack up in comparison to the arts and sciences? What credibility does it have within the higher echelons of the University and what exposure and profile does it have within the University itself? These are questions that at the moment remain unanswered.

In order to respond to this challenge there is a need to raise Activate's profile within the university community and to have it recognized as a good example of the University's civic engagement commitment. This commitment is made explicit and is underpinned by a set of institutional values that include, integrity, credibility, openness, and success, within the wider university context. In terms of its civic responsibility, the University states that it will "make an impact on the intellectual, social and cultural life, and economic success, of the City of Glasgow, Scotland and beyond." Activate is indeed an example of this in action, though we tend to agree with Lorlene Hoyt (2013, 4) when she describes the "mismatch" between the rhetoric and delivery of institutional mission statements, such as the one cited above.

One reason for this is perhaps the lack of clarity and understanding that may exist when using terms such as "civic engagement" in the academy and elsewhere. For example the University may feel it fulfills its civic engagement responsibility through its service-learning programs. However the Community Development team has a different way of thinking in terms of what it means to engage with the community. Somerville (2011, 33) sums this up in his discussion about four different approaches to community engagement, "neo-colonial—'done to the community'; welfarist—done 'for the community'; collaborative—done 'with the community'; and self-organisation—done 'by the community.'" The Community Development team openly promotes both collaborative and self-organization approaches that are founded on "building active and sustainable communities based on social justice and mutual respect" (Lifelong Learning UK 2009, 4), while perhaps the University's approach is more akin to the neocolonial or welfarist methods.

This concurs with a paper developed by the Kettering Foundation, "Civic Capacity Research: An Analysis of Kettering Literature and Related Scholarship" which refers to "the common pattern of universities seeing community as the passive recipients of their services and information" (2011, 38). This highlights similarities to Freire's (1972) thinking in his discussion around banking education, where people are viewed as empty vessels to be filled with what others deem necessary. No account is taken of the skills, knowledge, and experience people themselves have.

Demand for Activate has increased due to the positive feedback from previous students. Though a great sign for the program, this means that the sustainability of Activate is an ongoing challenge in terms of maintaining affordability for community partners to continue funding the courses and providing additional resources to support the students. Dealing with student expectations and support needs can be time-consuming and demanding, especially as not many of the partner organizations have dedicated staff whose roles include supporting students during and after the course. This responsibility is often picked up by the university tutor; however, this is not sustainable in the long term. Therefore, the challenge is to find a way to have a "joined-up approach" between all those involved, thus ensuring we have a robust all-round process that meets the needs and expectations of students while minimizing strain on participating organizations.

A final challenge we see is how to build on the success of the program and getting the time to consider what's next beyond Activate. We believe there is real potential in doing this; however, this requires a conversation that includes many voices, including Activate students, university faculty and administration, community members, and community partners. As a starting point we might consider drawing from the research and subsequent report collated by the university Community Development team. This report was undertaken at the request of key community partners in the East End of Glasgow, who have become a think tank for developing an Active Communities program. The players included other voluntary organizations, the university, local authorities, further education colleges, and housing associations. Essentially, this was to be about providing a real opportunity to build out the Activate initiative in support of a more strategic and developmental approach to strengthening existing community networks. It would be a community-led initiative established to meet the expressed needs and aspirations of local communities that are frustrated by the lack of local people applying for, or employed in, senior positions within the public, voluntary, and community sector organizations. This would see the beginnings of a "grow your own" process within the East End. The report from the University recommended the following:

- Increased resources for participation and capacity building are built in as part of the requirement for program funding.
- A designated engagement budget to provide practical support to initiate and deliver modest tangible projects that meet local needs.
- Partner organizations identify and designate suitable posts for inclusion in the "jobs bank" in support of positive action.

The report highlighted some opportunities, which included the following:

- A real opportunity exists to demonstrate a clear commitment to better coordinate and support community engagement in community planning while acknowledging the diversity of local communities. The Active Communities program is a long-term investment in the benefits of capacity-building measures—"grow your own" role models.
- The Active Communities program can be targeted at specific communities: geographical, ethnic minority, young people, the disabled, or lone parents. Basically, it presents a measurable opportunity to address issues of equality around engagement in community planning specific to local circumstances.

The report also highlighted some challenges, which included the following:

- The challenge for others and ourselves to listen to the experiences and ideas of the people who live in or are part of disadvantaged communities and find solutions that deliver services which meet their needs and aspirations.
- Engaging communities is not an easy option. Meaningful community engagement

involves compromise, shared decision-making, learning to cope with diversity, shifts in organizational cultures, dealing with conflict, mutual accountability, and revisiting priorities and timescales. Real or perceived, regeneration agendas are often seen as set in advance of community participation.
- A challenge is to develop and deliver a flexible, transitional training and employment scheme that will help lift people caught in the "benefits trap" out of unemployment and into meaningful education by maximizing existing partner resources (Jordan, Purcell, and Whelan 2004).

Unfortunately, due to a number of factors outside the control of the community or the University, the Active Communities program never materialized. However, now might be the time to reengage with the literature to rethink the "what next" stage, thus embedding Activate as a core activity within the community capacity agenda in local communities.

Successes

The Activate course has been hugely successful in human, economic, and social terms. It has also been significant in promoting stronger communities and improved networks. In this chapter we have also presented evidence of a culture shift and the destigmatization of individuals and communities who have been continually labeled as "disadvantaged." One of the most successful aspects of the program is the difference that it is making to community members. There is strong evidence of increased social capital and empowerment of individuals, community organizations, and the community itself. Both university and community partners have recognized the strengthening of relationships and community networks in dealing with local issues.

As we have mentioned, the economic impact on local communities has increased substantially, as many students have managed to secure sessional, part-time, or full-time employment. Rosie's story demonstrates that nothing is impossible or out of reach given the right set of circumstances. The story of another local woman provides another example of the successes birthed by the Activate course. She undertook the course at the same time as Rosie and went on to graduate with a BA in community development. She went on to work in her local community, where she helped establish a new center as a legacy hub of Glasgow's 2014 Commonwealth Games. She was elected as a local Labour councillor in Glasgow City Council elections and continues to work in the East End community.

Today more than one thousand students have come through the program; and approximately 42 percent of them have gone on to study at either a further education college or the University. Many more of them continue volunteering and participating in local community activities after completing Activate. Geographically the program has been delivered across the west coast of Scotland and recently was invited to the east coast. Activate has worked with over twenty-five different community-based organizations in the delivery of the program and has sustained relationships with around twelve organizations, notably ng homes.

Activate award evenings are hugely significant events for those who successfully complete the course. They are held at the University in the majestic Bute Hall, where students receive their awards in front of family and friends, who then get the opportunity to share in the celebration of achievement. This is significant in helping to break down the ivory tower concept, as it brings people into the "space of the University," dispelling some of the myths and perceptions previously held by people who feel that university is "not for the likes of them."

At an institutional level, Activate has now been included in the widening participation strategy for the 2014–2015 outcome agreement between the University and the Scottish funding council. This should provide leverage for future discussions. The development of the partnership with Further the Education: Glasgow Kelvin College is a huge boost in terms of student progression. As more and more students progress, their potential for employment is increased tenfold; and with additional money in their pocket, the impact on the local economy is boosted. Activate now has its own "homegrown" tutors, such as Rosie, whom Antonio Gramsci would refer to as "organic intellectuals." Gramsci (1971) said that all men were intellectuals but not all men have the function of intellectuals in society, demonstrating a belief that people have the capacity and capability to think. The issue then becomes how to harness those capacities and provide opportunities for them to further develop.

We collect feedback and evaluations for each course delivered, and the overriding word is that increased "confidence" enables people to participate in local organizations and to think beyond the impossible. Having the confidence to ask questions and keep asking is something that a lot of Activators speak about. The notion of having a voice and not being afraid to use it is a really powerful message that comes through the evaluation process. People are talking about things that are really important to them and are no longer being herded like sheep into spaces they do not want to go to.

And finally we believe there has been a "culture shift" within neighborhoods and communities on how they view themselves: from having low expectations and being pessimistic, they now see things as "a glass half full." There is clear evidence of a "can do" attitude developing and examples of people across age groups, social backgrounds, and cultures working together on community programs. The "asset-based approach," championed in Scotland by Sir Harry Burns, is evident here.[2] He draws on the concept of the asset-based approach to health improvement, developed by American sociologist Aaron Antonovsky. His concept of *salutogenesis*, which he describes as the creation of positive health and well-being, seems to offer the most coherent and evidence-based approach to these efforts. A key aspect of Antonovsky's theory is the idea that having control of one's life and circumstances is health enhancing. Central to the asset-based approach is the idea of helping people to be in control of their lives by developing the capacities and capabilities of individuals and communities. It draws on existing approaches that foster effective and appropriate involvement of the people and the professionals who serve them.[3] This approach links closely to the process undertaken in both the Activate course and ng homes' everyday activities.

Implications for Scotland, Glasgow, and the University

When people care enough to act, change will occur. . . . think about the unrecognised capacities in every community, find them and provide opportunities for people to offer them. Relationships build a community, we need to build them and utilise them, put citizens at the centre and engage them as actors, not recipients.

—Dr. Harry Burns, "Making It Happen" conference, Dundee, 2010

Scotland has a population of just over five million. The political landscape of the country has changed dramatically since the opening of its own Parliament in 1999 with the ability to govern, to some extent, the needs and aspirations of its people. Fundamental responsibility on areas of national security, taxation, and social security still lies with the Westminster national government in London. The Scottish independence referendum held on September 18, 2014, produced an extremely high turnout in voting, with more than 86 percent of those eligible to vote doing so. The result favored staying part of the United Kingdom. However, voters claimed responsibility for setting their nation's course, their "political will" sending a clear message that change is needed (Mathews 2002, 2). This prompted a "vow" from those in leadership positions within the main three political parties in Westminster to devolve more powers to the people of Scotland.

The Scottish government is committed to the people of Scotland having a greater say and a part to play in how local services are planned and delivered, partly demonstrated through embedding an asset-based approach in government policy. They believe local people should be recognized as critical to the regeneration of the most disadvantaged communities. This bears fruit through a variety of policies and strategies developed by the Scottish government. The most recent and noteworthy include the Single Outcome Agreement, the Christie Commission, and the Regeneration Strategy.[4] Moreover, national and local delivery organizations across Scotland are developing asset-based approaches as a means to tackle perennial social problems and "wicked issues." Scotland's former chief medical officer, Sir Harry Burns, has been a strong advocate of the asset-based approach to health improvement. In response to the Christie Commission, he noted in his 2011 annual report:

> I proposed that asset based approaches may provide the necessary step change in health creation which Scotland needs to accelerate gains in healthy life expectancy across the population. . . . There is willingness in Scotland to embrace new thinking in our efforts to narrow health inequalities, and make Scotland a better place to grow and develop. If we can capitalise on this positive mind-set, we can make changes which may result in significant improvements to the health and wellbeing of all Scots (24).

Glasgow

The Activate course operating within North Glasgow and beyond has begun to break through into the ways that communities operate and empower people to act. It provides the space for people to come together to discuss deep-rooted issues in a safe and encouraging learning environment. The diversity of the students allows for a "joined-up approach" and introduces students to collective working, problem-solving, and the ability to effectively use their voices for positive change. Students are introduced to community development values, which are woven through the interactive group work sessions. As a community partner, ng homes sees the relevance and the impact of Activate in building stronger people and communities, and is committed to providing and sourcing additional funds for the course to continue.

Looking beyond the current geographic community, we seek the opportunity for Activate to cut across civil society by entering into the sphere of local government and other public bodies. For example, approaches have been made to Scottish Prison Service and Glasgow City Council to collaborate.

University

The University prides itself on being an international institution with a worldwide reputation for delivering excellence in teaching and research. Activate, and all that it stands for, has played its part in contributing to this claim. However, the impact of the course has been felt much closer to home—right on the doorsteps of the institution, in the surrounding communities that have felt like the poor relative in the relationship. This is changing as more communities and individuals feel confident in bridging the gap between "town and gown," and the institution needs to be in a position to respond to their needs. We are beginning to see the seeds of this process emerging as negotiations are taking place to extend campus facilities into the East End of Glasgow in the near future. Therefore, we perceive Activate and those students and organizations that play pivotal roles in the East End as the drivers of this new initiative and the catalyst for the engagement process in the wider community. They will take their seat at the table with confidence and ensure that local perspectives and experiences are valued in the same way as other, more formalized, modes of knowledge production.

Conclusion

We hope that this chapter has demonstrated to the reader *new ways of seeing the world* through the untapped skills, talents, and gifts that people who live in areas designated as poor and disadvantaged have to offer if given the opportunity. This concurs with McKnight and Kretzmann who state: "Labeling people with the names of their deficiencies (i.e. their needs) causes us to miss what is most important to them, opportunities to express and share their gifts, skills, capacities and abilities" (1993, 4). We believe that Activate provides the platform for these opportunities due to its commitment to honoring the skills, knowledge, and experience that people bring to the course. Activate will continue to be a vital component in building the capacity of individuals. It remains a powerful element in not only breaching the ivory tower, but in providing a "new way of thinking and being in the world."

NOTES

1. This program looks at issues related to food justice and food insecurity (linking to the environmental issues relating to food waste and social issues of food need and food poverty), working collectively with the community to redistribute food and work in partnership for sustainable solutions.
2. Sir Harry Burns, previously chief medical officer for Scotland and a champion of the asset-based approach is now professor of global health, University of Strathclyde.
3. Bengt Lindstrom and Monica Erikson, *Contextualising Salutogenesis and Antonovsky in Public Health Development*, May 2006, http:www.assetbasedconsulting.net/uplodads/publications/A.
4. The Single Outcome Agreement of 2007 identifies fifteen national outcomes to manage progress in disadvantaged communities. The establishment of the Christie Commission in 2010 aims to improve public service delivery. The Regeneration Strategy promotes well-being by way of a stronger focus on community-led economic development initiatives.

REFERENCES

Antonovsky, A. 1993. Complexity, conflict, chaos, coherence, coercion and civility. *Social Science Medicine Journal* 37: 969-981.

Beck, D., and Martin, H. 2005. Co-investigation of social capital. Conference paper.

Boyte, H. 2004. The necessity of politics. *Journal of Public Affairs* 7(1): 75-85.

Burns, H. 2010. *Chief medical officer annual report 2010: Assets for health*. Scottish Government: APS Group Scotland.

Christie, C. 2011. *Commission on the future delivery of public services*. Scottish Government: APS Group Scotland.

Creighton, S. 2008. The scholarship of community partner voice. In D. White, ed., *Higher education exchange*. Dayton, OH: Kettering Foundation Press.

Dzur, A. 2013. "Trench democracy: Participatory innovation in unlikely places?" *Boston Review*, October 11.

Fallon, J. 2011. Speech at Talloires Leaders conference, Madrid, Spain, June 14-16.

Freire, P. 1972. *Pedagogy of the oppressed*. Trans. M. B. Ramos. Harmondsworth: Penguin.

———. 1976. *Education: The practice of freedom*. London: Writers and Readers.

Gramsci, A. 1971. *Selections from the prison notebooks*. New York: International Publishers.

Grisham, V. L., Jr. 1999. *Tupelo: The evolution of a community*. Dayton, OH: Kettering Foundation Press.

Hoyt, L. 2013. *Transforming cities and minds through the scholarship of engagement: Economy, equity and environment*. Nashville: Vanderbilt University Press.

Jordan, L., Purcell, R., and Whelan, L. 2004. *Taking the new and challenging road: The activate course in the eastend of Glasgow, 2005-2006*. Glasgow: University of Glasgow.

Kretzmann, J., and McKnight, J. 1993. *Building communities from the inside out: A path toward finding and mobilizing a community's assets*. Evanston: Asset-Based Community Development Institute, Institute for Policy Research, Northwestern University.

Ledwith, M. 2007. Reclaiming the radical agenda: A critical approach to community development. *Concept* 17(2): 8-12.

Lifelong Learning UK. 2009. *National occupational standards for community development*. London: Lifelong Learning UK.

Mathews, D. 2002. *For communities to work*. Dayton, OH: Kettering Foundation Press.

———. 2012. *What kind of democracy informs community development*. Dayton, OH: Kettering Foundation Press.

National Health Service Greater Glasgow and Clyde. 2014. *Building momentum for change report*. Director of Public Health Biennial Report.

Putnam, R. 2000. *Bowling alone: The collapse and revival of American community*. New York: Simon & Shuster.

Somerville, P. 2011. *Understanding community*. Bristol: Policy Press.

University of Glasgow. 2010. *Glasgow 2020: A global vision*. University of Glasgow Strategic Plan.

Amplifying Community Voices in South Africa: Nurturing Transformative Leaders through Dialogic Action

Joseph Francis and Hlekani Muchazotida Kabiti

Amplifying Community Voices is a community engagement program born out of the need for an educational approach with the potential to effectively liberate individuals and communities from their inherent belief that they are not able to self-drive development. It helps individuals discover their inherent power as leaders of positive social change and connects their work and life experiences to community empowerment. Amplifying Community Voices, which should also be viewed as a socioeconomic emancipation process, is based at the University of Venda, in rural South Africa. Its philosophical underpinnings have been actualized for a decade, contributing to lasting social and economic change in rural areas of the Vhembe District of South Africa. This social experiment seeks to help transform the way local government facilitates public participation, prioritizing strategies of integrated development planning that are people-centered and people-driven.[1] In addition, we are convinced that the Amplifying Community Voices approach will appeal to development practitioners who believe in *Putting the Last First* (Chambers 1983). Moreover, the work draws inspiration from *The Pedagogy of the Oppressed* (Freire 1970) in that it takes the experience of marginalized populations as the starting point for building civic and educational competencies. Before delving into the central tenets and practice of Amplifying Community Voices, we find it necessary to first share Hlekani's story.

Hlekani's Story: "Maintaining Cool Heads in the Face of Provocation"

I would like to share an Amplifying Community Voices experience from 2013 that caught me and fellow engaged students completely by surprise. As members of the ACV Students Association, we always brag about how well trained we are to engage even the most hostile, disadvantaged, or desperate communities. We engage them in order to make sure that those in positions of power hear the voices and concerns of communities they are leading. Because ACV has carried out this work for almost a decade, we are now renowned and well respected by virtually all the communities we work with.

It was a Sunday morning. Six of us were deployed to facilitate a public feedback session on the results of a community development planning process that we had spearheaded for about four months in a semirural area of Thulamela Local Municipality. A middle-aged woman opened the community gathering with an eloquent prayer. After that, the program director of the community engagement workshop welcomed all the people present. As soon as he had finished explaining the purpose of the day, a group of young men roared in disagreement. Many other community members, young and old, joined in arguing that the program director had hijacked the workshop and "squeezed the university students in" so that they could "conduct their never-ending research." The young men's frustrations, in particular, boiled over. They demanded that we leave immediately. They threatened to do us harm. The fact that most of us were not fluent in the local Tshivenda language seemed to make the inflamed situation worse. The young men demanded that we put away our cameras. However, before we could do that, we were forced to erase all the photographs that we had taken despite the informed consent we had secured for the community engagement gathering. We complied. What else could we do? We feared for our safety and lives.

A fellow student tried to explain why we were there. The angry and evidently drunk group of young men were not prepared to listen. In our confused and perplexed state, we had to think on our feet and quickly. I whispered to my colleagues that we had to hold our peace and leave with our sanity and dignity intact. We quietly walked away, our proverbial tails tucked between our legs. Although foul and vulgar language continued to be hurled at us with careless abandon, we remained calm and disciplined. In this moment I realized how well our leaders in the Amplifying Community Voices program had prepared us to think on our feet and maintain cool heads in the face of provocation.

We walked approximately 5 kilometers back to the university campus, carrying our equipment. That was the only option since the bus that delivered us to the meeting had departed and was not due back for hours. As we walked together, we reflected on what had happened. Local leaders had invited us. We had planned the gathering with them and adhered to all the respected protocols. Our feelings were mixed. They included feelings of shock, disbelief, frustration, and embarrassment. I wondered, could we have done more to make sure that most community members understood the scope and purpose of our work? Some students expressed resolve and a desire to return another day to continue with our community development work. This experience was a golden lesson for us. We knew that community engagement was not always a walk in a tranquil park of lush green grass. This experience taught us that one can never be fully prepared for what might happen while facilitating community-engaged development work.

There are still many unanswered questions regarding what triggered that particular outburst and how it could have been avoided. Was it that our team was predominantly female and the patriarchal community felt offended but did not want to voice their feelings in the group? Was it due to the fact that most of us were not fluent in their language? Were we victims caught in the crossfire of ongoing infighting in the community? What type of leadership is required to deal with the type of behavior we encountered?

This firsthand story is an interesting case of what might happen in the course of facilitating community development. It poses many questions on transformative leadership for development, conflict management, and social cohesion in a broad sense, among others. In this regard, transformative leadership requires "thinking on our feet." As alluded to, this was experienced in the course of advancing the philosophy and practice of facilitating the realization of people-centered development through Amplifying Community Voices.

University of Venda and Strategic Intent

The University of Venda is a small (about fourteen thousand students in 2016), rapidly growing institution located in Thohoyandou town of Vhembe District, Limpopo Province of South Africa. It is located about 150 kilometers south east of Beitbridge, which is South Africa's major border with Zimbabwe, and also 180 kilometers from Polokwane, the capital city of Limpopo Province. The university was established in 1982 to serve the predominantly Venda and neighboring Gazankulu homelands. Its core business of teaching, research, and community-engaged work is implemented in eight schools: Agriculture, Education, Environmental Sciences, Health Sciences, Human and Social Sciences, Law, Management Sciences, and Mathematical and Natural Sciences. The Institute for Rural Development (the Institute) is the flagship unit tasked with spearheading the University's agenda of combating poverty and underdevelopment. It aims to promote the realization of the university's vision, namely, "be at the centre of tertiary education for rural and regional development in Southern Africa." Central to this mandate is the belief that the vision can only be achieved if our approach to development adheres to our broader, institute slogan, namely, "Taking the university to its rightful owners—grassroots communities."

Amplifying Community Voices: Context and Purpose

Amplifying Community Voices is a people-centered rural development initiative that the Institute established in 2006. Pioneering work was undertaken in Wards 1, 17, 29, and 37 of Makhado Municipality until 2009. Thereafter, in response to requests from other communities, it was introduced in the Masia, Ngovhela, and Sinthumule Traditional Authority areas. In addition, it was partially applied in Wards 2 and 11 of Thulamela and Mutale municipalities in the Vhembe District, respectively. In total, Amplifying Community Voices has so far been implemented in more than ninety villages of Makhado, Mutale, and Thulamela municipalities.

Amplifying Community Voices is an experiment in learning by doing that seeks to enhance civic participation in decision-making when formulating municipal integrated development plans and budgets. This is in response to poor civic participation, which is increasingly becoming a pressing national issue, as indicated in the National Development Plan Vision 2030. Simultaneously, Amplifying Community Voices serves as a multifaceted "laboratory" in which students acquire hands-on experience in engaging various interest groups in rural communities. Students cofacilitate meetings where residents make decisions in a democratic manner on issues that affect the livelihoods of local people. Many of the causes of local poverty and entrenched "wicked problems" have their roots in the apartheid system. Finding solutions to these challenges demands that we be guided in our action by, and take seriously, the experiences of those who have suffered the most. Thus, it was not surprising that the Reconstruction and Development Program of 1994 stated that "no political democracy can survive and flourish if the mass of our people remain in poverty, without land, without tangible prospects for a better life. Attacking poverty and deprivation must therefore be the first priority of a democratic government."

It is imperative to examine the Institute within the context of the expected roles of a university in socioeconomic transformation and development. Youtie and Shapira (2008, 1188) explained that a university should move from being a "knowledge factory to a knowledge hub, to advance technical innovation and economic development in its region." With this aspiration in mind, let us explain the relationship between the country's history of apartheid and the University of Venda's efforts to find solutions to rural development issues.

Apartheid was a territorial system that segregated people based on ethnicity and race. Systematically implemented in South Africa prior to the attainment of democracy in 1994, it entailed promoting separate and marginal development in areas that were coined *Bantustans*, where the majority Black population was confined. This meant that social cohesion rarely materialized, in line with the principles of divide and rule. The marginal development promoted in Bantustans such as the former Venda Republic, where the University of Venda is located, incubated poverty, which now characterizes most of such historically disadvantaged rural areas (Triegaardt 2006; Westaway 2012). Most worrying is the fact that the apartheid government nurtured a culture of dependency whereby ethnic groups in the former Bantustans "look to the government for help or blame the government for their problems" (Barker et al. 2013). After the attainment of democracy in 1994, successive governments adopted various legal frameworks aiming to promote public participation and deepen democracy. The purpose of such laws was to realize the ideal that the "People Shall Govern," as stated in the African National Congress's Freedom Charter of 1955.[2] This mantra was reaffirmed in the Constitution of the Republic of South Africa of 1996. Legislation such as the White Paper on Local Government of 1998, the Municipal Structures Act of 1998, and the Municipal Systems Act of 2000, among others, creates an enabling environment for civic participation to take root. However, these legislative frameworks have yet to be fully understood, internalized, and embraced by the nation, in particular at grassroots level. Instead, persistent and violent service delivery protests have now permeated the fabric of communities in both rural and urban areas.

A casual analysis of the sentiments that protesters express seems to reveal a deeply entrenched dependency syndrome, a sense of entitlement, and lack of ownership of development initiatives implemented in local areas. The spread of violent protests to rural areas is a cause for concern. As if not to be outdone, in 2015 and 2016 students in South African universities almost paralyzed the higher education system through what is now popularly referred to as the "#feesmustfall" movement. These developments clearly highlight the need, more urgent than ever before, for approaches to grow and develop responsible, transformative leaders. It is in this context that Amplifying Community Voices, which is explained in detail in the next section, should also be viewed.

Approach to Community Engagement

The following excerpt from Paulo Freire's *Pedagogy of the Oppressed* informs the philosophy and practice of Amplifying Community Voices:

Leaders who do not act dialogically, but insist on imposing their decisions, do not organize the people—they manipulate them. They do not liberate, nor are they liberated: they oppress (1970, 178).

A series of workshops that involved local municipal and community leaders led to the birth and adoption of Amplifying Community Voices. It is an engaged, age- and gender-sensitive approach that creates spaces for children (seven years old and older), youth, adults, the elderly, and community leaders to interrogate pressing issues and make collective decisions about how to address them. Involving these interest groups in a step-by-step decision-making process creates a culture of engagement within villages (Francis and Kabiti 2014). This leads to the crafting of community development plans that typically address issues such as weak social cohesion, water and sanitation challenges, inadequate education and skills development, poor health provision, weak governance, social protection, local economy, housing, and transportation. In general, the program is designed to help cultivate positive attitudes and behaviors that enhance the chances of integrating community development plans into formal governance units, including wards and municipalities. This approach reinforces and realizes the vision of our university and the vice-chancellor: to be "at the center of tertiary education for rural and regional development in Southern Africa" and "to develop responsible citizens who will impact positively on the growth and development of South Africa."

Social Preparation for Engagement

Amplifying Community Voices is both a program and a process. The Amplifying Community Voices process pays special attention to the roles and personal experiences of students. As shown in figure 1, the first step is social preparation. To prepare for community entry, a vital component of Amplifying Community Voices, students participate in a series of activities. First, traditional and democratically elected leaders in each village are engaged by way of phone calls, written letters and emails, meetings, and workshops. The purpose of the initial engagement is to secure permission to carry out the planned work. Through workshops, awareness of the planned work is raised, contentious issues are clarified, and compromises reached. Above all, collective decisions on the nature and form of the planned work are made.

The most significant result of this stage is the commitment that community leaders make to support the program and collaborate. Implementation plans are jointly developed, and the roles of each party are negotiated and agreed upon. All these activities are necessary because both traditional and elected leaders wield considerable power in their communities. Failure to effectively engage and secure their support or commitment invariably makes it almost impossible to mobilize the participation of people who reside in areas under their jurisdiction. Once the community leaders grant permission to implement Amplifying Community Voices, the members of each village are then mobilized to participate.

Once awareness of Amplifying Community Voices is adequately raised, local community leaders facilitate the election of four to six interested, responsible, trustworthy, hardworking, and committed members of their villages to serve as "foot soldiers." These individuals are community representatives at the village level who volunteer to champion development and serve as agents

Figure 1. Reflection Circles Depicting Various Interest Groups

SOCIAL PREPARATION
Community entry, recruitment of village-based "foot soldiers," training "foot soldiers" and students to facilitate participatory decision-making in communities, community mobilization

DAY OF ENGAGING COMMUNITY
1. Opening (Singing National Anthem)
2. Welcome Remarks by a Community Leader
3. Completing Attendance Register
4. Introductions
5. Purpose of Engagement
6. Forming Breakout Groups for Facilitated Reflection Circles
7. Reflection Circles

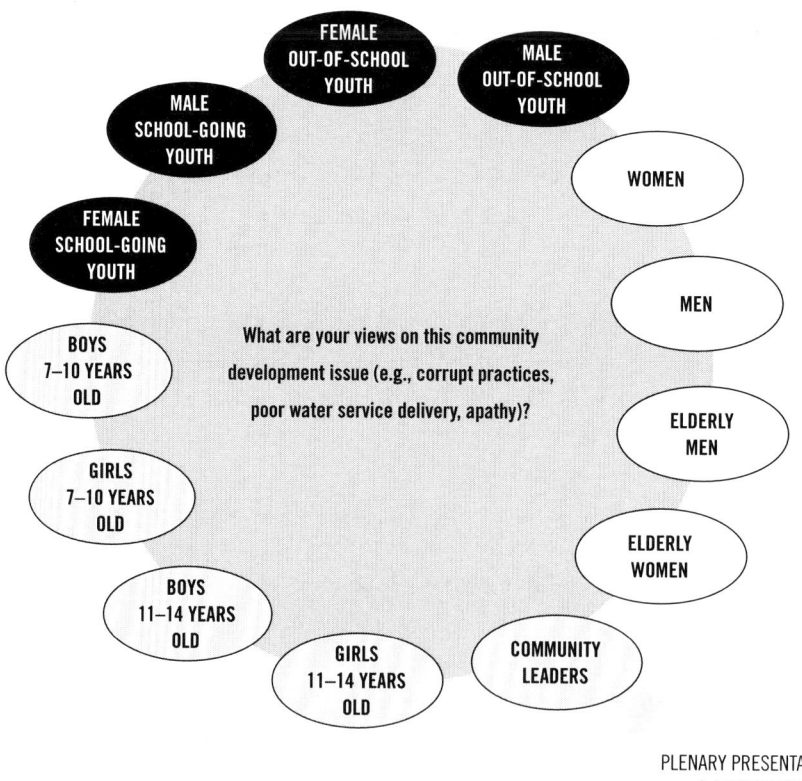

PLENARY PRESENTATION & DISCUSSION

CLOSING REMARKS | VOTE OF THANKS & ANNOUNCEMENTS | *MAZWIWA* (ADDRESS BY THE LEADER) | SUMMARY OF WAY FORWARD

of change (Francis et al. 2010). This village development cadre works closely with the university faculty and students to facilitate effective implementation of Amplifying Community Voices. In the village, they work closely with leaders to ensure that community members are well informed and motivated to participate.

Community Mobilization

In government-led processes, the meaning of "community" is not neatly defined. In contrast, the "community" as defined by Amplifying Community Voices includes anyone at least seven years old who resides in a particular area, such as a village. The interest groups that are mobilized to ensure inclusive decision-making and a sense of ownership of the community development agenda are shown in figure 1.

Multiple methods are used to mobilize the various groups within villages. For instance, letters are sent to key people in the village who are regarded as opinion leaders by virtue of their knowledge and influence. Notices are posted in public places such as communal water collection points, church buildings, public transport shelters, community halls, sports fields, and schools. Word-of-mouth is a common means for mobilizing the public. Announcements are made at meetings. In some villages, leaders send people to invite community members using a loud hailer. These methods have succeeded in disseminating information about planned engagement sessions to varying degrees. What is paramount in the process is that village residents take responsibility for the actions used to mobilize the community. We believe this approach is "handing over the baton stick" for championing sustainable rural development. By so doing, university faculty and students nurture motivation and a sense of ownership of the development agenda in the community. This is a significant departure from the tendency of some development agencies to create new "fissures and battlefields" to the detriment of local leadership and positive social change. Our experiences have revealed that a typical development agent would play a facilitating role in all the activities while working with the people, which is disempowering.

Although the methods explained above have been widely used, with mixed results, social media are virtually transforming the way residents are mobilized to participate in their development work. Messaging systems such as WhatsApp and Facebook are increasingly gaining popularity, especially among children and youth. In the process they are expanding the available modes of organizing and, in a way, turning all of their users into organizers.

Training Students and "Foot Soldiers"

Another crucial preparatory activity is the training of students, faculty, and the village development cadre so that they engage communities in a democratic manner. Students and the village development cadre who serve as facilitators participate in various workshops before being deployed into communities to fulfill designated roles. At the beginning of each year, new students participate in a workshop designed to orient them to the philosophy, values, practice, and achievements of Amplifying Community Voices. Poems, songs and dance, drama, experiential stories by returning students, cartoons, lectures, group discussions, questions, and videos of previous years' activities are used to tell the Amplifying Community Voices story. Considerable time is spent explaining the Amplifying Community Voices fourteen-point Charter of Positive Values and the Students Association constitution, which are both covered in detail later in this chapter. Workshops emphasize the importance of investing time and focused attention on peer-learning, establishing networks that enhance self-discovery, personal and collective development, and effective communication.

After the initial student and village development cadre orientation, more training workshops are held. In the workshops, the students and village development cadre are trained so that they acquire knowledge and skills for facilitating multiple stakeholder platforms. There is special emphasis on making collective decisions, community mobilization, stakeholder mapping and analysis, as well as participatory research methods and techniques. Introducing and deliberating about concepts such as community, engagement, and community development ensures that program members share a common understanding. Sessions are planned such that they enhance students' and the cadre's knowledge and appreciation of local culture, and teach facilitation protocols for rural community development in the Venda- and Tsonga-speaking areas. Most of the communities where Amplifying Community Voices is implemented speak these two vernacular languages.

Students who participate in community-engaged activities also undergo relevant pre-event orientation. Quite often, the students and mentor faculty meet community leaders and the village development cadre to jointly plan the events. They make decisions about the specific objectives, stakeholder roles, and the approach to be followed. Logistical issues and obligations are also clarified. Thus, the preengagement orientation is essentially a coaching and mentoring platform for students, faculty, and community members. Only those students who participate in the preengagement orientation sessions are assigned roles to play during the community engagement events.

Reflection Circles

Intergenerational deliberation is an essential component of Amplifying Community Voices. It is achieved through "ventilation platforms" that bring people of various ages and status in society together in a village assembly (figure 1) to democratically deliberate on issues of common interest. The platforms take many forms, including workshops, debates, and "reflection circles." University students from various disciplines organize and manage the reflection circles together with the initial village development cadre. A reflection circle is a modified focus group discussion, designed to eliminate power imbalances that are usually evident in collective decision-making experiences. A typical reflection circle breakout group consists of eight to twelve members of the same sex, age group, and/or status in a community of place, such as a village (see figure 1). This disaggregation originates from the realization that such cohorts are likely to have perspectives that differ from others.

In the reflection circles, no one takes a symbolic leadership seat, which helps to level out power relations. Sitting in a circular arrangement ensures that all the members have an opportunity to hear each other well and can easily contribute on the subject matter of interest (Francis et al. 2010; Moyo, Francis, and Ndlovu 2012). The success of a reflection circle depends on a number of factors. Some that we have identified are the interest that participants have in the issue being discussed, participant turnout, intergenerational representation, and the ability of facilitators to manage the planned deliberations.

Age and gender differences do not matter when establishing community leaders' reflection circles. Community leaders' reflection circles are crucial to ensure genuine democratic expression. Mixing community leaders with other villagers might stifle participation, because of fear of victimization by people who occupy powerful positions. In the reflection circles, students and the village development cadre work together to create an enabling environment for deliberation and decision-making on issues of mutual or community interest. As facilitators of reflection circles, they ensure that the participants in each discussion group appoint a moderator and a scribe. The chairperson leads the discussions. She or he ensures that issues are focused and authentic deliberation takes place. As the deliberations within the group unfold, the scribe records the ideas that are agreed upon. In most cases, the scribe presents the group's report during a plenary session. During the deliberations, students and the village development cadre look out for individuals with domineering tendencies as well as those who are withdrawn. Failure to manage such group dynamics might result in a few persons making decisions on behalf of others, which defeats the underlying purpose of public participation. Over the past few years of facilitating reflection circles, we have observed that children are among the most honest and reliable participants. Invariably, they innocently divulge information and issues that adults often shy away from and conceal. We believe that the adults' inclination toward a "conspiracy of silence" might help explain why sustainable development remains elusive to this day. Furthermore, we suspect that some development plans and programs implemented over the years in many parts of the world might have been constructed using half-truths and falsified information, thereby making them irrelevant.

Development of Transformative Leaders

Overall, Amplifying Community Voices aims to nurture a critical mass of university students and the village development cadre into people-centered and development-oriented leaders. In the process, space is created for interested students and the cadre to acquire a wide range of skills, including, but not limited to, the following: community mobilization; facilitating decision-making platforms involving children, youth, adults, and community leaders; inclusive community development planning; team building and teamwork; communication (report writing, public speaking, and dissemination of information); event management; community-based action research for development (data collection and analysis, writing scholarly papers); and project planning, implementation, monitoring, and evaluation.

At its inception in the year 2006, not more than ten students actively participated in Amplifying Community Voices. In the subsequent years, the number grew steadily until 2010, when an exponential growth in student numbers challenged Amplifying Community Voices' leaders to devise strategies to make student participation more meaningful and manageable. In 2012, participating students decided to establish a body, Amplifying Community Voices Students Association, to marshal and coordinate their community-engaged work. This was a product of a series of engaged workshops in which the students collectively discussed issues and made decisions. Thereafter, the Students Association was officially recognized and registered as a bona fide student body at the University of Venda. The specific objectives of the Students Association are stated in its constitution.

The association aims to nurture a critical mass of leaders and managers among students who advocate for and champion the participation of rural communities in their own development. This is achieved through creating opportunities for members to:

- Promote responsible citizenship through improved understanding of community development among students and youth in rural communities;
- Represent and promote the interests and responsibilities of students actively involved in Amplifying Community Voices;
- Learn about and contribute to community development, ensuring that they acquire more skills that would help them develop into wholesome individuals and teams;
- Practice good governance and adhere to participatory and nondiscriminatory principles as stipulated in the rules and regulations governing Amplifying Community Voices and the University of Vend;
- Set up similar rural school-based chapters within implementation sites of Amplifying Community Voices; and
- Foster viable working relations with similar associations and local statutory and nonstatutory bodies.

In 2016, 165 undergraduate and graduate students drawn from all the eight schools of the University were registered members of the Students Association. Apart from its constitution and Amplifying Community Voices Charter of Positive Values, rules and regulations governing the operations of the University of Venda's student organizations guide the Students Association's work. An eight-member management committee, which is democratically elected annually, is tasked with the responsibility of leading the Students Association. Any bona fide member of the association can be elected to any position in the management committee. However, students not performing well in their degree studies are automatically excluded because they are deemed to be already under pressure of work and thus might not perform to expectation. Also, this promotes the development of a culture of excellent academic performance. The management committee is composed of equal numbers of male and female students. To ensure that there is continuity, at least five members should be in their earlier years of studies. Soon after its establishment, the management committee forms various subcommittees, through which the core business of the Students Association is carried out. The Students Association's constitution stipulates that the following working committees are established: event management, communication and marketing, and disciplinary. Each registered member of the Students Association is expected to participate in at least one working committee. Active participation in all the activities of the student body is encouraged. This is done to encourage members of the Students Association to learn as much as possible through the engaged work.

Student Leadership Development Process

Central to the Students Association's work is the dream of developing leaders who are not resistant to change. This entails systematic nurturing of the students until they summon adequate confidence,

Figure 2. Ladder of Resistance to Change (Modified)

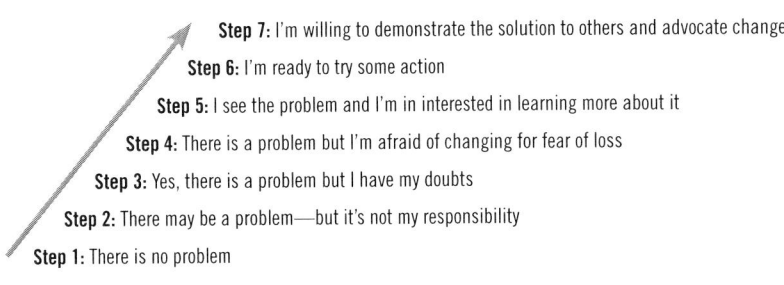

Step 7: I'm willing to demonstrate the solution to others and advocate change
Step 6: I'm ready to try some action
Step 5: I see the problem and I'm in interested in learning more about it
Step 4: There is a problem but I'm afraid of changing for fear of loss
Step 3: Yes, there is a problem but I have my doubts
Step 2: There may be a problem—but it's not my responsibility
Step 1: There is no problem

Source: Srinivasan 1990.

zeal, and energy to advocate for change when faced with a community challenge. The Students Association's implementation plans, developed at the beginning of each year, contain activities and exposure opportunities with potential to assist individuals move up the modified Srinivasan (1990) ladder of the resistance-to-change continuum, as shown in figure 2.

As members of the Students Association get the opportunity to plan and manage events and facilitate the mobilization of various interest groups in villages, they identify and communicate with relevant stakeholders and make logistical arrangements. Providing opportunities for students to play these roles helps them gain self-confidence because they work closely with community leaders, many of whom they rarely have the opportunity to meet otherwise. Community leaders may include the village development cadre, traditional leaders, municipal leaders, or senior managers in municipalities. During each engagement session, students work closely with the community leaders to make sure that the program runs smoothly.

The experience of facilitating community deliberations is crucial for nurturing transformative leaders for development. A leader for development should be an active listener who processes what she or he hears before making decisions or taking action. Such a leader must also be very observant and only talk when necessary. Thus, a typical Amplifying Community Voices facilitator should be caricaturized as an individual with a very big head, huge ears and eyes, and a tiny mouth. Facilitating discussions involving a wide cross-section of children, youth, adults, and community leaders helps to develop these skills. During facilitation, the students ensure that none of the discussants' ideas suppress those of others. By doing so, the students learn about group dynamics and how to handle them in a nonconfrontational way. Successful facilitation of the engagements makes the students gain self-confidence, gain skills in diplomacy and also helps them to network. Over the years, the Amplifying Community Voices experience has helped students learn how to work with elderly people, traditional leaders, persons in positions of authority in municipalities, and senior managers in both the public and the nongovernmental spheres. Reflecting on his experience, a first-year student pursuing a bachelor of science in agriculture at the University of Venda said:

> You know what, people who I have interacted with always talk about how shy I am. It's true that I am shy, which is why I never dreamt that one day I would facilitate an engagement in which there are more than seventy participants of all ages. Today, I have done just that. I was obviously nervous at the beginning,

which I believe is normal. My experience today is like being baptized. . . . I feel that I must do it again and again. What makes this even sweeter is that I was not going to get this opportunity through my degree studies. I am happy to have discovered that in me lies a lot of untapped potential.

During engagements, students collect various types of data together with community members, and process and analyze it before writing reports. Most of the engaged research is carried out in order to understand better the communities Amplifying Community Voices works in. The engaged nature of the data collection process makes it possible to unlock and deliberate on issues in depth, ensuring that most participants' views are considered. Apart from collecting data through reflection circles, the students take photographs and videos of the engagements. Informed consent is always secured before recordings. After the engagements, they write individual and group reports. The reports include a description of how the engagements were facilitated, challenges faced, and lessons learned in the process, among other components. The outline of the Amplifying Community Voices engagement report also compels the students to reflect on the significance of the work they will have been involved in, taking into account their degree studies, the University, and rural communities. This is designed to develop the students' analytical skills in line with the Amplifying Community Voices director's usual challenge when engaging students: "As university students, you should not regard yourself as well-educated and a leader if you cannot answer two crucial questions: Why am I involved in this work? Yes, this is what we found out, but so what?" Being able to identify shortcomings in one's own practice and taking corrective action after critical reflection are crucial for developing transformative leaders. Continuous reflection and action planning precipitate continuous improvement.

Some faculty and students participating in Amplifying Community Voices have published scientific papers on various aspects of completed work. Other notable academic outputs of the Amplifying Community Voices program include, as of the year 2015, more than twenty-five undergraduate or honors degree research projects, five master's theses, and two doctoral theses. More than twenty papers have been presented in both national and international conferences. All these achievements highlight the fact that Amplifying Community Voices provides a unique platform for developing a critical mass of engaged scholars, leaders, and people-centered development practitioners. The following verbatim quote from a member of the village development cadre in Ward 29 of Makhado Municipality, where Amplifying Community Voices was pioneered, lends weight to this argument:

> This is the only university initiative I am aware of which treats everyone involved in it as equals. Where else have you ever seen a common, uneducated person like me who stays in a poor village given the opportunity to present a paper in a conference? Just imagine . . . presenting a paper and rubbing shoulders with professors! I presented mine and was amazed by the interest shown in the work. It boosted my confidence, ego, and the view that we are doing a very good job.

Mobilizing Student Peers to Participate

Continuously spreading the word about Amplifying Community Voices on the university campus is necessary to recruit new students. Student leaders conduct outreach by posting notices in strategic locations on campus, informing and inviting students to participate in the program. We know that word of mouth affords potential members an opportunity to ask questions and receive answers, enabling them to decide whether to become members. Since 2013, social media platforms such as WhatsApp and Facebook have gained prominence as tools that are effective for recruiting students and constantly communicating with existing members. Furthermore, the Students Association adopted a highly publicized monthly cleaning initiative and started radio talk shows as strategies for popularizing its activities and Amplifying Community Voices. This is strengthening the visibility of ongoing work and positively profiling both Amplifying Community Voices and the Students Association.

Knowledge and Skills for Transformative Leadership

Students who participate in Amplifying Community Voices gain knowledge and learn to appreciate cultural norms, values, and tradition. The latter includes dress code and community-respected protocols. This knowledge makes it easier to build trusting and respectful relationships between the students and community members. Increasingly, it is becoming evident that this broadens participants' learning horizons. It allows them to enjoy the benefits of associating themselves with this laboratory of sociopolitical experimentation where participatory action research techniques and tools are applied in situ. Linking what they are taught in classroom and applying the knowledge in real-life situations cements student learning. They improve their communication skills through active listening. The use of vernacular languages that are not familiar poses one of the biggest challenges for a majority of the students. This is particularly daunting when metaphors and idioms are used that even some local residents cannot comprehend.

Creating space for students to coplan and facilitate some activities included on scheduled community engagement programs sharpens their public speaking skills. This is useful especially when they eventually get opportunities to engage in public debates and also present scientific papers at conferences and seminars. Compelling the engaged students to prepare pre- and postevent reports improves their event management and writing skills, and promotes learning from each other, team building, and ability to work as a team. Also, they become better community-based researchers. The students are always encouraged to include photographs to enrich their individual and team event reports. This encourages them to improve their abilities to take photographs, besides developing their imagination and creative capacities.

Development of Interpersonal Bonds

One of the most evident positive, though unintended, consequences of implementing Amplifying Community Voices has been the development of strong interpersonal relationships among faculty, students, and residents of rural communities. Friendships and acquaintances continue to be born. As this unfolds, the seemingly thick walls that surround some leadership institutions have been somewhat destroyed. The roles of university faculty and students in societal transformation and development have been demystified. Evidence of the maturation of the strong relationships among faculty, students, and rural community members includes the observed exchange of gifts such as fruits, vegetables, grocery items, and even money. Moreover, we have observed that some visit each other in their respective homes, in addition to attending wedding ceremonies, funerals, and other social events. We find this fascinating because of their value in entrenching Amplifying Community Voices in rural society and also reconfiguring and strengthening the actualization of the principles of *ubuntu* (humanism). Thus, it can be argued that the implementation of Amplifying Community Voices is producing positive results that far exceed the initial dream or project plans. We always reminisce about the question, how does one report about these outcomes in reports to funding bodies? Furthermore, how can these positive attributes be measured?

It is imperative to stress the fact that the students who join the Students Association are drawn from a wide cross-section of academic disciplines, sociocultural settings, primary spoken languages, and countries. The success of Amplifying Community Voices depends on how such assets are harnessed and interwoven to ensure that there is social cohesion, camaraderie, and harmony within the established teams. As they implement the program together and with the community, students learn to work in teams, to respect time, authority, each other, and to celebrate the strength that their diversity imparts to them. Regularly, students participating in Amplifying Community Voices reflect on their progress, taking stock of their efforts and success in working with people in challenging circumstances. The tensions sometimes arising from gossip and falsehoods peddled among the students, community members and even faculty constitute one of the major threats to smooth implementation of Amplifying Community Voices. What is fascinating about such experiences is that they present opportunities or case studies that we can use to analyze what happens when the students become development practitioners after graduating from the University.

Reflection Methodology

Nurturing transformative leaders through community-engaged work requires preparation for action and reflection. Unlike curriculum-based learning, in which the participants are assessed to determine knowledge mastered and skills acquired, community-engaged development work depends on how much one can learn from the engagement and apply in real-life practice. It is possible that some students might remain deeply involved in Amplifying Community Voices but never learn much from it. In order to address this challenge, reflection sessions are organized after each engagement, aiming to distill lessons learned. The reflection sessions are crucial colearning platforms, which remain very popular because of the participatory nature of how they are facilitated.

Reflection helps Amplifying Community Voices student participants to enhance their learning. A modified Gibbs (1988) reflective learning cycle (figure 3) is used to guide individual and team reflection.

Before a student writes analytical reports describing the issues discussed within a reflection circle, she or he writes a personal experiential report. This systematic reflection facilitates and enables learning to take place by revisiting the lived experiences. It allows the student to think about what was learned and appreciated, the new skills acquired, the challenges faced, and how the latter can be avoided in future. With their personal reflections in hand, all of the students participating in the same engagement come together to prepare a consolidated, composite team report. The team's report is prepared using the same outline as the personal reflection record. Preparing the joint report enhances colearning and helps participants to understand how future engagements can be

Figure 3. Reflective Learning Cycle

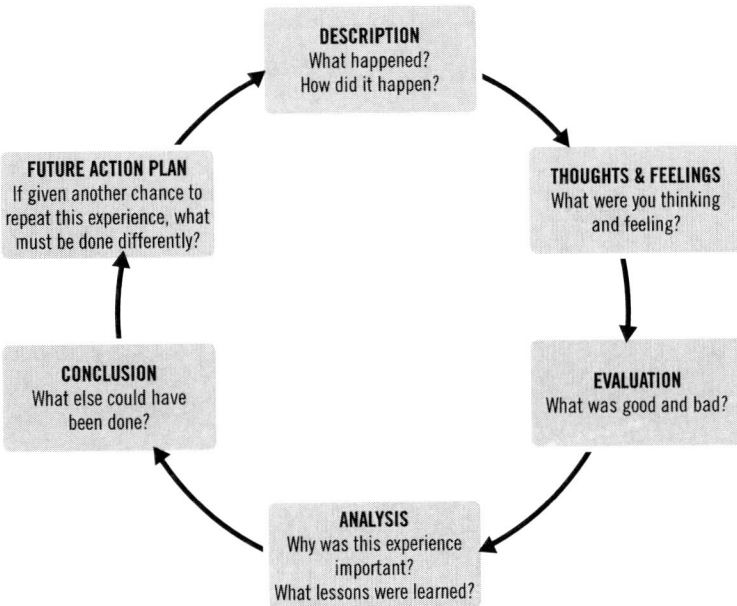

managed to achieve better results. The team's report writing is a melting pot of ideas. Perspectives from various academic disciplines are brought to the fore and interrogated intensely. For an idea or perspective to find its way into the team's report, the student who proposes it has to convince his or her peers it is an important contribution. Through this negotiation process, students develop important conflict resolution and communication skills. In what follows we present some excerpts from students' reflections that highlight nurturing character of Amplifying Community Voices.

Adivhaho Makhado graduated in the year 2014 with a bachelor of arts in media studies. While a student at University of Venda, Adivhaho was also a member of the Students Association's communication and marketing committee. He shares his reflections regarding his participation in Amplifying Community Voices:

> From what I understand and experienced in ACV, a true leader should be a good follower as well, and one of the most fundamental human characteristics is to be satisfied. No one wants to be a failure in life. God did not give us life to be failures. I am happy and convinced that I am one of the heroes of ACV. I did not join ACV and spend two years in it for material gain. I was there to acquire unique knowledge and skills, which I did. Thanks to ACV for grooming, molding, and shaping me into a new, actually different Adivhaho Makhado. This could not have been achieved because of my genetic composition but through hard work and diligence.

In 2012, Hlekani served as the Students Association deputy chairperson before being elected as chairperson in 2013. The reflections on her experiences during her tenure as a leader of the Students Association provide some insights into what the leadership of an engaged student body entails.

Serving as the chairperson of the Students Association for two years exposed me to immeasurable, life-changing experiences and skills. This position was a huge responsibility because it brought an extra load on my academic work. In addition to the skills which the other students usually gain, I learned to be more responsible and accountable even for things that were not of my own making. Serving in this position taught me to embrace failures and appreciate the efforts we made as we tried to succeed. The position made me realize that failure results from doing something. The most challenging part was to keep the other members of the management committee motivated and active because their withdrawal would mean an additional load on me. The ability to resolve disputes which arose within the association was another huge skill I acquired. There were many such cases, I must say.

Kevin Lubisi successfully completed studies toward a bachelor of arts honors degree in applied anthropology. Overall, he was a member of Amplifying Community Voices for four years. He served as the chairperson of the Students Association in 2014. Reflecting on his association with the program, Kevin said:

We sometimes encounter problems with the community members we work with. Some threaten us or resort to unconstructive criticism that we find difficult to understand. Sometimes we also feel pained by wastage of funds when community leaders postpone engagements at the last minute and fail to communicate with us in time. Nevertheless, we continue to exercise patience when this happens because we believe it is part of our learning experience.

Tebogo Mokganyetji is an Amplifying Community Voices student alumnus who has worked as a consultant and also for some nongovernmental organizations in Limpopo and Western Cape Provinces of South Africa. Currently, she is a PhD student at the University of Cape Town. The following sentiments extracted from one of her contributions on Amplifying Community Voices are very revealing:

I watched community members interrogate practices, development plans, and procedures that were about them. It was for the first time in my life that I experienced communities carve their own development agenda. And to this day, I am grateful for the experiential learning platform. I learned that being literate or one's educational status does not dictate how an individual can contribute and make a difference in their communities. For me that was a sacred lesson. Contrary to the general view in South Africa, not all communities wait for aid! Although people can use the help received, they achieve what they can with the little they have or own. This is an important lesson that all students must learn, at least before they graduate out of tertiary institutions. That way, we do not waste time reinventing the wheel but rather get down to work.

We introduce an outsider's reflections as well. From June to August 2015, Amplifying Community Voices hosted a graduate student intern from the University of Virginia in the United States. Daniela Eppler's reflections confirm that indeed Amplifying Community Voices is developing a cadre of transformative leaders. She writes,

Most students in my master's program in the United States want to better society in one way or another, but they have a great focus on the money they can earn in the process. Their work is very profit-oriented. At the University of Venda, through the ACV program in particular, I watched faculty and students alike engage in work that did not necessarily profit them directly; but they took part in this work for the benefit of others involved. Observing the type of hard work that was put in to this type of work made a lasting impact on me, as I hope to have that type of character and those types of values as a professional as well.

Notable Achievements

One of the most refreshing achievements of Amplifying Community Voices is that some former students are initiating community-based initiatives and organizations, aiming to combat pressing socioeconomic issues. For example, one student established a community newspaper that now captures and shares stories of the Giyani area of Limpopo Province. The newspaper serves as a platform for marketing local products and talent. On the eve of launching the newspaper, the founder invited the Amplifying Community Voices director to join the event. He wrote:

> It is not always that we celebrate someone's life when s/he is still with us on earth. As I write this invitation, my heart is filled with pride and joy because I am taking the ACV program to benefit my own people, just like you did when you initiated it in Makhado Municipality. I cannot believe that those weekends we spent with you in the villages of Wards 1, 17, 29 and 37 of the Municipality planted the seed that has now germinated and is growing so well in Giyani . . . it will be a great pleasure to have you here when we announce to the world the arrival of this baby in our community.

Another alumnus of Amplifying Community Voices, who participated in it for about three years, is Leonard Chihovo. He is a young Zimbabwean who studied at the University of Venda and graduated with a bachelor of arts in youth in development in 2013. In 2015, he wrote to the Amplifying Community Voices director to share his success stories since leaving the University. The following excerpt was taken from one of the reflective stories, in which he appreciated the experiential learning platform that Amplifying Community Voices created for him and other students.

> Today, I am a proud founder of the Transformative Youth Development Association here in Harare, Zimbabwe. Its ideologies were concretized and inspired by my participation in ACV. Before its registration, a constitution was required. The constitution drafting process and finalization was directly inspired by the one we did for the Students Association in 2012. My organization is making giant strides. For example, we have so far trained more than 100 peer educators in high schools and also for highly renowned NGOs such as SOS Children's Villages Zimbabwe and Tariro Trust. You might not believe it but it's true that the facilitation and administrative skills that have so far helped me achieve this were acquired through my involvement in ACV work.

The birth of the Students Association remains one of the most significant milestones in the life of the ACV program. It is serving as a vehicle that spearheads student involvement in engaged work. Today, it is a university-recognized and formally registered implementation arm of the ACV. Partially, it implements civic responsibility-building activities such as cleaning campaigns, career guidance in schools, and periodic donations of goods and services to the less privileged members of society. Moreover, the Students Association members volunteer to educate community members of all ages about the meaning (from a developmental perspective or orientation) of the bill of rights enshrined in chapter 2 of the country's constitution, the African Union Charter, and the Sustainable Development Goals (which replaced the Millennium Development Goals) that world leaders adopted in September 2015.

Other activities that the Students Association runs each year are celebrations of national holidays and other significant days, namely Youth, Mandela, Women's, and Heritage Days. Invariably, children, youth, adults, and community leaders are engaged so that they share perspectives on the significance of the days in question. This makes the days and platforms created coteaching and colearning opportunities, in addition to being moments that nurture social cohesion. It is vital to point out that social cohesion is a fundamental ingredient of sustainable development.

Vhembe District and its constituent municipalities recognize the innovative nature and ability to deepen democratic participation of local citizens in governmental decision-making processes. For example, in 2013 Amplifying Community Voices was adopted to engage communities in Makhado, Mutale, and Thulamela Municipalities when formulating local economic development strategies. In the process, the Local Government Sector Education Training Authority released approximately ZAR 2 million (US$150,000) to train 350 local people. To date, 152 people have completed training in basic research, facilitation, and institutional arrangements for local economic development. Among them are traditional leaders, ward committee members, community development workers, and municipal officials.

We believe that all that we have shared so far is a testimony to the power that Amplifying Community Voices wields. We are not aware of any engaged program that has ever yielded a student body that advances a critical component of the university core business such as community engagement, which most universities still find extremely difficult to institutionalize (Hall, Nongxa, Muller, Favish, and Slamat 2010; Mtawa, Fongwa, and Wangenge-Ouma 2016).

It is exciting and highly motivating to note that besides nurturing students who are making inroads in society, others are being elected to the Student Representative Council in this university. Currently, five members of the Students Association hold various portfolios in the Student Representative Council structures. These developments, though not deliberately planned, are likely to significantly reconstruct and transform the terrain of student politics. Student protests in South Africa surrounding any issue often turn violent. Negotiation seems not to be a favored option when students engage university leaders and management. A lot of "hot air is blown," which usually poisons negotiation platforms.

This argument implies that decisions made on issues affecting students are rarely well informed by voices of reason. We find this to be a worrying trend because the same student leaders grow, develop, mature, and eventually take up positions in various spheres of government, business, and civil society. Because of the dearth of experience and tools that help them lead or manage their institutions or organizations in a less confrontational way, it is likely that they would refine and sharpen coercive means of decision-making and action. Such a style of leadership or management only breeds and promotes hostile reaction from those being led, thereby manufacturing pockets of dissent, disharmony, and even hostile conflict. If not addressed, this might turn out to be one of the major threats to the country's fermenting democracy.

The fact that Amplifying Community Voices is a national and international award-winning initiative deserves recognition. In the year 2008, the program received a silver award in the Impumelelo Innovation Trust competition in recognition of its work on deepening municipal governance through the intergenerational approach. Its potential to considerably influence how public participation is deepened during integrated development planning makes it stand out in the local government sphere. The other award was third place in the international MacJannet Prize for Global Citizenship in the year 2011. Both awards helped to rejuvenate Amplifying Community Voices and also, we believe, turned the heads of the University's leaders, resulting in tangible support.

Presumably, the observed natural permeation of Amplifying Community Voices into the Student Representative Council will refresh student politics at the University of Venda and beyond in a way that promotes peaceful and meaningful collaboration between parties. If this happens, such transformative leadership might be embraced in other South African universities and colleges, especially in the aftermath of the "#feesmustfall" student movement that almost paralyzed higher education in 2015 and 2016.

Institutional Support as an Enabler of Successful Implementation

Although we have so far highlighted a wide range of achievements, inclusion of Amplifying Community Voices program in the University of Venda's strategic plan for 2016–2020 as a flagship initiative stands out. During the embryonic stages of Amplifying Community Voices, it was extremely difficult to implement community-based activities. This was mainly due to a poor understanding of what engaged work actually meant and how it fit into the broader agenda of university transformation and development. However, in 2007 the University of Venda mission and vision changed. The new mission and vision, crafted with the aim of enhancing the university's relevance to rural and regional development as it transformed itself into a comprehensive institution that offered both academic and vocational programs, considerably reconstructed conditions for embracing the promotion of community engagement as a critical component of the core business.

Institutional Bottlenecks

Students who participate in Amplifying Community Voices find it difficult to balance time between community-engaged work and their degree studies. Carrying out this type of work during weekdays is virtually impossible because of stiff competition for time with degree studies. Rural community-based work involves and demands considerable planning with respect to protocol, content, communication, mobilization of target participants, and logistics prior to engagements. After engaged work, students enter and analyze the data collected, synthesize the results, and write reports. This is a challenge because the students do not get any academic credit for this highly demanding work.

Invariably the Amplifying Community Voices team is compelled to carry out massive recruitment and training to replace students who leave the University upon completing their studies. Also, although interest and level of student participation is usually high at the beginning of the year, it significantly diminishes as students' academic loads become heavier.

Another challenge is that some faculty and students who occupy key decision-making positions do not seem to adequately understand or appreciate the nature of work that student-based community engagement organizations are involved in. By virtue of being a recognized student organization at the University, the Students Association should benefit from the funds allocated to the Student Representation Council (SRC) annually. Yet over the years attempts to access the funds to implement community-based work have been in vain. In 2014 one member of the management committee of the Students Association described experiences that provide some pointers on the underlying reasons for the SRC's reluctance to release money to support community-engaged work.

> As agreed in our last Students Association Management Committee meeting, I met the SRC minister of finance after being referred to him by the director of Student Affairs and also discussing everything with the head of Student Governance. It took me almost two weeks to secure an appointment with him. When we eventually met, he told me that university funding that the SRC manages is meant for activities that take place on campus only. The money is also not supposed to be used to pay for food for students when they run off-campus activities. In addition, the bus we hire should not be used to transport people in the rural areas where we are working. Colleagues, all I am saying is that I am stuck. To say I am very disappointed is an understatement.

The negative attitude and mind-set displayed by the SRC highlights the need for revisiting university rules and regulations to make it possible to carry out unhindered community-based work. Presumably, including community engagement on the orientation program for new student leaders elected to serve on the SRC might help build the desired mind-set and unlock the support needed for rural community-based work.

Community-Based Obstacles

Most communities where Amplifying Community Voices is implemented experience considerable challenges with respect to delivery of basic services such as clean water, sanitation, and transportation. Quite often, the residents direct their frustrations and anger at Amplifying Community Voices students. Despite our best efforts to explain over many years why we are working with the community, the mistaken belief persists that faculty and students from the University are part of a governmental effort.

Communities are frustrated by poor service delivery and unfulfilled promises from leaders and institutions. A villager once alleged that "after one university carried out its medical trials here, people got sick and we had to take care of those people. It only shows that university people do not care at all." Mounting frustrations and prior negative experiences leave community leaders and residents asking the question: "What is in it for us?" This issue is particularly daunting in relation to Amplifying Community Voices' emphasis on self-drive and self-reliance. We do not have handouts. Nor are we interested in approaching villagers in a manner that suggests we have something to give them that they do not already possess. Our experiences of working in the rural areas of Limpopo Province have convinced us that handouts from the government and nongovernmental organizations precipitate and entrench a growing dependency syndrome in many rural areas, including those where residents had been previously renowned for being self-reliant. This implies that as long as no effort is taken to mitigate this growing pattern, sustainable development will forever remain elusive and a pipe dream.

Amplifying Community Voices is implemented in areas under the jurisdiction of traditional leadership, which is patriarchal in nature and, to an extent, also conservative. In order to ensure that smooth working relations with local residents are developed, one must thoroughly understand the societal "dos and don'ts" associated with the different communities. There are many dos and don'ts that dictate how and when activities are supposed to be undertaken, including the roles that various stakeholders should play. Because of this challenge, the contributions of some community members and even students are often curtailed.

Despite the various attempts made to create an enabling environment for students to champion engaged work with minimal involvement of faculty, some communities find this extremely difficult to accept. Apparently, the community members and their leaders do not trust students. Nor do they believe that the students can carry out any meaningful activities without faculty supervising them. Past experiences of bad student behavior and irresponsibility seem to fuel the skepticism and discomfort of the communities.

Individual Characteristics: Students and Faculty

Many students and faculty who join Amplifying Community Voices seem to lack commitment and self-drive. Some become members of the development crusade hoping that there will be monetary benefits along the way. When they realize that no such benefits are forthcoming, they drop out. Because numerous interrelated workshops are run with the aim of nurturing self-propelled, assertive leaders who believe in the centrality of people-centered development, dropping out negates the goal of reaching a critical mass of such change agents. However, Amplifying Community Voices continues to draw inspiration from Margaret Mead (renowned American cultural anthropologist), who argued that hope and power do not lie in the numbers of people involved in a change process. She pointed out that we should "never doubt that a small group of thoughtful, committed citizens can change the world; indeed, it's the only thing that ever has." Thus, even though some students and faculty abort their participation in Amplifying Community Voices, there are others who help achieve set goals. Often, once challenges are identified, they are deliberated on and collective decisions on how to address them are formulated. This learning-by-doing, "thinking on our feet" approach helps keep Amplifying Community Voices committed to its underlying principles and values contained in the Charter of Positive Values that members crafted and adopted in August 2010.

Future of Higher Education Community Engagement in South Africa

The experiences highlighted in this chapter suggest that there is a huge potential for Amplifying Community Voices to transform student and rural community life as well as leadership. It offers a path to building lasting bridges among the multiple leadership institutions based in rural areas.

Such social cohesion is necessary because it is the primary building block and glue of vibrant and healthy communities, collective decision-making, and, ultimately, sustainable growth and development. We are convinced that sustainable development will forever remain elusive without strong community-based institutions that are aware of, and practice, what they are mandated to do, while recognizing and respecting the people they lead. Chambers (1983) advocated for a paradigm shift in development, pointing out that it is necessary to "put the last first." He suggested that in order to do this, it was crucial to answer such questions as these: Whose reality counts? Who constructs that reality? Who acts on that reality? Who is in control of the "development" process?

Amplifying Community Voices' intergenerational approach addresses all these key questions through robust engagement of various interest groups. Prior to convening the reflection circle-based deliberative engagements, considerable time is invested in creating awareness of the intentions of Amplifying Community Voices and securing the commitment of community-based institutions to be integral players during implementation. These efforts effectively hand over ownership of program implementation and its associated results to the local leaders.

There is no doubt that Amplifying Community Voices' engaged character and its patience in building lasting and trustful relationships among faculty, students, and residents of villages in rural areas provide substance to the concept of civic or public participation. In addition, it deepens democracy in a country in which "developmental local government" is the torch that guides local social change. As explained in South Africa's White Paper on Local Government of 1998, developmental local government encompasses a commitment to working with citizens of the country and community leadership institutions to craft sustainable strategies for meeting people's social, economic, and material needs, thereby improving their quality of life.

The Amplifying Community Voices approach will go a long way in helping universities to take their rightful place in contributing to the realization of the fundamental imperatives that underpin public participation. The mandates are codified in the White Paper on Local Government of 1998, Municipal Structures Act of 1998, Municipal Systems Act of 2000, National Development Plan Vision 2030, and South African Policy on Post-School Education of 2013. The potential for Amplifying Community Voices to strengthen ward committees' capacity to serve as effective public participation vehicles is huge. These arguments must also be viewed in conjunction with the fact that the South African Higher Education Community Engagement Forum is seeking ways to better contribute to the implementation of various policies and legislations, among which the National Development Plan Vision 2030 is the most prominent.

NOTES

1. Integrated development planning is a nationally mandated requirement of rural urban planning in South Africa that was instituted after the demise of apartheid to ensure a more equitable pattern of development.
2. A set of freedom demands that the African National Congress (current ruling party in South Africa) and its allies in the struggle for democracy adopted at a Congress of the People, June 25–26, 1955.

REFERENCES

Barker, D., Brace, E., Bravo, M. F. P., Catalano, J., Cirillo, M., Corbel, N., Diebel, A., Francis, J., Gaber, E. B., Hoyt, L., Ornelas Newcomb, A. Kabiti, H., Keegan, M., Koh, J., Layden, M., Martin, H., Naidoo, L., Putu, T., Wilson, M., and Zulkifar, P. 2013. Group meeting. December 16–20.

Chambers, R. 1983. *Rural development: Putting the last first.* New York: Routledge.

Hall, M., Nongxa, L., Muller, J., Favish, J., and Slamat, J. 2010. *Community engagement in South African higher education.* Pretoria, South Africa: Council on Higher Education.

Francis, J., Dube, B., Mokganyetji, T., and Chitapa, T. 2010. University-rural community partnership for people-centred development: Experiences from Makhado Municipality, Limpopo Province. *South African Journal of Higher Education* 24(3): 357–373.

Francis, J., and Kabiti, H. 2014. Amplifying community voices for people-centered development in South Africa. Unpublished paper, Venda, South Africa, June 12.

Francis, J., Mamatsharaga, P., Dube, B., and Chitapa, T. 2011. Making youth voices count in development programming in Makhado Municipality, Limpopo Province. *Journal of Geography and Regional Planning* 4(5): 297–304.

Freire, P. 1970. *Pedagogy of the oppressed.* London: Penguin.

Gibbs, G. 1988. *Learning by doing: A guide to teaching and learning methods.* Oxford: Oxford Further Education Unit.

Hoyt, L., and Newcomb Rowe, A. 2015. *Leaders in the civic engagement movement.* Medford: Talloires Network.

Mbati, P. 2014. Interview by Lorlene Hoyt, Medford, Massachusetts, June.

Moyo, C. S., Francis, J., and Ndlovu, P. 2012. Grassroots communities' perceptions relating to extent of control as a pillar of women empowerment in Makhado Municipality of South Africa. *Gender and Behaviour* 10(2): 4864–4882.

Mtawa, N. N., Fongwa, S. N., and Wangenge-Ouma, G. 2016. The scholarship of university-community engagement: Interrogating Boyer's model. *International Journal of Educational Development* 49: 126–133.

Srinivasan, L. 1990. *Practical ways of involving people: A manual for training trainers in participatory techniques.* New York: United Nations Development Programme.

Triegaardt, J. D. 2006. Poverty and inequality in South Africa: Policy considerations in an emerging democracy. Annual Conference of the Association of South African Social Work Education Institutions, September 18–20, University of Venda, Thohoyandou, South Africa.

Westaway, A. 2012. Rural poverty in the Eastern Cape Province: Legacy of apartheid or consequence of contemporary segregation? *Development Southern Africa* 29(1): 115–125.

Youtie, J., and Shapira, P. 2008. Building an innovation hub: A case study of the transformation of university roles in regional technological and economic development. *Research Policy* 37(8): 1188–1204.

The Refugee Action Support Program in Sydney, Australia: A Bridge between Cultures

Loshini Naidoo and Eric Brace

> The Refugee Action Support tutors helped me; they said "keep going, keep going," and I soon realized I could carry on. They helped me all the time, with essays and assignments, and taught me how to cope.
> —Al Sina Hassan, 2012

Al Sina Hassan is a young man of Afghani background, forced to flee his country due to its ongoing conflict and the persecution of his people. He had dreamed of becoming an engineer or doctor since he was seven years old. At the time, living in Iran, far from his country of birth, it seemed like an impossible dream. He and his family had no place to call home, and their journey would span many years and places, not uncommon for refugees who are resettled in Australia. In 2007, Al Sina and his family arrived in Australia and faced the challenges inherent in making a home in a foreign place. There was a new language to be learned, complex institutions to navigate, jobs to be found, identities to negotiate, and past traumas to confront. None of these challenges are easy to overcome.

Al Sina Hassan is presently studying mechanical engineering at the Western Sydney University, though, not long ago, he was a high school student navigating exams, course selections, and more. The epigraph from Mr. Hassan comes from a newspaper article highlighting his success and the success of a program known as the Refugee Action Support program (Han 2012). With resilience and concerted support of family, the community, schools, and forward-thinking programs like the refugee program, Mr. Hassan is able to take steps toward his aspirations. In doing so, he and his family teach many lessons to those in the Australian community, and to those university students who are involved as "tutors" in the refugee program.

The refugee program is built on a simple premise. Trainee teachers from the University are recruited to provide one-on-one and small-group language and literacy support on a weekly basis for students of refugee background at selected schools throughout the year. The aim of the program is twofold. First, it seeks to facilitate this extra learning assistance and mentoring for young refugees—like Mr. Hassan—within the first three years of their resettlement in Australia. This aim, at first glance, appears to be the program's sole objective. However, the program also provides a platform for the preservice teachers (the "tutors") to learn *about* their students, to learn *from* their students, and to perceive schooling and the broader social context from the unique perspectives within the refugee community.

The reciprocal nature of these relationships provides spaces where young people find camaraderie, discuss goals, and develop key cultural understandings. As one classroom teacher attests, "With the [Refugee Action Support program] the kids [students] have really got a voice now. It has been everything that I wanted to be able to achieve rather than just a literacy and numeracy program" (classroom teacher, 2010). In turn, the tutors develop an awareness and understanding of the strengths and challenges of students of refugee background within schools. One Refugee Action Support tutor noted:

> I begged to be accepted [as] a tutor in [the program]. . . . Coming to Australia as a migrant, I had a really tough time growing up. Australia is a great country with lots of support and resources, but if you don't speak the language, if you don't know what the culture is about . . . it is very difficult. . . . [Being a Refugee Action Support tutor] is about being able to be a bridge between cultures and communities. It's a learning process for me. It's helping someone learn. It's not about teaching. It's about helping someone learn.

The Refugee Action Support Program

The Refugee Action Support program was launched in 2007 through a partnership between Western Sydney University, the New South Wales (NSW) Department of Education and Communities, and the Australian Literacy and Numeracy Foundation. The partners share a commitment to facilitating support for the education and resettlement of refugee youth in Greater Western Sydney. Though each partner understood the need, they could not implement the refugee program on their own. It was essential for the partners to propose collaborative solutions, consider limitations, and implement a program that was both sustainable and effective.

The resulting program is an academic English language and literacy tutoring initiative in which university education students are recruited and trained to provide one-on-one and small-group support for recently settled[1] students of refugee background who are enrolled in years 7–11 at participating schools.[2] Each tutor engages in sixty hours of activity in a given semester, which equates to tutoring four hours per week for twelve weeks plus an initial twelve-hour training session delivered by the University, the Department of Education and Communities, the Literacy and Numeracy Foundation, and the NSW Service for the Treatment and Rehabilitation of Torture and Trauma Survivors. In addition to the initial training, tutors receive ongoing supervision from school staff, four weeks of professional experience in the classroom, related university coursework, certification, and course credit.[3] Therefore, community engagement is positioned as central—not peripheral—to the professional and civic development of preservice teachers. A cohort of tutors is recruited each semester.

A salient feature of this program is the University's commitment to community engagement. It does not see itself as existing solely within the boundaries of its campuses, as if separated from its surroundings. It sees itself as integrated with, concerned about, and reflective of the environmental and cultural diversity of the western suburbs of Sydney. Western Sydney has a high culturally and linguistically diverse population and has been a significant destination for refugee resettlement. Almost two thirds of Australia's newly arrived refugee and humanitarian entrants settle in the region. Typically, refugees settling in Greater Western Sydney arrive from Sudan, Iraq, Afghanistan, and Sierra Leone.

Notably, students enrolled in NSW public schools reflect a significant diversity of cultural, linguistic, and socioeconomic backgrounds. In 2014, 774,700 students were enrolled in over 2,200 NSW government schools. Of the total enrolment, 242,850 students identified as having a language background other than English, which comprises approximately 32 percent of total students. Of those, 138,487 (or 18 percent) were identified as needing English as an Additional Language or Dialect (EAL/D) support, and 7,448 were refugee students. Each year government schools enroll more than 1,300 refugee and humanitarian entrant students. Of the total population of refugee students enrolled in public schools in the state of NSW, 81 percent of refugee students are attending schools located in Greater Western Sydney.

Since 2005, the University has developed the Schools Engagement strategy to raise aspirations and transition students of low socioeconomic background to the University; implement a system for tracking and improving community engagement; establish leadership positions across Western Sydney University's schools and faculties to coordinate engagement activities; and change the management and structure of the Office of Engagement. The University currently engages with organizations and individuals in the Greater Western Sydney region on a variety of community- and school-based projects. The embedding of community engagement in learning and teaching, research, and institutional collaborations has made the University an "engaged university" (Watson et al. 2011).

The philosophy underpinning the University's approach to community and regional engagement is the link between its mission in the region (the "why" of community and regional engagement), the University's Making the Difference: 2010–2015 strategy and regional priorities (the "what," or focus, of community engagement), and the operational framework (the "how") for community and regional engagement. The University has found this to be a compelling model for mobilizing institutional capacity, as it recognizes the contributory nature of engagement, and the fact that engagement is a fluid and evolving phenomenon, rather than a particular outcome at one point in time (Western Sydney University 2012, 102–103).

By including university students (trainee teachers) in this commitment to collaborating with the local refugee community, the University's School of Education and its community partners (the Department of Education and Communities and the Literacy and Numeracy Foundation) aim to support the educational opportunities for young people of refugee background. As mentioned earlier, the reciprocal nature of this program also contributes to the development of future educators who would exhibit active and responsible citizenship, as well as an increased awareness of principles concerning social justice and equity that are essential for both teaching and learning. Such experiences and related university coursework emphasize that learning is highly dependent on the development of trust, rapport, and critical understandings of diversity.

On one hand, the Refugee Action Support program has become a valuable contribution to the learning support for refugee youth, particularly in the postcompulsory years of education and training (Olliff 2010). The refugee program aims to provide effective, individualized support for refugee students as they grapple with the language, literacy, knowledge, and cultural demands of schooling by providing them with regular access to a skilled tutor-mentor. The program has become a space where tutors can model, discuss, and negotiate a range of knowledge and skills. Additionally, the program is a valuable component of teacher training that prepares individuals to be responsive and sensitive to the learning needs of a diverse range of students (Ferfolja 2009; Naidoo 2012). Participating university students extend the values of social inclusion and social justice presented within university coursework and apply their understanding in the field.

The refugee program tutoring sessions occur one day per week for four hours when all tutors allocated to the school are present and supported by a senior teacher. Four high schools participated in the initial 2007 program. In 2014, eighteen high schools participated in the Refugee Action Support Partnership in Greater Western Sydney through the University. The number of tutors at a school can range from four to twelve or more. This creates a "learning center" environment through which tutors support students in both classroom and out-of-class contexts, such as the library and in an after-school homework center. In a typical tutoring environment, "Students all addressed the tutors by their first name [which assists] in reducing the power differential between tutor and student, which [is] so important in developing a positive dynamic in the workings of the center" (Ferfolja and Naidoo 2010, 13).

It is important for the university students and the school students to notice the changes that occur when one is able to renegotiate learning spaces, particularly in fast-paced environments of the modern classroom and school. Observations of these insights have been gathered through focus groups and interviews with the tutors, school students, and school staff that have formed the basis of program's initial evaluations (Ferfolja et al. 2007; Ferfolja 2008; Ferfolja et al. 2009; Australian Literacy and Numeracy Foundation 2010; Ferfolja and Naidoo 2010). Tutors notice that "it's more like we are a group of students all working together rather than teacher-student" (Refugee Action Support tutor, video interview, 2008). In these spaces, the tutors react and respond to the needs of their students. The students have a certain degree of control and have the ability to seek clarification that may not be possible in the typical classroom setting. As one student noted, "The first week, we just want them to sit next to us and really help. But after that, you can do it by yourself, and I'm okay I can do it by myself. . . . And at the end they can check your work" (participating high school student, 2010). Teachers notice how the impact of the tutor-student relationship extends beyond academic success: "Access to a caring adult . . . interested in them and their learning has meant that [refugee] students have built their confidence and made them think more about what they want to achieve . . . and has made them more resourceful" (classroom teacher, interview, 2009).

Reciprocally, tutors acknowledge how the program fosters cross-cultural understandings that serve as tools that help them become better teachers and members of the community. A Refugee Action Support tutor noted:

> You get to grow in the way that you interact with students. You also get to experience their cultures in many ways, the way they view things, the experiences they go through. . . . Some [of] it is very beautiful.

. . . At the end of Ramadan, [the students] cooked a massive feast and invited us [the tutors] to lunch. We sang. We danced. It was the most amazing experience I had at university.

History and Activities

The initial discussions around the refugee program commenced in late 2005 and continued into early 2006. The program's development coincided with the respective partners (the University, the Department, and the Foundation) each independently consulting with schools, community groups, and youth/service agencies about implementing initiatives to assist with the settlement and education of young refugees of African background in the Western Sydney area. The community and the partnering organizations recognized that adolescent refugees, particularly unaccompanied minors, are at a particular educational disadvantage as they are placed in classes that reflect their chronological age, yet their literacy and numeracy abilities may be well below the academic requirements of their year (Ferfolja and Naidoo 2010). This is compounded by other factors such as having experienced psychological trauma (Foundation House 2005; Strekalova and Hoot 2008); having to adapt to the expectations and culture of a formal education system, knowledge of which is taken for granted by those already teaching and learning in the system; having to deal with material, personal, and cultural loss; and having to adapt to an entirely new social, economic, and cultural system. In spite of the challenges, young people of refugee background often hold high aspirations of educational success and demonstrate significant levels of resilience (Brown, Miller, and Mitchell 2006).

Racism also prevails (Brown, Miller, and Mitchell 2006; Strekalova and Hoot 2008). The predominant narratives in popular and political culture need to be combated. Newspaper headlines —such as "No Apology for Linking Africans to Crime" (Roberts 2006), "African Refugee Program 'a Failure'" (Parnell 2009), "Most Think Refugee Level Is Too High" (Grattan 2008), and "Minister Cuts African Refugee Intake" (Farouque, Petrie, and Miletic 2007)—served to generate contempt for refugees in the broader community rather than compassion and support. Spurious claims linking African youth to increases in crime were found to be without basis by the Australian Human Rights and Equal Opportunities Commission (Roberts 2006). Despite the overt racism in popular politics, it is important that schools are seen as "stabilizing features in the unsettled lives of refugees. They provide safe spaces for new encounters, interactions and learning opportunities" (Matthews 2008, 32).

In 2005, the University was in the early stages of consulting with the Sudanese community for a project known as the Sudanese Language and Literacy Alliance initiative. The Department of Education and Communities was allocating additional resources for the creation of refugee student support officer positions throughout the state as well as providing additional funding to schools that had higher proportions of students of refugee background. The Literacy and Numeracy Foundation was in discussions with the Department and local community agencies, such as migrant resource centers, about the prospects of establishing additional language and literacy tutoring for young people of refugee background. Each partner had a vested interest in working together to facilitate additional support for students of refugee background due to the cultural and linguistic diversity of the communities of Western Sydney.

In 2006, representatives from the Foundation met with representatives of the University to mutually explore ways to support the development of language and literacy skills of young Sudanese refugees in Western Sydney. The School of Education course Professional Experience 3 was identified as the subject through which preservice teachers could be engaged to provide refugee students with additional academic language and literacy support. Professional Experience 3 is a mandatory community engagement course whereby university students earn credits for completing sixty hours of activity in the community.

In mid-2006, a steering committee was established with representatives of the NSW Department of Education and Communities, the Australian Literacy and Numeracy Foundation, the University, and selected schools. The University's representation included Professor Vickers, Associate Professor Loshini Naidoo, and Dr. Tania Ferfolja. The Department was represented by its Multicultural Programs Unit, which was headed by Hanya Stefaniuk. Eric Brace and the Foundation's executive director, Mary-Ruth Mendel, represented the Foundation. A pilot program, funded by a discretionary grant from the NSW education minister, was launched in 2007 that involved four schools and would be known as the Refugee Action Support program. Community liaison officer(s) were appointed to assist schools and tutors in working with parents/caretakers of targeted students as well as providing important cross cultural training to tutors and school personnel.[4] In the pilot year, thirty-five tutors were recruited to support sixty-five students across the four schools. Funding was allocated to schools to provide relief time to coordinating teachers, to the Foundation for tutor training, to regional staff to pay the community liaison officers for their time, and to the University to conduct evaluation activities. Each partner was required to provide a substantial amount of in-kind support, as the financial contribution covered only a portion of real costs.

The steering committee negotiated guidelines that identified each organization's role in the initiative as well as how the tutors', students', and teachers' time would be allocated. The creation of the guidelines created a substantial amount of productive tension as each partner advocated for the people it represented. For instance, the Department of Education and Communities and schools were committed to supporting a program that would primarily benefit refugee youth. They wanted the support available to be substantial. They feared that the university students might become involved for only a few hours, and that this involvement would place additional demands on schools. They also wanted assurance that the program could be sustained after the pilot phase. Meanwhile, the University wanted the program to respect the limits upon what could be asked of university students. It wanted the program to have robust teaching and learning outcomes, and expected that the program could contribute to the body of research in this area. The Literacy and Numeracy Foundation shared many of the objectives that the school and the Department had, though it also wanted the program to be a viable model that could be shared with and applied to different contexts.

The initial evaluation—conducted by the University's Centre for Educational Research—reported that tutors benefited from the activities and that 75 percent of participating youth improved at a significant or greater degree in language and literacy skills. Improvements were more pronounced for those students who attended most regularly, and it was recommended that the program expand in 2008 with minor modifications (Ferfolja et al. 2007). In 2008, the guidelines were streamlined under the direction of the steering committee. The program adopted what is now the current model of two tutor cohorts per year, each serving for twelve weeks and providing support one day per week for four hours each week. Eight schools became involved in 2008, and that year's program and associated evaluation were funded through the Westpac Foundation. Over eighty tutors were involved to support over two hundred young people across the eight schools.

In subsequent years, the programs would come to be funded through support from the NSW Department of Education and Communities (2010–present); the Australian Department of Education, Employment and Workplace Relations under the Schools Assistance (Learning Together—Achievement Through Choice and Opportunity) Act of 2004 (2010–2011); various grants from the philanthropic sector (including the Verizon, Paul Newman, Collier, and Mary MacKillop Foundations); and through in-kind support provided by staff at the University, the Literacy and Numeracy Foundation, the Department of Education and Communities, and participating schools. Despite ongoing support for the initiative, changes within the NSW Government relating to the education-funding model will be a factor that the partnership must address for the continuing sustainability of the initiative.

Since 2007, the program with Western Sydney University's Faculty of Education (Secondary) has involved over six hundred tutors who have collectively provided over thirty thousand hours of support to well over one thousand young people. The program has been replicated in rural locations with the support of Charles Sturt University (Wagga Wagga and Albury, NSW), and the program expanded into primary schools in 2010. These developments were facilitated through findings from university-led evaluations. Case studies of effective refugee program schools have provided further support to improving the initiative (Ferfolja and Naidoo 2010; Naidoo 2012). In 2014 alone, eighteen high schools and eleven primary schools in urban and rural locations hosted three hundred tutors who provided support for more than six hundred children and young people that year. Over the course of the program's history across all sites and partnerships, approximately fourteen hundred university students have been involved.

The Refugee Action Support program is a depiction of community engagement in which concerted and strategic efforts are made to work together on an issue of local concern. It demonstrates how universities and schools are not isolated, separated institutions, but are "democratic institutions where the efforts of individuals can improve literacy within diverse learning communities" (Prosser and Levesque 1997, 34). In the process, the participating university students are immersed in viewing educational practice from new, broader perspectives that engage them in the politics of access, equity, and diversity.

Developing Civic Capabilities

The preceding sections have shown how Refugee Action Support as a school-university-community partnership program was created to reflect the partners' commitment to community building and civic vitality. This section will show how the integration of the refugee program into the learning of preservice teachers exposes them to the lived educational experience of diverse others, so that participation becomes an effective mechanism for civic education by meeting real community needs.

For nearly a century, democratic theorists have argued that civic dispositions develop through practice and experience (Dewey 1921; Freire 1972). They underline the importance of the dialectic of reflection and action, theory and praxis; thus, opportunities to engage with the community serve an educative function that helps develop the identities of democratic citizens. It is through opportunities to engage with others in the community (schools, the workplace, civic and nongovernment agencies) that people learn the capacity for self-governance.

By aligning educational objectives with community needs, community engagement is meant to enhance reciprocal learning. Bringle and Hatcher (1995, 112) assert that community engagement activities are a way "to gain further understanding of course content, a broader appreciation of the discipline, and an enhanced sense of civic responsibility." In Australia and at the University in particular, the term "community engagement" is preferred to "service-learning" because it is believed that community engagement is more closely linked to Boyte's (2004, 82) notion of political involvement. In community engagement, staff, community members, and faculty are part of the conversation to produce strategies for positive social change. Collins (2010, 11–12) stated that the notion of community implies a "major vehicle that links individuals to social institutions," and is "central to how people organize and experience social inequalities." It is therefore a catalyst for "strong, deep feelings that can move people to action."

"Service," on the other hand, is perceived to be closely aligned with deficit thinking and values of philanthropy, power differentials, and exploitation. According to Boyte (2004, 82), "The history of the word is associated with terms such as 'servile,' 'serf,' and 'servant.' It conceives of people without credentials as needy clients to be rescued or as customers to be manipulated" (Boyte 2008, 107–112). He goes on to say that if students are to develop their "political sensibilities, we need to change the now dominant view of civic learning as community service or service-learning . . . understanding education should be about transformation, the 'reworking' of ourselves and our contexts" (Boyte 2008, 107–112). Fox (2002, 7) suggests focusing on "learning as a form of service rather than on learning by way of service" to emphasize the importance of reciprocal learning as a key learning outcome of service exchange. "An *organizing* approach is what we need to develop, if we are to think and act politically" (Boyte 2004, 84). This is a counterresponse to a service model that supports the notion that the sharing and exchange of ideas can lead to a level of cultural understanding that bridges current cultural divides (Porter and Monard 2001). The refugee program is, in effect, an organizing approach as it develops the civic capacity of all participants.

Professional Development

The significance of the refugee program for the development of civic capabilities is that the content of the Diversity, Social Justice, and Equity teaching unit that all refugee program tutors study is intended to engage preservice teachers in a broad examination of "social justice." In this training, students examine strategies and pedagogies that work for teaching marginalized and disadvantaged students in particular and explore what works in addressing social and educational problems. Mills (1959, 4), in writing about the sociological imagination, said that the link between individual lives and social forces tailored "the kinds of people they were becoming." The sociological imagination transforms passive citizens into active individuals engaged with public issues. For Boyte (2004, 12), "Democratizing education [goes beyond Dewey] in the sense of its reconnection with the political life of communities, and in the sense of educational and learning activities as sites for democratizing the larger society . . . to the extent that education becomes a medium for developing bolder, more confident, and more political citizens." Thus, the curriculum should be under review throughout and contribute to a critical reflexivity that in effect sustains the dialectics touched upon here. By working with refugee youth in schools who were considered to be "at risk," preservice teachers in the refugee program were able to subject their individual and shared understandings to critical review. Dzur (2008, 121) believes that the way to sow "the seeds of a more deliberative democracy" in universities and communities is "by cultivating norms of equality, collaboration, reflection, and communication."

The development of the interrelationship between theory and praxis in the Diversity, Social Justice, and Equity unit through community engagement provides crucial learning opportunities for pre-service teachers. They develop an awareness of the importance of combining academic learning with issues relating to education in the community, and they become active agents in their own professional development. Academic learning becomes more real and builds a sense of citizenship in preservice teachers. The link between theory and praxis allows preservice teachers to gain an understanding of course content, a broader appreciation of social justice issues, and an enhanced sense of civic and social responsibility. The active construction of knowledge leads to a deeper understanding of the course objectives, which are designed to introduce preservice teachers to the roots of social differences and social inequalities, and to motivate and inspire engagement through critical pedagogy. Preservice teachers hence cultivate the knowledge, skills, and dispositions to empower themselves as future teachers able to develop social justice projects in their future schools. A former refugee program tutor notes:

> I wouldn't be where I am today, not just in regard to my position [but] in regard to the fact that it has made me more aware of what some of these students have gone through. I believe a lot of the refugee program teachers come out better people and a lot more understanding. Your awareness increases. The program gives us that opportunity to be more realistic [about] what goes on in schools. We are seeing a lot more refugee students coming through. The refugee program is the pinnacle of it all. It helps us realize where we can go with these students.

Accordingly, community engagement becomes a site of knowledge production with the reflective student journals that students are asked to keep throughout the program. This journaling process transforms experience into knowledge and brings it into the public domain, linking community engagement to civic engagement. By integrating subject content with community engagement, the program more fully links abstract theory and concrete practice, which can then achieve the highest degree of reciprocity. For teacher education programs it is important that the moral and civic values and strategic judgments, which are acknowledged as belonging to the profession, are themselves "democratized." This is akin to Dzur's (2008) assertion that democratic professionalism is not seen as occasional individual heroism but rather as an institutionalized approach to ethics and practice. A preservice teacher attests:

> I do have an interest in refugee stuff and so I'm pleased to have ended up in [refugee program] to get a broader perspective on refugee issues and what it's like to teach kids who've come from a refugee background.

Community-oriented problem-solving opportunities in the teaching of the diversity subject content and the refugee program allow preservice teachers to be self-reflective. In the process, preservice teachers integrate and apply knowledge to real-world situations. This enhances their civic, social, and political participation as individuals and as a group in a democracy. "Recognizing the community issues that affect schools can promote community mobilization for education, and that mobilization can strengthen democratic practices, build stronger public relationships, and reinforce norms of cooperation" (Mathews 2014, 158). This infusion process also requires that educators critically examine the curriculum and revise it as needed to make issues of diversity central, rather than peripheral. Boyte and Kari (2000, 40) assert that the meaning of "citizens" draws from the "public work" tradition of democracy: "public problem solvers and co-producers of public good." This tutor's reflection indicates an orientation toward democracy and recognition of how their careers as future teacher professionals interact with the public:

> When I saw this I thought, "what's it going to be like for those kids coming to Australia, what's going to be in their memories of where they've come from?" ... How do you, as a teacher, deal with that emotional baggage, help them to then start learning again?

A fundamental feature of the Refugee Action Support program is the deliberate development of commitment, knowledge, and skills for the public good. Tutors commit to tutoring over a semester, making real commitment to people and issues in communities. The intentional training, including individual and group observation sessions, equips tutors to become more engaged citizens. The program then becomes a civic engagement lens that focuses on public aspects of academic and professional knowledge. So in addition to preparing future teachers by exposing them to diversity, social justice, and equity, the refugee program enhances professional development in preservice tutors by instilling self-confidence, patience, and responsibility.

According to Freire (1972), people participate in history when they produce culture; that is, when they critically reflect and act upon the crucial themes of their times and through that process contribute to new meanings. Written reflections from preservice teachers at the conclusion of their participation in the refugee program indicated improvements in self-confidence, patience, and responsibility. Their professional development was enhanced by greater awareness of career options, and an appreciation for the importance of civic responsibility, and "giving back." It is the capacity for dialogue that contributes to critical consciousness and hence the development of civic capabilities. According to a preservice teacher, "I think for some of them [the homework center] was the only place in the school that they felt safe enough to express an opinion or ask a question or, you know, just be counted."

Gallego (Vickers 2007, 207) found that when student teachers participated in community-based service-learning as a parallel practicum experience, they developed the ability to stand aside from the "naturalized" practices of schools. This distance allows student teachers to critique traditional practices and contrast them with the kinds of learning environments they encounter in alternative out-of-school settings. While such engagement is confrontational, it allows teachers to gain an understanding of the contexts of the students' lives (Dunkin 1996). This understanding helps teachers develop flexibility in their teaching that accommodates and supports diverse student perspectives and sensibilities. According to Vickers (2007, 213), the recognition by student teachers of the legitimacy of marginal students' views about "school" is described here as a "reversal of the lens": "I think that's what I learned—how as teachers, we need to really, not just teach skills but make sure that students understand."

As teacher educators, Allard and Santoro (2004, 14) suggest that "part of our role is to offer experiences to our students that enable them to understand and examine their own positioning within and through current discourses." Seeking to disrupt notions of self by stepping outside the center and trying to see life from the margins may serve as "a starting point for developing understanding and insights into taken-for-granted beliefs about culture and class" (Allard and Santoro 2004, 14).

Freire (2004, 74) also stresses the importance of engaging students in a curriculum that "challenges them to build a critical understanding of their presence in the world." Refugee program tutors came to understand students who inhabit a social world that is sometimes far removed from their own. One notes:

> I sort of gathered that many migrants are, you know, are sort of multilingual, and their first language might be different. They have to navigate around languages to be able to make sense of certain things.

The refugee program suggests an image of the society that students will graduate into, and of the kinds of contributions they can make to that society. These notions are embedded implicitly in the interactions between educators and students. Refugee program tutors, as a result of the community engagement activity, begin to seriously think about their philosophy of teaching and the social conditions of schooling. Many, we have observed from extracts provided, see a much larger function of teaching that transcends institutional walls. This practical experience is a stepping stone to developing theoretical competence in citizenship and civic education. Tutors move from the "what" of teaching to the "why" of teaching, and in this way develop a sense of what it means to educate for democratic citizenship.

The focus on the development of civic capabilities and knowledge through the refugee program indicates that preservice teachers involved in the program are socioculturally conscious. That is, the teachers recognize that there are multiple ways of perceiving reality and that these are influenced by one's location in the social order. They hold affirming views of students from diverse backgrounds, seeing resources for learning in all students rather than viewing differences as problems to be overcome. Teachers see themselves as both responsible for and capable of bringing about educational change that will make schools more responsive to all students; understand how learners construct knowledge and feel capable of promoting learners' knowledge construction; know more about the lives of their students; and use the knowledge about students' lives to design instruction that builds on what they already know while stretching them beyond the familiar (Villegas and Lucas 2002, 21). It means that the "One size fits all" approach to teaching is not in the best interests of students, especially refugee or newly arrived migrant students whose first language is not English.

Interpreting the world for others, and doing it well, requires not just a skill set but also a knowledge of how interpretation is done, of the cultural fields in which it is done, and of the other possibilities of interpretation that surround one's own. Finding a place not only refers to a physical bit of land, it also refers to what gives people an identity; if "it is not grounded in a common ethnicity, religion or language, it must be grounded in shared ideals, a shared vision of the society it is striving to create" (Dummett 2001, 7). In schools—for instance—students of refugee backgrounds "are continuously contested, imagined and reimagined, transformed and negotiated, both by their members and through interaction with others. The identity, and so the meaning, of any culture is, thus, aspectival rather than essential" (Peters 2010, 21). Tutors become partners in the navigation of new identities and new rules. A 2007 preservice teacher reflects:

> Students who attend now are able to complete their assignments and are gaining additional skills from working one-on-one with tutors. Last term Hassan Ali received a merit certificate at the school merit assembly for the quality of his work.... Students have a point of reference for their literacy problems and a chance to achieve in tasks that would not have previously been available to them.

Fostering a University Culture of Engagement

Sullivan (2000, 20) states that "campuses educate their students for citizenship most effectively to the degree that they become sites for constructive exchange and cooperation among diverse groups of citizens from the larger community." This has been an important place-marker for the University "as it has sought to build the mechanisms and relationships that deliver on mutual benefit and a sense of reciprocity" (Western Sydney University 2012, 7). Accordingly, concepts of engagement are part of the university mission and integrated across the curriculum and research activities. Professor Barbara Holland, at the time the WSU pro-vice-chancellor (engagement), said in 2010 that the refugee program "links teaching and research approaches to urgent community issues. It enriches the lives and futures of our students through community-based learning." Additionally, the National Protocols for Higher Education also argue that all public universities in Australia have an obligation to

> engage with the community to enhance material, human, social and/or environmental wellbeing of the community; equip the community with social, cultural and international knowledge, skills and attitudes to improve the quality of life for all citizens; and contribute to a democratic, equitable and civilised society. (Ministerial Council 2006, 3)

As previously stated, the regional characteristics of Greater Western Sydney determine the nature of the University's engagement with the region. Greater Western Sydney is Australia's third largest economy. Over the next fifteen years six hundred thousand people are expected to settle in Greater Western Sydney (Western Sydney Regional Organization of Councils 2011). Greater Western Sydney is a socioeconomically disadvantaged area that historically suffers from systemic underinvestment in social infrastructure, particularly in regards to quality educational and cultural facilities. In particular, the culturally and linguistically diverse and refugee populations in Greater Western Sydney have been identified as a specific population group in the region that faces significant and ongoing socioeconomic inequities. Among them are low incomes, low levels of educational attainment, and high unemployment (Western Sydney Regional Organization of Councils 2011).

The body of knowledge that emerges from the Refugee Action Support program helps facilitate the University's transformative change, which is based on emphasizing quality, engaged civic leadership. With such knowledge, the University is able to reconstruct and dignify the learning and teaching experiences of the school and university community. This makes it possible for preservice teachers and refugee students to acquire perspectives on teaching and learning that allow them to critically examine the role society has played in their own self-formation. Boyte and Fretz (2010, 72) state that community-organizing practices can be a way of "building public relationships across lines of difference, creating free spaces for people to work publicly with others and understanding and embracing the messiness of change." The refugee program was embraced and supported at the University as a part of its academic teaching and learning structure, thereby creating a sense of ownership that led to the success of the program. By articulating a vision of community engagement that is consistent with the needs of a changing demographic, as well as planning strategic initiatives to build human and community capacity, the University as a stakeholder in education has improved the learning and research that it facilitates. Furthermore, the program has helped strengthen the University's presence in the region and contributed to the creation of future leaders and agents of social change.

Essentially, the application of knowledge gained from the refugee program led to the cultivation of a community of educators and learners who disseminate information, assess concerns of all participants in the planning process, and anticipate opportunities for transformation. The sharing of responsibility among stakeholders—realized through task rotation, sharing skills and information through consistent meetings and workshops, and regular evaluation—has been an important participatory function of the program. According to Fisher (1993), professionals who are more closely embedded in local knowledge and who research issues from community interests are apt facilitators of participation and deliberation, and can serve as bridges between expert and public discourses. Therefore, equality among stakeholders is an important underlying strategy indicating that all stakeholders, formal and informal, are given the opportunity to develop leadership abilities. Ward and Vernon (1999, 36) note:

> By inviting the community service agency to have a voice and become an active partner in the academic service-learning process, higher education can more fully realize its public service and outreach mission, actualize a social change model for service-learning, and achieve the ideals of the engaged campus.

There are greater opportunities for social participation by parents too as they become involved in activities through people like community liaison officers who provide bilingual and bicultural support for parents and school personnel. The literature on community building (McNeely 1999) implies that community building itself will increase civic capability. This is reinforced by social capital theorists (Putnam 1993; Putnam 2000), who see civic engagement as an incidental by-product of informal voluntary association participation. The shift from "organizational structures" to "citizen participation" also shows the shift from politics as ideology to politics as community. According to Walker-Dalhouse and Dalhouse (2009, 333):

> When two elephants fight the grass suffers. This Sudanese proverb asserts that parents and teachers are major figures in the lives of children. If there is discord between them for any reason then the children

will suffer. Consequently, both teachers and parent's support [is] needed for refugee students to achieve academic proficiency.

Making and Sustaining Partnerships

The relevance of broad partnerships between nongovernmental organizations, community liaison officers, local governments, and universities in the development of educational initiatives to improve the efficiency and effectiveness of the delivery system cannot be underestimated. Such partnerships—unlike the traditional technocratic, top-down approach—can increase the control of people over development processes; uncover more resources from a wider range of actors; increase program demand, relevance, efficiency, and sustainability; and develop new knowledge, skills, and attitudes in those participating in the process. To do this, educators in higher education institutions like universities must prepare professional teachers to develop, lead, manage, teach, work within, and influence society's institutions, including the most basic foundation of education. Besides training future teachers, schools of education at universities strongly influence the learning framework of the education system.

The Refugee Action Support program has been able to establish itself as a sustainable program for a range of reasons; however, it must be noted that such sustainability is achieved through the dedication of individuals and the commitment of institutions. Consequently, prospects for sustainability can weaken if a program is not able to adapt to changing political, institutional, and individual conditions. The program has benefited from the mutual partnership of the University, the Department of Education and Communities, the Australian Literacy and Numeracy Foundation, schools, and community agencies, such as the NSW Service for the Treatment and Rehabilitation of Torture and Trauma Survivors. No one partner would have had sufficient resources to implement, monitor, and sustain the initiative individually. By establishing a partnership between government, universities, schools, and community agencies, we were able to allocate resources and workload across the participating organizations. The partners also each bring their own insights into the opportunities, limitations, and future changes from within their respective sectors: university, government, schools, community, and philanthropy.

Through the course of the program, each partner has also played a role in contributing resources that the other partners could not otherwise access. For instance, in the pilot phase of the program, the Literacy and Numeracy Foundation was able to source philanthropic funds that allowed the program to provide sufficient results in order to sustain a case for further government investment. Meanwhile, the University has been able to source research funds to document the program and themes pertinent to the program. These research funds would not be accessible to the other partners. More importantly, the government partner, the NSW Department of Education and Communities, had been able to allocate a portion of ongoing funding to schools for the program, and—while recent policy changes will alter how this funding is distributed in the future—the ongoing commitment and in-kind support from government partners has been vital to the sustainability of the initiative.

Let us not forget that the initiative was born out of community consultation, professional collaboration, and capacity building with community members and school staff. Many of the original individuals continue to take an interest or a role in mentoring the university students and school students involved in the initiative. At the start, these individuals shared a similar agenda and were jointly seeking similar goals and outcomes, which tended to sustain the relationship at times when institutional changes may have otherwise frustrated efforts. Creating trusting and communicative relationships is important in sustaining such a partnership. The early efforts of the steering committee, which met quarterly until 2011, provided a platform for shared leadership, decision-making, conflict resolution, resource management, knowledge exchange, shared learning, and capacity building. Evaluation was a key priority for the committee, with formal research evaluations conducted in the first four years of the program, and ongoing monitoring in the subsequent years. A commitment to continuous assessment of the partnership itself, as well as the outcomes generated, is seen as a vital factor for program sustainability (Holland 2005).

Further factors have contributed to the program's sustainability. As emphasized earlier, the tutoring activities are incorporated into the teaching and learning activities of preprofessional development at the University so the activity is *central*, and not *peripheral*, to university practices. The steering committee was able to establish clear guidelines with a regular schedule, and the University involves a consistent number of tutors each semester. Therefore, participating schools were able to anticipate the number of tutors and could incorporate the role of the tutors within their broader instructional plans (Ferfolja and Naidoo 2010). As a consequence, the program offers schools and students the flexibility to mold the activities to the unique and diverse school culture and requests from students, which encourages schools and students to take ownership of the initiative.

Furthermore, many of the schools have gone on to employ past tutors as graduate teachers, who are—in turn—able to maintain teaching and learning relationships with their students and their families/caregivers. While there is no formal documented evidence to indicate exactly how many tutors have been employed by the schools, the majority of the past tutors have indicated that the schools have employed them either permanently, on contract, or casually. These graduate teachers hence commence their careers in whatever capacity with a strong awareness and commitment to the needs and aspirations of students of refugee background and, therefore, are attractive early professionals for schools working with diverse student populations in the communities of Greater Western Sydney.

Perhaps one of the early lessons was to acknowledge the limitations of the program and to work within those limitations. The original community consultation identified a key need that was not being met in a concerted way: academic language, literacy, and learning support for adolescents of refugee background. While other features could be incorporated into the program—such as university campus visits, arts initiatives, and career/postschool mentoring—these activities were considered to be supplementary aspects of the program. When resources or opportunities have been available, such enrichment activities have been offered or organized. A clear, strategic mission is therefore essential to the success of the program.

Successes

Overall, preservice teachers have demonstrated a greater sensitivity toward diverse cultures and refugees in particular, questioning the stereotypical beliefs about refugees and asylum seekers as portrayed in the Australian media and social imagination. The sensitivity toward other cultures also means that preservice teachers develop a deeper understanding of teaching strategies and pedagogies for teaching students from diverse backgrounds and, in this case, supporting the unique needs of refugee students. Firstly, the refugee program *develops self-confidence in preservice teachers*. In the caring, safe learning environments in the tutoring centers, preservice teachers were able to spend more individual time with students. This allowed tutors to tailor teaching strategies to specific students' needs, thereby producing better outcomes for the refugee students. Second, preservice teachers become *aware of bias and prejudices*. Preservice teachers were "transformed" in significant ways and found particular benefits when they were matched with tutees that were significantly different in terms of ethnicity, culture, and socioeconomic status.

The research also found that students developed new understandings about their preconceptions and stereotypes of marginalized and disadvantaged communities. Finally, as preservice teachers become more skilled and confident at reflection, they *consider more innovative and strategic ways of reflecting on practice*, particularly in teaching refugee students. Preservice teachers become committed to collaboration and reform in their own classrooms, schools, and communities, raising the quality of teachers going out to teach in schools. What this means in practice is that when preservice teachers become teachers with classrooms of their own, they will have the experience and knowledge they need to create an inclusive classroom environment.

It is apparent through the research and evaluation undertaken as part of this project that initiating a community engagement program like the refugee program requires preservice teachers to move outside their comfort zone. This leads to personal growth in the preservice teachers who serve as tutors and forces them to rely on self-knowledge and self-esteem to handle the particular situation. It also leads to a growth in self-confidence and a heightened sense of social responsibility. Finally, the refugee program assists students in developing the resilience that they bring with them from their home countries.

An effect of this community engagement program on refugee background students is improved literacy and increased comprehension and writing skills. This leads to improved grades, self-confidence, and growth in self-esteem, and develops students' academic growth, as indicated by such student reflections as these: "They helped us so much and helped to write essays, how to do everything and now I can do" and "It [the experience] makes you more confident as well. If they believe in [me] why can't I believe in myself?"

Most important, however, is the development of resilience in refugee students. It is important to note that resilience is not a fixed attribute, but an alterable set of processes that can be fostered and cultivated (Masten 1994; Padron, Waxman, and Huang 1999):

> Everything was hard, the studying is hard as well, but I've always been through it. I always got high marks and my last record I got 98 as an average in year 6.

This has important implications for the understanding of resiliency, in that it can be cultivated and improved by social and educational interventions. Therefore, by building connections to the outside community, the program gives students support from additional directions and encourages them to develop resolutions to issues that reestablish a sense of personal control. Wilkinson et al. (2012) suggest that development of a positive self-image is vital to maintaining the "can do" attitude that underlies a successful strategy for resilience. This is reiterated by a teacher at one of the schools participating in the refugee program, who said:

> A raising of their skills gives [the students] that confidence, improved self-esteem. You know, you can attack problems better when you feel better about yourself and you're a bit more confident to risk take. That's what the students gained: confidence.

Challenges

Implementing a community service-learning program is not without its challenges. Firstly, it requires a significant commitment of time and resources from the partners to create unique service experiences that are relevant, meaningful, and in line with the institutions' mission. Considerable time and resources must be devoted to orientation, training, and organization of preservice teachers and school students. Compounding these issues is the fact that teaching staff are not always adequately compensated in terms of workload sharing. Nongovernmental organizations must also invest a fair amount of time in the program, which is not worthwhile if there are insufficient payoffs for the organization. Second, not all preservice students are able to participate in the refugee program, and intake is limited to the numbers that can be offered a teaching placement at participating schools. Further, while most preservice teachers are reliable tutors, there are those who are less committed and fail to attend tutoring sessions or follow up on tasks. In most cases this creates an administrative inconvenience for school and university conveners of the program.

Third, while most of the schools in the program show a considerable level of commitment to the program, there are those schools who believe that the service does not complement their immediate needs despite having a large refugee student cohort at the school. Accordingly, teachers at the school thought the additional formal evaluation of preservice teachers at the end of the program to be a burden. In addition, the expansion of the program has meant that each school receives less individual consultation than in the early stages of the program when there were more opportunities to consult with school staff in order to workshop the role of the tutors at the school and determine what spaces to make available. The program has been able to provide support for more students through its expansion; however, if the program is to expand or be maintained at its current level, the challenge of maintaining consistency across the network will be an important one to address.

Conclusion

This chapter has drawn on salient points in the development of civic capabilities among university preservice teachers and high school students of refugee background involved in the Refugee Action Support program. The background information on the history and context for the program shows how it developed in collaboration with the community. Together, they adopted the goal of empowering refugee students affected by historical, political, educational, social, and economic challenges through academic literacy support. While the program is well connected to the University's academic curriculum, it was largely the community that defined the service that was required. For preservice teachers involved as tutors in the refugee program, it means being actively engaged in social and civic transformation, through their own lives and through their work as tutors for refugee youth. Both the University and the schools partnered with a nongovernment organization to design a program that improved the educational opportunities of those most at risk in society, and did so in a way that was mutually beneficial to all involved. The learning is reciprocal, the service informed, and delivery of the support truly meets the needs of the community, the students, preservice teachers, and the institutions.

The University however, despite being globally engaged and highly responsive to regional needs and partnerships, occupies an ambivalent space in terms of internal teaching and learning goals. Despite responding to the changing external environment of the university, internally, knowledge remains largely discipline based, showing little interplay with external dynamics and imperatives. This was particularly evident in the examination of existing pathways that support the transition of refugee background students into tertiary education (Naidoo et al. 2014). Although there are examples of exemplary high school practices to support transition to university, these pathways are not systemic and are too often dependent on the knowledge, excellent practice, and goodwill of individual schools and universities and their staff. Furthermore, while many refugee background students have high aspirations for educational attainment and a strong desire to succeed academically, and demonstrate desirable attributes such as high levels of resilience and problem-solving capacities (Naidoo et al. 2014), these individuals face unique hurdles that must be addressed. Specifically: forced migration, interrupted schooling, and significant differences in teaching pedagogy represent major barriers to mainstream pathways to higher education.

University staff view tutoring and mentoring of refugee background students as an important way to transition these students to university; but at the tertiary level, many staff feel ill-equipped to support refugee background students and feel that it may be outside their role and responsibility as academics (Naidoo et al. 2014). This issue raises questions about whether the provision of support is an abrogation of an academic's duty working in an increasingly diverse student demographic. For instance, what is a university staff member's responsibility when a student is frequently missing lectures or tutorials due to housing stress, the need to put food on the table, or major caring responsibilities? (Naidoo et al. 2014, 12). Second, there is a contrast between the sheer visibility and greater levels of learning support provided for international students at university (whose fees are a crucial part of university funding, particularly in an increasingly deregulated environment) and the lack of targeted and specific programs for young refugee background students (Naidoo et al. 2014, 12).

This issue raises the question of how equitably different types of students can be treated given straitened times for universities. It also raises the question of whether finances may be playing a far greater role in allocation of resources than concerns for equity and access. Finally, it is difficult to establish what number of refugee background students who achieve their goal of transitioning to university remain at university or complete their university studies. Data, for example, on refugee background student retention, goal attainment, and degree completion are not readily available or accessible at tertiary institutions to verify completion and retention rates (Naidoo et al. 2014). To address refugee background students' access and transition to education, it is important to refocus and address some of the crucial challenges and questions raised in this chapter. This implies that institutions need to go beyond discipline-based, piecemeal, and deficit approaches to student difference in favor of teaching and learning that is of mutual benefit to constituents inside and outside the institution.

NOTES

1. Students are able to receive support from the Refugee Action Support program during the first three years after arrival in Australia. The most important support is provided when young people make the transition from the Intensive English Centre to the mainstream high school. After arrival into Australia—in general—young people on a humanitarian visa are enrolled in an Intensive English Centre for six to eight months, where they receive targeted language support in a responsive student-centered environment. Intensive English Centers are often located on a mainstream high school campus. The transition to the busy, competitive contexts of middle and senior school can be challenging for students of refugee background who have experienced significantly disrupted education. Supporting the successful transition to school and to postschool options is essential.
2. A similar program to support primary-aged children of refugee background was launched in 2010; however, the present chapter will focus predominantly on the program in high schools.
3. Participation in the refugee program satisfies the university students' mandatory Professional Experience 3 course requirement in the master of teaching degree at Western Sydney University.
4. Financial support for community liaison officers ceased at the end of 2009.

REFERENCES

Allard, A., and Santoro, N. 2004. Making sense of difference? Teaching identities in postmodern contexts. Paper presented at the Australian Association of Research in Education Conference, Melbourne.

Australian Literacy and Numeracy Foundation. 2010. *Refugee Action Support: Final report, 2009*. Sydney: Australian Literacy and Numeracy Foundation.

Boyte, H. C. 2004. The necessity of politics. *Journal of Public Affairs* 7: 75–85.

———. 2008. Against the current: Developing the civic agency of students. *Change: The Magazine of Higher Learning* 40(3): 8–15.

Boyte, H. C., and Fretz, E. 2010. Civic professionalism. *Journal of Higher Education Outreach and Engagement* 14(2): 67–90.

Boyte, H. C., and Kari, N. N. 2000. Renewing the democratic spirit in American colleges and universities: Higher education as public work. In T. Ehrlich, ed., *Civic responsibility of higher education*. Westport, CT: American Council on Education / Oryx Press.

Bringle, R. G., and Hatcher, J. A. 1995. A service-learning curriculum for faculty. *Michigan Journal of Community Service Learning* 2: 112.

Brown, J., Miller, J., and Mitchell, J. 2006. Interrupted schooling and the acquisition of literacy: Experiences of Sudanese refugees in Victorian secondary schools. *Australian Journal of Language and Literacy* 29(2): 150–162.

Collins, P. H. 2010. The new politics of community. *American Sociological Review* 75(1): 7–30.

Dewey, J. 1921. *Democracy and education*. New York: Macmillan.

Dummett, M. 2001. *On immigration and refugees*. London: Routledge.

Dunkin, M. 1996. The future of teacher education in the USA: The third Holmes Group report. *Teaching and Teacher Education* 12: 561–566.

Dzur, Albert W. 2008. *Democratic professionalism: Citizen participation and the reconstruction of professional ethics, identity and practice.* University Park: Pennsylvania State University Press.

Farouque, F., Petrie, A., and Miletic, D. 2007. Minister cuts African refugee intake. *The Age*, October 2.

Ferfolja, T. 2008. *Refugee Action Support (RAS) Program.* Research evaluation 2008. Penrith, NSW: Western Sydney University.

——. 2009. The Refugee Action Support program: Developing understandings of diversity. *Teaching Education* 20(4): 395–407. doi:10.1080/10476210902741239.

Ferfolja, T., McCarthy, F., Naidoo, L., Vickers, M., and Hawker, A. 2009. *Refugee Action Support (RAS) Program.* Research Evaluation 2009. Penrith, NSW: Western Sydney University.

Ferfolja, T., and Naidoo, L. 2010. *Supporting refugee students through the Refugee Action Support program: What works in schools.* Penrith, NSW: Western Sydney University.

Ferfolja, T., Naidoo, L., Vickers, M., and McCarthy, F. 2007. *Refugee Action Support (RAS) Program: Interim Report.* Penrith, NSW: Western Sydney University.

Fisher, F. 1993. Citizen participation and the democratization of policy expertise: From theoretical inquiry to practical cases. *Policy Sciences* 26: 165–187.

Foundation House, Victorian Foundation for Survivors of Torture. 2005. *Survivors of torture.* Http://www.foundationhouse.org.au.

Fox, D. J. 2002. Service learning and self-reflectivity in rural Jamaica. *Practicing Anthropology* 24(2): 2–7.

Freire, P. 1972. *Pedagogy of the oppressed.* New York: Continuum.

——. 2004. *Pedagogy of indignation.* Boulder, CO: Paradigm Press.

Grattan, M. 2008. Most think refugee level is too high. *The Age*, August 5.

Han, E. 2012. Refugee students get helping hand to fulfil their educational dreams. *Sydney Morning Herald*, May 7.

Holland, B. A. 2005. Real change in higher education: Understanding differences in institutional commitment to engagement. In A. J. Kezar, T. C. Chambers, and J. C. Burkhardt, eds., *Higher education for the public good: Emerging voices from a national movement.* San Francisco: Jossey-Bass.

Masten, A. S. 1994. Resilience in individual development: Successful adaptation despite risk and adversity. In M. C. Wang and E. W. Gordon, eds., *Educational resilience in inner-city America: Challenges and prospects.* Hillsdale, NY: Lawrence Erlbaum.

Mathews, D. 2014. *The ecology of democracy: Finding ways to have a stronger hand in shaping our future.* Dayton, OH: Kettering Foundation Press.

Matthews, J. 2008. Schooling and settlement: Refugee education in Australia. *International Studies in Sociology of Education* 18: 31–45.

McNeely, J. 1999. Community building. *Journal of Community Psychology* 27(6): 741–750.

Mills, C. W. 1959. *The sociological imagination.* Oxford: Oxford University Press.

Ministerial Council on Education, Employment, Training and Youth Affairs. 2006. *Report of national meeting.* Brisbane, Australia, July 6–7.

Naidoo, L. 2009. Refugee-centred education: Critical theory in praxis. In B. H. Stroud and S. E. Corbin, eds., *Handbook on social change.* New York: Nova Science.

——. 2012. Refugee action support: Crossing borders in preparing pre-service teachers for literacy teaching in secondary schools in Greater Western Sydney. *International Journal of Pedagogies and Learning* 7: 266–274.

Naidoo, L., Wilkinson, J., Langat, K., Adoniou, M., and Cunneen, R. 2014. *Supporting school-university pathways for refugee students' access and participation in tertiary education.* NSW: WSU Printery.

NSW Department of Education and Communities. 2011. *Freedom from fear: Supporting refugee students and their families: Lessons from refugee support initiatives in the South Western Sydney region of schools.* Greystanes, NSW: NSW Department of Education and Communities.

Olliff, L. 2010. *Finding the right time and place: Exploring post-compulsory education and training pathways for young people from refugee backgrounds in NSW.* Sydney: Refugee Council of Australia.

Padron, Y. N., Waxman, H. C., and Huang, S.-Y. L. 1999. Classroom and instructional learning: Environment differences between resilient and nonresilient elementary school students. *Journal of Education for Students Placed at Risk* 4(1): 63–81.

Parnell, S. 2009. African refugee program "a failure." *Australian*, February 2.

Peters, M. A. 2010. Wittgenstein as exile: A philosophical topography. In M. A. Peters, N. C. Burbles, and P. Smeyers, eds., *Showing and doing: Wittgenstein as a pedagogical Philosopher*. London: Paradigm Publishers.

Porter, M., and Monard, K. 2001. Ayni in the global village: Building relationships of reciprocity through international service-learning. *Michigan Journal of Community Service Learning* 1(1): 5–17.

Prosser, T. M., and Levesque, J. A. 1997. Supporting literacy through service learning. *Reading Teacher* 51(1): 32–38.

Putnam, R. D. 1993. *Making democracy work: Civic traditions in modern Italy*. Princeton, NJ: Princeton University Press.

———. 2000. *Bowling alone: The collapse and revival of American community*. New York: Simon and Schuster.

Roberts, G. 2006. No apology for linking Africans to crime. *Australian*, April 4.

Strekalova, E., and Hoot, J. L. 2008. What is special about special needs of refugee children? Guidelines for teachers. *Multicultural Education* 16(1): 21–24.

Sullivan, W. M. 2000. Institutional identity and social responsibility in higher education. In T. Ehrlich, ed., *Civic responsibility and higher education*. Phoenix: Oryx Press.

Vickers, M. H. 2007. Reversing the lens: Transforming teacher education through service learning. In S. B. Gelmon and S. H. Billig, eds., *From passion to objectivity: International and cross-disciplinary perspectives on service learning research*. Charlotte, NC: Information Age.

Villegas, A. M., and Lucas, T. 2002. Preparing culturally responsive teachers: Rethinking the curriculum. *Journal of Teacher Education* 53(1): 20–32.

Walker-Dalhouse, D., and Dalhouse, A. D. 2009. When two elephants fight the grass suffers: Parents and teachers working together to support the literacy development of Sudanese youth. *Teaching and Teacher Education* 25(2): 328–335.

Ward, K., and Vernon, A. 1999. Community perspectives on student volunteerism and service learning. Paper presented at the Annual Meeting of the Association of the Study of Higher Education, San Antonio, TX.

Watson, D., Hollister, R. M., Stroud, S. E., and Babcock, E. 2011. *The engaged university: International perspectives on civic engagement*. New York: Routledge.

Western Sydney Regional Organisation of Councils. 2011. State Election: Issues Papers. Http://nla.gov.au/nla.arc-c10741.

Western Sydney University. 2012. *Review of community and regional engagement.* Sydney: Western Sydney University.

Wilkinson, J., Major, J., Santoro, N., and Langat, K. 2012. What out-of-school resources and practices facilitate African refugee students' educational success in Australian rural and regional settings? *Research Institute for Professional Practice, Learning and Education Report*, March.

The Kampung Tekir Project in Seremban, Malaysia: Worth all the Difficulties That We Have Encountered Thus Far!

Koh Kwee Choy and Wong Chin Hoong

It was Saturday July 28, 2007. Early that morning, I assembled with approximately one hundred medical students and staff of the International Medical University (IMU) in Malaysia. I talked to the group about the historical significance of this day: IMU would "adopt" Kampung Tekir (kampung is the Malay word for "village"). The adoption signified the beginning of a relationship between the village and IMU.

As representatives of IMU, we wore our IMU T-shirts proudly, but more than that, we felt excited about making a difference for the Orang Asli people (Orang Asli is the Malay word for "aborigines"). The students had a mixture of roles that day: performing health screenings, delivering talks, distributing gifts, and engaging the villagers in fun and educational activities. Looking around, I felt affirmed by the presence of supervising IMU faculty members.

Our forty-minute bus journey to Kampung Tekir took us to the fringe of a large palm oil plantation. From there, we had to switch to a carriage pulled by a four-wheel-drive tractor provided by the plantation. We made our way along a dirt road dotted with numerous waterlogged potholes. The village itself seemed hemmed in by the vast expanses of the surrounding palm oil plantation, while behind it the comforting presence of the forest periphery gave some measure of solace. Once in Kampung Tekir, we saw an eclectic mix of concrete and wooden homes, some better built than others, perhaps reflecting different levels of affordability. A few homes had motorcycles, even fewer had cars parked outside. The children played among the wildlife—it was interesting to see them running around with their household cats and dogs only to be "interrupted" by the occasional iguana. There was an abundance of local fruits within the village. Against the backdrop of long-standing religious tension between Muslims and Christians in Malaysia, I was pleasantly surprised to see that both a church and a mosque coexisted within the village!

By 9:00 a.m., we had set up in the local multipurpose hall or "Dewan Serbaguna" (in Malay). We were joined by members of the dental team from the hospital, representatives from a local pharmaceutical company, and personnel from the palm oil plantation. As popular Malay songs started to play in the background, the villagers started to arrive. During the health screenings, the *villagers were also entertained by various acts and events catered for all age groups. Villagers played games, participated in a lucky draw contest, competed in a karaoke singing competition, watched a dressed-up clown, and played a soccer match, which all helped to build relationships between the villagers and IMU. IMU students also ventured throughout the village, distributing brochures and getting to know the villagers.*

As we anticipated, the villagers were shy and hesitant to step forward. Most did not talk much when approached, but the few that engaged with us were friendly. Other villagers could be seen watching everything from a distance. Some were shutting themselves into their homes as we approached. I wondered how much of their difficult history—the dispute about landownership and Islamization policies—had made them suspicious of us (see Toshihiro 2009; Nicholas, Engi, and Teh 2010; and Nicholas 2000 for further information on these issues). Perhaps this was part of their personality and culture, but I could not be certain at that point. Our efforts eventually paid off, as by the end of the day sixty-nine adults and forty-five children had attended the event. We had the opportunity to share with them through educational talks about hygiene, drug and smoking addiction, and the use of contraception. In prior meetings with village authorities, we had been informed that these were issues of concern for the villagers.

The day culminated in a cordial afternoon tea. There was a sense of camaraderie as speeches were given by the IMU president, Tan Sri Abu Bakar Sulaiman; the village Tok Batin *(the traditional village head); and the village* Penggerak *(a Malay word for "actuator," the government-appointed officer who oversees the welfare of Muslims in the village and the government-sanctioned process of Islamization within the village [JAKIM 2013]). IMU distributed prizes for those villagers who won various events throughout the day; there was even a special prize for the oldest and youngest person screened that day! The occasion was also celebrated with a soccer match between the villagers and IMU, which IMU lost badly. More important than our loss on the pitch was what we gained from the day's efforts. The camaraderie and trust we built would pave the way for long-standing cooperation between the various stakeholders in the project. Finally, the relationship was affirmed as Tan Sri passed a memorandum of understanding to the Tok Batin, signaling the start of a relationship between Kampung Tekir and IMU for the years to come.*

—Dr. James Koh, the IMU Cares Kg Tekir Coordinator, 2006–2013

IMU Cares

Community engagement activities have been one of the core activities of the University from the moment that the International Medical College (IMC) was established as the first private medical college in Malaysia in 1992 (IMC was granted university status and became the International Medical University in 1999). Major community engagement activities under the IMU Corporate Social Responsibility (CSR) program were initially carried out via the Students' Affairs Department of the university and the Student Representative Council (SRC). On January 9, 2008, Dr. Mei-Ling Young, the university's provost and one of the founding members of IMC, replaced the word "Corporate" with "Community" to better reflect the University's focus.

Until 2001, there were many community-directed activities in IMU, organized by various individuals, departments, and even schools. Many of these activities were less structured, usually ad hoc, and had only short-term objectives. In 2002, all community-directed activities were consolidated under the banner of IMU Cares, and eventually major CSR activities were assimilated under the banner of IMU Cares as well.

IMU Cares is a highly structured entity within the University's organization. The philosophy of IMU Cares is to help create "a community of scholars and professionals committed to serving society, promoting the development of students to reach their true potential to become competent, ethical, caring and inquiring citizens, and visionary leaders." All IMU Cares programs must have the essential elements of clearly defined outcomes that benefit the community and clearly defined learning outcomes for staff and students, must carry out research, and must be conducted in a manner that is consistent with the highest standards of professionalism and ethics. Today, under the leadership of Professor Kok Hai Ong, the director of external affairs of IMU, more than fifty community engagement projects are operating actively under the banner of IMU Cares.

In conjunction with the fifteenth anniversary of IMU in 2007, the University set in motion a plan for each of its three campuses to "adopt" a village as part of its CSR program. In Seremban, the Kampung Angkat (Malay for "Adopted Village") Project (KAP) in Kampung Tekir was the outcome of that plan. The KAP project in Kampung Tekir was eventually assimilated under the banner of IMU Cares to become one of its major community engagement projects. The project came to be known as IMU Cares Kampung Tekir.

IMU Cares Kampung Tekir

The vision for IMU Cares originated from Tan Sri Abu Bakar Sulaiman (TSAB), president of IMU since 2001. He believes that the teaching of medicine should shift from institution-based teaching to community-based teaching. He envisioned the establishment of an adopted community where a long-term base can be set up by IMU within the community. IMU students and staff would use the base for teaching-learning activities and service opportunities. More importantly, TSAB's vision was that at the end of five years, there should be mutual benefit, with both villagers and IMU growing and benefiting together from the relationship.

From Vision to Mission

In the fall of 2006, Professor Kandasami Palayani (who was dean of the IMU Clinical School in Seremban at the time) assigned Dr. James Koh (then a lecturer in the Department of Internal Medicine) the mission to form a working group comprised of academic and corporate staff. This group's goal was to locate a suitable village near the Clinical School in Seremban for adoption under the IMU CSR program that would be launched the following year in conjunction with the fifteenth anniversary of IMU. The location, demographics, and needs of the village were to be identified and in line with IMU's institutional philosophy, that is, that of a medical university.

The project team ultimately was made up of a physician, a surgeon, a pediatrician, a family medicine specialist, two gynecologists, five community nurses, two corporate staff, and an IT expert. They held several meetings to outline the objectives of the project. In the end, eight key objectives were identified, namely: identify a suitable village for adoption by IMU for a period of three to five years; identify and engage the relevant stakeholders in the project; identify the needs in the village through engagement with the village community; determine how IMU, as a health education institution, can contribute to meeting the identified needs over an extended period of time; determine the desired outcomes for IMU students and staff through participation in the project; determine the desired outcomes for the community through this project; identify sources of funding to facilitate long-term sustainability of the project; and aim for integration of the project into the curriculum of the various schools in the university.

The team initially identified three villages within a distance of less than twenty-five miles from the Clinical School—Kampung Lukut, Kampung Chua, and Kampung Tekir. The first two were predominantly fishing villages located along the coastal town of Port Dickson, nineteen miles away from Seremban, while Kampung Tekir was an aboriginal village. The findings of these three villages were submitted in a proposal to the dean on March 29, 2007.

From Mission to Implementation

On April 13, 2007, the dean, in an email to the heads of departments of the Clinical School, formalized the appointment of Dr. James Koh as the coordinator of the KAP projects in Kampung Tekir and Kampung Simpang Enam in Batu Pahat, a town 120 miles away from Seremban where the IMU Clinical School in Batu Pahat was located. The email also formally recognized the adoption of Kampung Tekir by the Clinical School in Seremban. Kampung Tekir was chosen based on two identified need groups: health care needs (e.g., relative lack of health care accessibility; a large number of children in the village with health concerns such as malnutrition, head lice infestation, poor eyesight, and poor dental hygiene; and unknown health status of adult population in the village) and social needs (e.g., children born out of wedlock, alcoholism, chronic smoking, glue sniffing among the teenagers).

The driving force and heart of IMU Cares is Professor Kok Hai Ong, the current director of external affairs and one of the founders of IMU, who has a distinguished career as a scientist-cum-entrepreneur spanning more than four decades. Professor Ong believes IMU leaders are obliged to inculcate into their staff and students the spirit of serving and giving to society because it "is an expected requirement of our profession as healthcare providers" (Hoyt and Newcomb Rowe 2013).

On April 16, 2007, Professor Ong presented a working paper entitled "Community Involvement and Social Responsibility" at the University's eighteenth Academic Council Meeting. Professor Ong addressed three core issues in his presentation, namely, Where are we now? Where do we want to go? and How do we get there? He informed the Council that the work of adopting a village in Seremban had begun. His working paper outlined the aim of integrating the KAP program into the curriculum and increasing faculty participation in CSR activities. To achieve this aim, Professor Ong recommended three proposals: formalizing the integration of the CSR activities into the curriculum; the provision of an annual budget allocation for CSR activities; and the participation in CSR activities as one of the criteria for annual appraisal of IMU staff.

Between April and July 2007, several meetings were held between the KAP working group led by Dr. James Koh and relevant stakeholders. On May 28, 2007, in a meeting between the working group and Encik Sturi, the village chief (Tok Batin); the latter formally accepted IMU's proposal to adopt his village and provide a mobile health clinic to the village and periodic health talks on issues relevant to the village's needs. The inaugural health-screening event by IMU in the village was held on July 28, 2007, signaling the beginning of a five-year relationship between the Clinical School in Seremban and Kampung Tekir.

Funding

Although IMU Cares receives a sizable budget allocation for its community engagement projects, the owners of these projects are encouraged to raise funds by engaging individuals or corporate bodies to be partners in the projects by providing funding, services, or expertise. In addition, IMU Cares organizes several major charity events every year to raise money. The annual charity golf tournament is one such example where funds are raised from corporate bodies that participate in the tournament. The annual IMU Chariofare is another hallmark charity event organized by IMU Cares that raises funds through a charity run and sale of food and beverages by IMU staff and students. The funds generated are donated to various organizations like orphanages and hospices, or channeled to fund IMU Cares projects. "It's a little like taking from the rich and giving to the poor," Professor Kok Hai Ong once remarked. In 2012, IMU became part of IHH Healthcare Berhad,[1] a leading international provider of premium health care services in Asia, Central and Eastern Europe, the Middle East, and North Africa. A sizable budget reserved for community services by IHH became another source of funding that IMU Cares could tap into. Having funding from various sources helped increase the potential for IMU Cares projects to make a difference, but probably a more significant benefit is the opportunity to move individuals and organizations into civic action.

IMU Cares Framework

IMU Cares has well-defined guidelines, known as the IMU Cares Framework, which all projects under its banner must adhere to in order to "maximize the benefits from the projects and to ensure the projects are carried out with clear-cut objectives and defined outcomes." A brief description of the IMU Cares Framework is summarized in figure 1.

Kampung Tekir and the Temuan People

Kampung Tekir is a small aboriginal village located about twelve miles away from the IMU Clinical School in Seremban. The village is nestled about two miles deep within a large oil palm plantation that belonged to the Sime Darby Plantations. In 2007, it was estimated that there were one hundred houses scattered over a large area in the village, with some of these houses accessible only by foot or by two-wheelers. Most of the houses were constructed using wood with several partial wood-brick houses and an even smaller number of brick houses. According to the Tok Batin, the population in the village at the time was estimated to be around four hundred with almost half of them being children below the age of twelve, although the official figure provided by the Jabatan Hal Ehwal Orang Asli (JHEOA; otherwise known as the Department of Aboriginal Affairs) was

Figure 1. The IMU Cares Framework

ITEM	DESCRIPTION
1. Compile background information about the project	Background information may include the physical layout, the organizational structure of the intended community, and establishing good working relationships with relevant stakeholders.
2. Submit project proposal for approval	A proposal based on the background information and aligned with the objectives of the university is written and submitted for approval. This step ensures adequate funding when the project is implemented.
3. Form the project team	The project team should be multidisciplinary in order to effectively meet the multiple needs of the community served.
4. Engage the stakeholders and identify their needs	Engagement of the stakeholders is critical to identify and prioritize their needs. The project team should choose needs that IMU can address effectively and have measurable outcomes.
5. Formulate the action plan for the project	The project team should formulate an action plan that includes the prioritized needs of the community, the resources needed, and a budget proposal to fund the project. The plan should also include a Gantt chart to map activities that will be carried out and the expected outcomes over a defined period of time. The stakeholders should be engaged in this process. Adjustments and refinement to the action plan can be made as the project proceeds.
6. Identify outcomes and how they will be measured	Outcomes should be quantified and measured in order to enable the project team to evaluate the impact, if any, of the project.
7. Empower the community	The project should empower the community in ways that can either elevate their personal development or that of their community. This may include the transfer and acquisition of knowledge and skills.
8. Research	Quantitative or qualitative research opportunities should be created within the project.
9. Experiential learning experiences for staff and students	Strong elements of reflection and sharing should be integrated within the project. They should be deliberately structured to allow opportunities for staff and students of IMU to benefit maximally from the experience of participating in the project.
10. Feedback sessions	Feedback sessions with the project team are held after each activity in the project. These sessions are invaluable for evaluating the project and considering changes or refinements to be made for subsequent events in the project.
11. Databases	Two types of databases are kept in projects under IMU Cares. The first relates to a database designed to capture the staff and students' roles in community engagement projects. The results of analysis of this database may be used in consideration for awards of excellence or distinguished participation. The second database captures the details of individuals in the community who have participated in the project. This database is useful for project leaders to measure and analyze outcomes within their particular project.
12. Reports	Reports help to capture events and experiences. They are also important for learning, project improvement, and for recording purposes to capture the historical involvement of individuals and institutions. The project leader's report is prepared after every community engagement activity, preferably after debriefing. This report should consist of descriptions of various activities carried out, photographs, data on outcome measures achieved, research progress (if any), and the budget expenditure to ensure financial accountability and transparency. Project reports are important for the central administration to monitor and integrate all projects. The other type of report is the student's report, which provides evidence of student participation in IMU Cares projects as required in the curriculum. The report should include a summary of the activities participated in by the students, their roles in the project, and reflections on their learning experience.

ninety-six families with a total population of 342 people. Back then, entering the village involved driving on narrow gravel roads on motorcycles, compact cars, four-wheel-drive vehicles, or tractors.

The Temuan[2] people are one of eighteen ethnic subgroups that comprise the Orang Asli. These ethnic subgroups are categorized into three main groups: the Negrito, the Senoi, and the Proto-Malay (see Toshihiro 2009 and Nicholas 2000 for an in-depth discussion of the various Orang Asli subgroups; also see Jabatan Kemajuan Orang Asli n.d.).

The majority of the Temuan people are found in the states of Selangor, Negeri Sembilan, and Pahang. Although traditionally they had engaged in hunting, gathering, and swidden agriculture,[3] their way of life has changed as a result of surrounding development, fostered in large part by government policies (Toshihiro 2009). Previously, the typical Temuan community would sit on the lowlands, but most are now located on coastal areas, hillsides, or edges of forests (Toshihiro 2009; Nicholas 2000). Currently, the typical Temuan community sits on the edges of forest reservations, usually surrounded by rubber or oil palm plantations (Toshihiro 2009). Dunn, in 1977, described this as "an island in an ocean of development." The boom in rubber plantations in the twentieth century resulted in the majority of Temuan switching to rubber tapping as a source of income (Toshihiro 2009).

The Temuan, like other Orang Asli, have been the victims of historical marginalization that centered on a contest for resources, eventually leading to loss of land, loss of autonomy, and widespread poverty. Their overall socioeconomic status, access to amenities, and health status still lags behind mainstream society in Malaysia (Nicholas, Engi, and Teh 2010; Chung 2010).

Typical for Temuan communities, Kampung Tekir has a paternalistic culture where the men work while the women stay at home. Most of the men earn money by working on small-scale agricultural enterprises, while others work in nearby factories and plantations. A government-funded primary school was built in the village. In 2009, there were a total of twelve teachers and forty-eight students in the school. Most of the children do not complete year 5 of education. Most of the villagers are Christians, with less than 10 percent belonging to the Muslim faith or practicing forms of ancestral worship.

The village's water supply is channeled directly from nearby streams using PVC pipes supplied by the state's Department of Aboriginal Affairs (JHEOA). Electricity supply is available only for limited parts of the village. There were no medical or antenatal clinics in the village prior to the IMU Cares initiative; the nearest health clinic was located about eight miles away from the village. Home delivery of babies assisted by midwives was still practiced, although most women in the village delivered their babies at nearby health clinics. New mothers were visited by community nurses from nearby health clinics twice after delivery.

The decision-making structure of the village is similar to other aboriginal villages in the country (figure 2). At the top is the JHEOA, which determines government-sanctioned policies that affect every aspect of the village. These policies are then implemented by the Village Development and Security Committee under the supervision of the Penggerak. In contrast, the Tok Batin probably has indirect influence on the policies implemented, particularly in policies affecting the ways of life and beliefs of the villagers.

Figure 2. Decision-Making Structure in Kampung

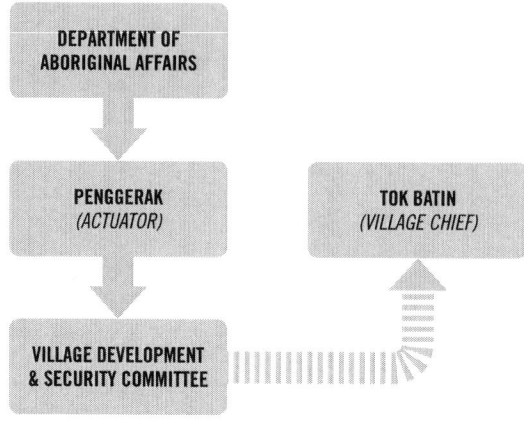

Stakeholders and Challenges in Gaining Legitimacy

Many stakeholders had to be engaged to ensure buy-in to the project, to seek approval, and to gain legitimacy.[4] This was probably the biggest challenge during the initial phase of the project. Because the executive power in the village belonged to Haji Kassim, the Penggerak who was appointed by the Department of Aboriginal Affairs (JHEOA), rather than the Tok Batin, who was the village chief, buy-in from the former was vital. While the latter warmly welcomed the idea of his village being adopted by a medical university, the former was more cautious and suspicious. Islam is the official religion in Malaysia, but the country's constitution allows the freedom to practice other religions. Nevertheless, many issues are viewed through the religious lens of Islam versus others, with many policies created and projects adopted in favor of the former. State officials viewed IMU, and its English name, with initial suspicion and distrust. Perhaps there was fear that IMU's involvement was a veiled attempt to disseminate Christianity.

Eventually, Haji Kassim was convinced of the viability of the project and the benefits to the village through a series of semiformal meetings held over several weeks, often in his or the Tok Batin's home. He was finally convinced that IMU's involvement was purely to provide health services that would benefit the villagers, IMU students, and staff, with no other hidden agenda. Approval from the Village Development and Security Committee was easy once these two community leaders had given their nod to the project.

The State Department of Aboriginal Affairs (JHEOA)

The next challenge was to obtain approval from the JHEOA. As with the Penggerak, initially the team from IMU was met with a less than cordial reception by officials in the JHEOA. The directors of the JHEOA initially resisted the idea of the project because they had erroneously believed that IMU had a hidden agenda, namely to proselytize the village under the guise of providing health care services.[5] The team took great pains to set up several face-to-face meetings with the relevant directors to help them understand the project better. Dr. James Koh recalls the first face-to-face meeting with the director of the state's JHEOA:

> I remember we had to make several appointments just to meet the state JHEOA director before we eventually met. His initial demeanor on meeting Gabriel Tan (who was a key player in the project team who facilitated many of the meetings with stakeholders) and I was that of veiled hostility, until I noticed the bulging tortuous blood vessels on his arms. I decided to change tact and asked about his health. I correctly ventured my impression that the director was on dialysis for kidney problems. He was taken aback by my observation and proceeded to share with me his struggles with his condition. Thereafter, he became considerably cordial and receptive to our proposal!

Official approval was finally granted when the directors were satisfied that the proposed project was genuine and without a hidden agenda.

The State Health Department, State District Hospital, and Community Health Clinics

Next, approval from the State Health Department was necessary in order for IMU to conduct health-related activities in the state. This was easily obtained by the project team once the department was made aware that the JHEOA had no objections to the project. Once the approval was obtained, university officials approached the director of the State District Hospital Tuanku Ja'afar Seremban (the only referral hospital in the state). They requested permission to allow hospital personnel to participate in planned events in the village, and for ill patients in the village to be referred to the hospital for specialized care. Once approval from the hospital director had been given, the family medicine specialists who were in-charge of clinics that had jurisdiction over the village were approached for permission to obtain supplies of basic medications from their clinics to be used in the village by IMU students and staff; and for permission to refer villagers with less severe illnesses not requiring hospitalization to be treated by the IMU team. Because prior approval was obtained from authorities higher up in the chain of command, it was relatively easy to obtain permissions from the respective specialists.

Oil Palm Plantation Company

In order to enter and exit the village, especially in large numbers, permission had to be obtained from the management of the oil palm plantation that encircled the village. In addition, IMU also needed their cooperation to help keep the community hall, where medical equipment was kept, from vandalism. In order to keep these items safe, IMU had invested heavily in the restoration of the community hall, including repairing its windowpanes, installing iron grills on the windows and doors, and repainting the walls, which were infested with poultry lice. Although vandalism of IMU property continued infrequently over the next few years, the losses were minimal. This was because over time the villagers slowly took ownership for the safety of IMU's property kept inside the community hall. Essentially, IMU property became community property because they realized the sustainability of the adoption project depended on the safety of the equipment entrusted to them. It was a calculated risk the project team took, and it paid off handsomely in fostering civic responsibility and a sense of partnership in the community.

Private Corporate Bodies and Other Companies

To encourage the participation of corporate enterprises in the Kampung Tekir project, the project team approached many large corporations. Chief among them were manufacturers of nutrition products and pharmaceutical companies, whose CSR vision, services, and products were in line with IMU Cares' philosophy. Most of these companies have annual budget and product allocations for CSR activities. The project team soon learned to engage these companies well in advance in order to procure their allocated budget and products.

Most of these companies were engaged by IMU on an ad hoc basis for their direct participation (for example, Colgate Palmolive provided a dental team in addition to dental hygiene products in one of the events in the village) or contributions in the form of sponsorship of prizes and gifts to be distributed in the village. However, with some companies, IMU managed to establish long-term partnerships. For example, Danone-Dumex partnered with IMU for two years to provide nutritional food products for the children in the village.

IMU Staff and Students

Initially only students from the School of Medicine in IMU participated on a voluntary basis in the IMU Cares project in Kampung Tekir. In late 2008, the project became integrated into the medical curriculum, thus making student participation in at least one project activity in two years mandatory. Each activity was well publicized on the University's website, drawing much attention to the project. Within a year, students from the School of Nursing and Department of Nutrition and Dietetics joined the project on a regular basis. Eventually students from the School of Dentistry and the Department of Chiropractic participated as well. Thus, IMU Cares Kampung Tekir evolved into a platform for interprofessional learning, harnessing the self-interests of each school collectively for the good of the community. Student participation was tracked via reflective reports and logbook entries.

In the first year of the project, the team, comprised of faculty members, organized the activities, while students merely participated. From the second year of the project, the roles were reversed. The IMU Student Representative Council (SRC) took over the organizing of the project, while the project team offered support and played advisory roles to the SRC. The project had become a student-driven project. Students who had participated in earlier health-screening events often returned to provide leadership and guidance to junior students or first-timers. This practice of peer mentorship was continued when IMU began its work in Kampung Sebir in 2013.

Participation of academic and corporate staff in the project was disappointing in the early days of the project. Few signed up because the activities were held on weekends and they believed community service should be voluntary. There were others who were interested but found themselves at a loss as to how they could contribute effectively on the ground. This was especially true for corporate staff. Staff participation increased dramatically after participation in IMU Cares activities was made a mandatory criterion for annual appraisal for remuneration and rewards. "Sometimes, we need to do a bit of arm-twisting in the beginning," Professor Kok Hai Ong once quipped when asked how IMU ensures full participation from academic and corporate staff at the ASEAN University Network's Second University's Social Responsibility and Sustainability Capacity Building Workshop on June 12, 2013.

Since 2008, "participation in a community engagement activity with a defined role" became a mandatory Key Performance Index (KPI) measure for every staff member of IMU. This criterion opened up the possibility for wider participation of corporate staff because they need not be physically on the ground participating at the events but can contribute in other defined roles behind the scenes such as report compilation, logistics, budgeting, and helping to source sponsors for events. In short, one of the measures of performance in IMU is the contribution of that staff member to the community, and IMU provides numerous means for staff to get involved.

Gaining Trust and Acceptance (July 2007–June 2008)

Analysis of the health-screening results from the first event revealed several unexpected health problems in the village. Between 30 and 35 percent of the adults were overweight, chronic smokers, had poor eyesight, and had anemia. About 5 percent of the adults had diabetes mellitus, and 6 percent consumed alcohol regularly. In the children, almost half of them were underweight, and most of them had head lice infestation and scabies. In other words, the adults had "urban" diseases, while the children had "rural" diseases. In addition, social problems were identified, including teen pregnancies, smoking initiation at a young age, unplanned pregnancies, glue sniffing, illiteracy, and drug abuse among the youths.

After several meetings involving all the relevant stakeholders, the team formulated a plan to help tackle the identified problems. In the first year, four events (including the inaugural event) were held in the village. In each event, the project team would use the same modus operandi; that is, a scaled-down carnival-like event held once every three months in the village. There were adult and youth health-screening activities in the community hall, the usual games and singing competitions, health talks delivered by students on topics relevant to the village's social needs, and conjoint communal activities between IMU and the villagers such as *gotong-royong* (Malay word for "coming together to clean up the surrounding areas").

The main objectives in the first year were to gain the villagers' trust and their acceptance of IMU's presence in their village. At the same time, the project team had hoped to capture the health data of at least 50 percent of the village population through the trimonthly health-screening activities. As usual, villagers identified with more severe illnesses were referred to either the hospital or the nearest health clinic, while those with minor ailments were treated at the community hall. By the end of the first year, IMU had only captured the health data of about 20–25 percent of the village population. Analysis and evaluation of the data revealed several patterns: less than 20 percent of the adults screened were men; most of the adults were busy working in the morning; youths tend to stay away from the IMU-organized activities; villagers living far from the community hall were reluctant to come for health screening; and recurrent lice and scabies infestations were seen in the children despite therapy.

Innovative Strategies, and Short-Term Gains (July 2008–June 2009)

Based on the identified needs and feedback from stakeholders, the project team decided to make changes to the way the health-screening activities were carried out. In order to get more adult males to undergo health screenings, the team decided to begin each health-screening activity in the afternoon rather than in the morning, as was the practice in the first year. In this way, the adult males in the village could be screened after they had returned from work in the late afternoon. In addition, the project team decided to modify the strategy for implementing health screenings. Instead of organizing four large, carnival-like health-screening events, as was done in the previous year, changes were made to the format for the second year. This time, three out of four events were on a much smaller scale and a large, year-end event was held instead. In the smaller-scale events, IMU students were divided into teams of five to six students, each led by a staff member.

One team would set up camp at the community hall within the village, while the rest of the teams were equipped with backpacks containing basic health-screening equipment. Each backpack was carefully prepared by the capable hands of Sister Rosalind Loo, a retired infection control nurse who had joined IMU as a nurse trainer in the IMU Skills Unit. Rosalind was one of the pioneer members of the original project team. These "mobile teams" were then instructed to walk to the fringe of the village and then backtrack from there. Their task was to visit every house they encountered on the way back and engage the occupants of the houses to provide health screening and health education, and help check the hygiene and sanitation standards of the area surrounding the houses. Villagers identified with health problems requiring treatment or referral to the nearby clinic or hospital were brought to the community hall, where the primary team was stationed. At the community hall, a proper examination of the villager was carried out and the appropriate course of action prescribed by the attending clinician / faculty member. Villagers who had serious ailments were referred to nearby health clinics or the hospital. The new approach worked very well, and by the end of the second year, the number of villagers screened increased drastically to about 50 percent of the village population.

To address the problem of undernourished children in the village, Dr. Cheong Wei Cheah, a pediatrician and a member of the project team, formulated a medium-term initiative called the Health and Wellness program that would be run concurrently with the Kampung Angkat Project—a project within a project. Dr. Cheah designed the project solely for children aged twelve and younger in the village. In his project, anthropometric measurements and assessment of the children's diet would be done at regular interval to enable proper monitoring of the physical growth of children identified with nutritional deficiencies. Faculty members from the Nutrition and Dietetics Department of IMU became part of Dr. Cheah's project to provide hands-on training to medical students on the know-how of anthropometric measurements and dietary assessment of children. Dr. Cheah's initiative was allocated a separate budget to work with. Dr. Cheah used his funds to acquire three netbooks, and with the help of the IMU IT department, a Microsoft Access–based health data tracking program was developed and installed in the netbooks to allow for easy data entry and recall on-site. The aim of the Health and Wellness project was to identify the nutritional needs of the children in the first year, and to formulate strategies to supplement the nutritional deficiencies in the children in the second year.

A simple strategy was employed to tackle the issue of recurrent head lice and scabies infestations among the children in the village. When a child was identified with the infestation, the students would accompany the child back to his or her home, carrying enough supply of head lice or scabies medications to treat the entire household as well as to provide advice to the child's parents on how to eliminate these parasites from the home.

The oil palm plantation management, realizing the frequency of the IMU Cares project in Kampung Tekir and perhaps its impact on the well-being of the villagers, decided to upgrade the access road into the village by building a tarred road to replace the uneven gravel access road. The road allowed IMU staff and students to drive directly into the village without the need to utilize the tractor-driven tram provided by the plantation or a four-wheel-drive vehicle. A local distributor of nutritional products began providing milk powder as diet supplement to children identified with nutritional deficiencies under the Health and Wellness program. Postevent feedback on the health status of the villagers by IMU to the Village Development and Security Committee and the Department of Aboriginal Affairs enabled them to take proactive steps to look after the health of those identified with illnesses. A salient example is the speed with which arrangements were made to transport villagers needing more specialized care to health clinics or the hospital.

The Year of Crisis and Crisis Management (July 2009–June 2010)

At the beginning of the year, a high-ranking official from the JHEOA paid a surprise visit to the village during one of the health-screening events held by IMU. Such surprise visits would become common in the years ahead. On that visit, the official was so impressed with the work done by IMU that she granted several requests made by the project team. One such request was the transfer of a vacant house located next to the community hall to IMU, to be used as a permanent base for the project. The house used to be the home of the former Penggerak, Haji Kassim, who had since moved out of the village in anticipation of his retirement. Further support was given in the form of two large makeshift tents for project use, as well as gifts to be distributed to the villagers.

Overjoyed by the news, the project team petitioned the dean of clinical school at that time, Professor Kew, who then approved an additional budget of MYR 2000 (about US$650) to repair the vacant house. The house would be used to securely store expensive medical equipment and medications belonging to IMU. It also allowed for more privacy when staff or students performed physical examinations on the villagers. The repair work was completed before the next scheduled health-screening activity in the village in July 2010.

However, several unexpected setbacks occurred in the third year that threatened to derail the entire project. The JHEOA abruptly withdrew permission for IMU to use the repaired vacant house as a permanent base without offering any reason for the decision. It was a huge blow to the project team, as it had hoped to establish a permanent presence within the village that even included plans for staff and students to stay in the house for longer periods of time in order to engage with the community in a more meaningful way. The sudden withdrawal of JHEOA's earlier permission may have been due to a belated realization that a permanent IMU base within the village might not be favorable to, or in line with, JHEOA's structure of administrations for aboriginal villages under its jurisdiction. However, the real reason may never be known.

After Haji Kassim retired as Penggerak of the village, his responsibility was taken over by Noel, the chairperson of the Village Development and Security Committee. A misunderstanding arose between Noel and Sturi, the Tok Batin of the village. The latter had accused the former of sidelining him in the decision-making process in matters related to the Kampung Angkat Project. Because of this misunderstanding, the health-screening event in July 2010 was severely compromised, as both parties refused to cooperate with each other. On that day the Tok Batin locked the community hall and refused to open the hall for health-screening activities, a sizable number of villagers were taken out of the village in a bus to attend a religious event, and although the JHEOA provided the promised tents, they were not erected by the villagers.

The project team had to step in and organize a reconciliatory meeting between Noel and Sturi for the sake of the project. A representative of the JHEOA and student leaders also attended the meeting, which eventually resulted in restoration of good ties between all stakeholders, particularly between the two leaders in the village.

Another major blow to the project occurred when Dr. Cheah abruptly left IMU. His resignation created a leadership vacuum in the Health and Wellness program and although staff from Nutrition and Dietetics stoically carried on the program for another year, the program eventually came to a premature closure, as no suitable replacement for Dr. Cheah could be found.

Another crisis that threatened the sustainability of the program occurred when the JHEOA received unsubstantiated complaints from unidentified people in the village who claimed that IMU was secretly proselytizing the villagers, attempting to convert Muslims to Christianity, under the guise of providing health-screening services. As a result, the project team coordinator, Dr. James Koh, was summoned to answer the accusation. Another meeting between the project team and a high-ranking official from the JHEOA was arranged and the official was reassured that IMU had no such ulterior motive. Nevertheless, as a precautionary measure, the official imposed three conditions in order for the project to continue: the details of each participant in future events had to be submitted to the department for approval; all project participants must wear T-shirts with the IMU logo displayed prominently; and each event must have the participation of several Muslim students. Failure to meet these requirements would lead to the withdrawal of JHEOA approval for the project. The last condition was probably an attempt to safeguard against perceived, but actually nonexisting, proselytizing by non-Muslim IMU students. The project team agreed to these conditions and the project was saved.

Although the project team was tempted to throw in the towel in the face of the nearly insurmountable challenges it encountered that year, the steady leadership and guidance of several key people in IMU's top management positions helped the team to assess each challenge objectively and navigate through each crisis successfully. Furthermore, the team was reluctant to renege on its five-year commitment with the village.

Thereafter, the project was back on track and steps were taken to provide solutions to the lingering problems in the village. To address the issue of teenage pregnancies in the village, Dr. Sheila Rani, a gynecologist and a member of the project team, together with other faculty members from her department, developed a community engagement workshop named the "Adolescent Sexual Health Module." The well-received module was designed as a face-to-face workshop to help adolescents understand issues relating to sexuality and making safe choices. Similarly, another community engagement workshop designed by Dr. Shane Varman, a psychiatrist from IMU, was conducted to help the villagers understand the dangers of alcohol and drug abuse.

Empowering the Community (July 2010–June 2011)

By the fourth year of the project, the presence of IMU staff members and students in the village had become a regular part of village life. It was common to see IMU staff members exchanging greetings with the villagers and chatting like old friends during the health-screening events held that year.

The health-screening events held that year were marked by a significant shift—instead of being solely student-driven, the events were organized by both villagers and students working together. Villagers were invited to play a larger role in the health-screening events; for example, taking charge of the logistical arrangements for each event and the preparation of lunch and afternoon tea. Previously, these tasks were handled fully by IMU participants.

Lillian Tai, who succeeded Gabriel Tan as corporate manager at the IMU Clinical School in Seremban, joined the project team. Lillian firmly believed that efforts should be made to help the aborigines in the village leave their culture of apathy and dependency. When seven adult villagers were identified with refractory visual impairment and needed prescription glasses, Lillian negotiated with a local optometrist who agreed to provide the glasses for the villagers at a discounted rate. On the other hand, the seven villagers were informed that they would be provided with glasses only if they were willing to contribute at least 10 percent of the cost. All seven villagers had lived with poor vision for years but did not see the need to wear corrective glasses. In reality, the 10 percent was negligible, but Lillian's approach helped the villagers to take ownership of their health. By the end of 2011, the project had provided health-screening services to an estimated 80 percent of the village's population.

Renewing the Cooperation (July 2011–2012)

The year 2012 marked the fifth year of IMU's presence in Tekir, the village it has adopted since 2007. The fifth anniversary was celebrated in a momentous, large-scale health-screening event. Held in July 2012, IMU's president, Tan Sri Abu Bakar Sulaiman, presented a plaque to the Tok Batin, Sturi, in a ceremony to reaffirm IMU's continued presence in the village for another three years. Months before the event, the Tok Batin, upon being told that IMU was nearing the end of its five-year presence in his village, expressed his desire for IMU to continue its work in his village for at least another three years. "We have benefited a lot from your presence," he told the project team in a meeting.

However, two new developments determined the future of the IMU Kampung Angkat Project in Kampung Tekir. In January 2010, the prime minister of Malaysia, Datuk Seri Najib Tun Razak, announced the formation of the Klinik 1Malaysia. This was a government-initiated program that set up clinics manned by medical assistants throughout the nation to provide affordable basic treatment for minor ailments to people. As a result of this initiative, from late 2011, a mobile 1Malaysia Clinic began operating in Kampung Tekir to provide basic health services on a Tuesday once every two months. The village now has what it did not have before—direct and easy access to health services; essentially offering the services IMU had provided for the prior four years. The impact of the 1Malaysia Clinic on IMU's work in the village was not immediately felt, but over time fewer villagers presented themselves for health screening during events held by IMU.

The other development was a formal request from the JHEOA for IMU to replicate its work in Kampung Tekir at another aboriginal village nearby, Kampung Sebir. The request came about because the department was alarmed at the high number of villagers in Kampung Sebir that suffered from asthma problems and skin ailments. They had reasons to believe that these ailments may be due to the close proximity of the village to a nearby quarry. Like Kampung Tekir back in 2007, Kampung Sebir had no easy access to health care services. IMU held its inaugural health-screening event at Kampung Sebir in late 2012, which was very well received by the villagers. It would be another year before IMU formally began providing regular health care services in Kampung Sebir.

In view of these significant developments, the project team deliberated at length and came to a decision. Rather than duplicating a health service that is now being provided on a regular basis by the 1Malaysia Clinic, the IMU Cares Kampung Tekir project would be brought to a close, while opportunities for engaging the community in areas other than health services should be explored. Meanwhile, resources and health screening services should be focused on Kampung Sebir instead. In early 2013, Dr. Sheila Rani succeeded Dr. James Koh as the coordinator of Kampung Tekir, while Dr. Chin Hoong Wong was appointed the coordinator for IMU Cares Kampung Sebir. In April 2013, the IMU Cares Kampung Tekir project was awarded the MacJannet Prize for Global Citizenship by the Talloires Network.[6]

Measuring Outcomes

One of the biggest obstacles the IMU Cares Kampung Tekir project team faced was the challenge of quantifying the outcomes of the project. While the outcomes from the participation of staff and students in the project could be somewhat measured using feedback, questionnaires, and postevent reflective writings done by the students (Koh et al. 2014); the middle- and long-term impacts on the students were less quantifiable. Nevertheless, several reflective exercises completed by former IMU students and staff that participated in the IMU Cares Kampung Tekir project provide qualitative evidence that the project positively influenced their outlook and perspectives, and helped them develop leadership qualities. What follows are several examples.

According to Dr. Albert Ling (IMU graduate, February 2014), his community engagement experience contributed to a sense of social responsibility:

> [The project] has definitely impacted me in a positive way. I learned about the lifestyle of (the) Orang Asli, their deficiencies in terms of infrastructure and formal education. I felt obligated to do something to help them more, perhaps organize monthly tuition for the children. Because of that, I am choosing the interiors of Sabah as one of my preferred place[s] for [an] internship.[7]

Dr. Gerard Geetham Sebastian (IMU graduate, February 2014) reflected on how the engagement experience contributed to the development of important skills:

I was very happy every time I was involved in Kampung Angkat because it helped me improve on my soft skills and also my leadership skills in planning, organizing, and carrying out the event. Besides that, the project also left me wondering [about] how the Orang Asli are left out in terms of health and education in Malaysia.[8]

Dr. Azreen Abdul Halim (IMU graduate, August 2014) adds:

During the program, I met a forty-two-year-old woman afflicted with scleroderma and learned about how she lived with the disease. I encountered the clinical signs of microstomia, sclerodactyly, and calcinosis for the first time. After the health screening, I also had to facilitate (the) children's telematch games. I felt very privileged to have gained these experiences, especially since there were many kind lecturers who guided us through the program and taught us about how to assess the patients correctly.[9]

Dr. Wan (Pam) Amni Zulfikar (IMU graduate, February 2013) discovers in herself the desire to have an impact on the world:

I have learned how to manage my time and improved my organizational skills best through this program. Each event took weeks of planning involving many meetings. I find joy in juggling work between hospital duties and event planning, as it was a welcome change to the daily routine of a medical student. Through this program, I also realized the wide disparity between the general public and the natives of Malaysia. Through (this program), I noticed the Orang Asli in Kampung Tekir had not caught up with the developments rapidly happening in our country in terms of health, education, transportation, etc. It was a shocking insight but I slowly came to realize that many of the villagers were comfortable with their lifestyle. They have grown accustomed to the simple aspects of their lives and most were comfortable in their current condition. I have come to realize through the IMU Cares Kampung Tekir program that I am a person who is passionate about effecting change.[10]

Dr. Sheila Rani Kovil George (consultant obstetrician and gynecologist and senior lecturer) speaks to both the development of vital skills and putting those skills to use to improve communities:

I learned about the Orang Asli and their socioeconomic and health-related problems through participation in the IMU Cares Kampung Tekir project. I have developed personal qualities such as teamwork, communication skills, leadership, and empathy. I think I am a better person in terms of understanding the Orang Asli and their issues. I feel motivated to help improve their living conditions. I am determined to link them with NGOs that can help them improve their living (standards), health, and social status.[11]

Last, Ms. Inthirah Narayanan (IMU corporate staff and member of IMU Cares Kampung Tekir project team) describes the engagement experience as an opportunity to learn to work across disciplines:

As a corporate support staff, I have gained insight into teamwork and volunteerism from my involvement in the project. It has also broadened my knowledge and skills, particularly in liaising with the Department of Aboriginal Affairs. I also became familiarized with medical terminology and health issues that used to be foreign to me. The project was a good one and encouraged interdisciplinary participation.[12]

Because the project is essentially student-driven, students are directly responsible for the planning of every aspect of each health-screening event in the village. This process includes forming a student committee and subcommittees, appointing student leaders, recruiting student volunteers, delegating responsibilities, preparing and delivering health talks in Malay, communicating in Malay with the community, prescribing medications (under supervision of a specialist), giving health advice in Malay, doing home-to-home visits, and coming up with creative ways to engage the community, especially the children. These activities help promote the development of leadership qualities, the spirit of volunteerism, empathy, effective communication skills, and foster civic engagement and professionalism in these students.

The health-screening events provide rare opportunities for IMU students and the community to mingle, thus helping to bridge a wide urban-rural divide. Students learn valuable lessons on Orang Asli culture, beliefs, and lifestyle from the community; and gain insight into the flora and fauna, such as the medicinal properties of traditional herbs, found in the jungles surrounding part of the village. Nevertheless, some of the objectives of the project were never fully realized. For instance, the project team had initially wanted to model the Kampung Tekir project after another similar project that was already running at IMU's campus in Batu Pahat, where medical students were "adopted" for a weekend by the families in the community. These "adopted" students were then exposed, albeit only for a weekend, to the life and culture of the village partly through a cultural show held at night where both students and villagers showcased the uniqueness of their cultures through songs and dance performances. Unfortunately, this strategy was not feasible in Kampung Tekir due to the nature of the village: houses are spread over a wide area in the village with poor communication and access between them, giving rise to potential security concerns.

Benefits and Challenges

The health status of the community in Kampung Tekir has been well documented throughout the five years of community engagement activities through the IMU Cares Kampung Tekir project. Analysis of the health data (e.g., blood pressure, blood sugar levels, blood cholesterol levels, body mass indexes, etc.) helped to guide the project team to plan relevant educational and health-related community engagement activities in the village. The data also allowed longitudinal tracking of the health status of the community as a whole.

However, tracking individuals in the community was challenging because many had similar names, had no identification cards, lived in unmarked houses scattered over a wide area within the village, and changed their phone contact numbers frequently (each prepaid phone number was replaced with another as soon as the credit stored in the card had run out). All of these factors made it extremely difficult for the project team to keep track of individual health outcomes. To overcome this, various tracking strategies were tried, including the use of appointment cards and photo identification, but these strategies were only partially successful. The villagers frequently lost their appointment cards, and many were unwilling to be photographed.

The community in Kampung Tekir benefited directly and indirectly from IMU's presence in their village in many tangible ways. Direct benefits included access to specialist care in the village as well as at the Hospital Tuanku Ja'afar Seremban, where many of IMU's faculty are also consultants or specialists, as well as easy access to basic medications for minor ailments provided by IMU. Indirect tangible benefits include direct access to members of parliaments or community leaders, as they were often invited by IMU to officiate at some of the large health-screening events in the village. This created opportunities for the Tok Batin to request the provision of basic amenities such as a piped, treated water supply and electricity in the village; a better access road to the village built by the management of the oil palm plantation surrounding the village; and infrastructure projects, such as a new community hall built in 2012 next to the old community hall to cater to the increasing needs of the village.

The frequent health-screening events in the village brought economic benefits to some of the individuals in the community, especially during the large-scale events. However, intangible gains for the community from IMU's presence in their village are harder to measure. Obtaining good quantitative and qualitative measures of the impact the project had on the community in Kampung Tekir is extremely challenging and frustrating for the project team. Most of the villagers, adults and children alike, were illiterate, and therefore the use of written questionnaires was not feasible. Furthermore, the villagers only spoke Malay, while most of the IMU staff and students were more proficient in English, giving rise to frequent miscommunications and misunderstandings because of the language barrier. That none of the members of the project team were social scientists or trained in qualitative research proved to be a major disadvantage to the project as a whole in terms of measuring and documenting impact of the project in the community.

"I want to study hard and become a nurse," said Aishah, a fifteen-year-old girl in the community after she observed how IMU nursing students served in the village—thus providing, perhaps, a rare glimpse into the intangible and hard-to-measure positive impact of the project on the community.

Conclusion

The IMU Cares Kampung Tekir project was a unique project—an aboriginal community with identified health-related needs required a degree of technical expertise, and IMU was able to provide the expertise to meet these needs; all while creating opportunities for students broaden their perspectives, raise awareness and consciousness of social injustices, and gain valuable field experience. How successful was the project in moving beyond service-learning and extending expert knowledge to build civic capacity in the community served and develop civic professionalism in IMU students? Was the project successful in departing from the prevalent culture of how members affiliated with institutions of higher learning often function—in isolation, exclusively, and with an aura of superiority in knowledge and therefore, decision-making? Was there a move to the kind of engaged scholarship that is "localized, relational, practice-based, actively collaborative, experiential and reflective?" (Boyte and Fretz 2010, 68–69).

The IMU Cares Kampung Tekir project contained most, if not all, the elements of community organizing principles, that is, "building public relationships across lines of difference, creating free spaces for people to work publicly with others, and understanding and embracing the messiness of change" (Boyte and Fretz 2010, 72). Relationships had to be built across the divisions of knowledge, culture and beliefs, economic status, language, and power structures between IMU and various stakeholders in order to ensure the sustainability of the project. These relationships have to be worked at continuously and strengthened over time with mutual trust and respect. Through the project IMU has been successful in moving some of these stakeholders into civic action.

The project provided opportunities for IMU staff and students to engage with the community in Kampung Tekir through collaborative activities. Faculty members and students were able to reflect on the "public meanings and possibilities of their own work," and thus help bridge the divide between civic theory and practice. This helped them to see civic engagement as more than voluntary activities for the occasional weekend (Kari 1999 described these principles in her defining work at the College of St. Catherine). Embracing change and the messiness of change were part and parcel of the organizing process of the project through the many challenges encountered by the project team, often forcing the team to reflect, innovate, strategize, and change. All this would not have been possible without the strong leadership and direction provided by the university's president, Tan Sri Abu Bakar Sulaiman; the university's provost, Dr. Mei-Ling Young; the director of external affairs, Professor Kok Hai Ong; the executive deans of IMU at the time, Professor Peter Pook and Professor Victor Lim; and the dean of Clinical School in IMU, Professor Kandasami Palayani.

Nevertheless, looking back in all honesty, the IMU Cares Kampung Tekir project *did* begin with a premise that completely violated the iron rule of the practice of civic professionalism: *Never do for others what they can do for themselves*! In the early stages of the program, IMU was *acting* on the community, rather than working *with* them! IMU was looking at the community in terms of their needs and deficiencies instead of recognizing their assets. This approach focused on individual or one-sided success at the expense of marginalizing the community from decision-making processes, rather than fostering collaborative work that brings about collective commonwealth. This "soft technocracy" (very well described by Boyte and Fretz 2010) resulted in further propagating and affirming the already prevalent culture of apathy and dependency in the community and a culture of detachment from the civic life of the community among IMU staff and students. A slow but perceptible change occurred as the project matured where IMU slowly adopted the role of catalysts and coaches to encourage democratic change in the community, rather than acting as mere service providers.

Did the community become empowered democratically over the five years? The short answer would be no. It would be unrealistic to undo the damage from decades of suppressive administrative policies imposed on the Orang Asli by the national government. Nevertheless, through the project, the community was able to exercise the "right and capacity to have some say in the decision-making processes that affect their lives" (Payne 1995, 68), and take responsibility for their own well-being.

IMU students who participated in the project were encouraged to develop a mind-set that would allow them to function as civic professionals. They had to abandon the "customer of the university" or "curious bystander" mentality and instead be totally immersed in the community. They had to develop the understanding that the community was "not a homogenous group of like-minded people" but rather a "heterogeneous group striving for collective self-interest in order to better their communities" (see Boyte and Fretz 2010, 75, for an in-depth explanation of this concept). Through interprofessional and intergenerational learning, the students recognize that the solution to any problems lies in collaboration, and oftentimes the desired change has to come from within the community itself. The development of the students as civic professionals was probably not fully achieved in this project because many students were involved in the project as a once-off engagement, rather than undertaking the sustained involvement needed to promote the qualities of an engaged civic professional. The new work in Kampung Sebir attempts to address this issue by encouraging long-term student involvement.

In the end, although the IMU Cares Kampung Tekir project may have started off on a "wrong foot" with regards to building civic capacity in the community and developing civic professionalism among IMU staff and students, it somehow *got things right* as the project matured. Peter Pook, vice president of IMU, responded to this chapter by writing the following note to Dr. Koh Kwee Choy:

> [My hope is that] reflecting through your chapter will give us more courage and conviction that projects such as Kampong Tekir and other IMU Cares [endeavors] provide opportunities for us, health care professionals, to [apply] our vocation to serve communities who are not as fortunate as [we are]. It is worth all the difficulties that we have encountered thus far!

NOTES

1. IHH Healthcare Berhad, http://www.ihh-healthcare.com/index.php.
2. The villagers of Kampung Tekir are comprised mainly of Temuan people. Overall, the Orang Asli make up less than 1 percent of the population of Malaysia. Previously, they were referred to (perhaps in derogatory fashion) as *Biduanda, Jakun, Sakai*, aborigines, and by other terms, mainly during the period of British colonization (Nicholas 2000).
3. This is a method of cultivation that involves burning and clearing forests for plantation. The ash provides fertilization and the burning generally eliminates weeds. Over time, fertility declines and a new area is sought and the cycle repeated.
4. Stakeholders include IMU (students and staff from various schools), the village (Tok Batin or chief, Penggerak or actuator), the Jawatankuasa Kemajuan and Keselamatan Kampung (JKKK), governmental bodies (Jabatan Hal Ehwal Orang Asli or JHEOA and Department of Aboriginal Affairs; Jabatan Kesihatan Negeri, Negeri Sembilan or JKNNS, and State Health Department; Director of the Hospital Tuanku Ja'afar Seremban, and family medicine specialists in charge of several health clinics near the village), as well as the oil palm plantation owner, pharmaceutical companies, and corporate bodies.
5. An important note to mention here is that since 2011, the JHEOA became known as the Jabatan Kemajuan Orang Asli (JAKOA, or Department of Orang Asli Development). For the sake of simplicity, the abbreviation JHEOA will continue to be used in this chapter.
6. Talloires Network is a global coalition of 332 community engaged universities in seventy-two countries. The MacJannet Prize is awarded for recognition of exceptional community engagement initiatives by institutions of higher learning from around the world. More information on the MacJannet Prize can be found at http://talloiresnetwork.tufts.edu/about-the-macjannet-prize/#.
7. Albert was the recipient of the Aflame Student Award for 2013, established in 2012 to acknowledge a graduating student's passion to do good for humanity (see International Medical University 2013). Albert was actively involved in charity and humanitarian work among Myanmar refugee children in

Negeri Sembilan, Hospice Negeri Sembilan, and community work among the Orang Asli in Tampin, Negeri Sembilan, Penampang, Sabah, and Hulu Langat, Selangor. Albert is currently the youth officer, Malaysian Red Crescent Society Seremban Chapter. Albert was awarded the Pingat Jasa Kebaktian (Meritorious Service Award) by the ruler of Negeri Sembilan on January 14, 2015, in recognition of his contributions to the community.

8. Gerard was the president of the Student Representative Council in IMU Seremban for the term 2012–2013 and an active member of the project team for IMU Cares Kampung Tekir.
9. Azreen was an active participant in the health-screening events in Kampung Tekir in 2012.
10. Pam was a member of the IMU Cares Kampung Tekir project team and a student leader. She participated in the deliberations in the first Regional Perspectives in Community Engagement meeting in Boston, December 2012, as a student leader in IMU. Pam has since graduated as a doctor and is working in the interior of Sabah, Malaysia.
11. Sheila has been the coordinator of IMU Cares Kampung Tekir since 2013.
12. Inthirah was an active member of the project team from 2010 and played a vital "behind the scene" role in the project.

REFERENCES

Boyte, H. C., and Fretz, E. 2010. Civic professionalism. *Journal of Higher Education Outreach and Engagement* 14(2): 67–90.

Chung, Y. F. 2010. The Orang Asli of Malaysia: Poverty, sustainability and capability approach. Master's thesis, Lund University.

Dunn, F. L. 1977. Secular changes in Temuan (Malaysian Orang Asli) settlement patterns, subsistence and health. *Malayan Nature Journal* 31(2): 81–92.

Hoyt, L., and Newcomb Rowe, A. 2013. Leaders in civic engagement series—December 2013. *Talloires Network Newsletter*. Http://talloiresnetwork.tufts.edu/wp-content/uploads/Dec-2013_LCEM_Final.docx.

International Medical University. 2013. IMU Aflame 2013 Student Award. Http://elearning.imu.edu.my/course/category.php?id=196.

Jabatan Kemajuan Islam Malaysia (JAKIM). 2013. Ijtimak Penggerak Masyarakat Orang Asli (PMOA) Peringkat Kebangsaan Tahun 2013. Http://m.islam.gov.my/en/ijtimak-penggerak-masyarakat-orang-asli-pmoa-peringkat-kebangsaan-tahun-2013-0.

Jabatan Kemajuan Orang Asli (JAKOA). n.d. Orang Asli Information. Http://www.jakoa.gov.my/en/orang-asli/info-orang-asli/suku-kaumbangsa/.

Jabatan Kemajuan Orang Asli (JAKOA). 2011–2015. Pelan Strategik Jabatan Kemajuan Orang Asli 2011–2015. Kuala Lumpur, Malaysia: Bahagian Perancangan dan Penyelidikan Jabatan Kemajuan Orang Asli.

Kari, N. 1999. Political ideas: Catalysts for creating a public culture at the College of St. Catherine. In H. C. Boyte, ed., *Creating the commonwealth*. Dayton, OH: Kettering Foundation Press.

Koh, K. C., George, S. R. K., Pak, J. W., Liow, Y. T., and Khor, J. X. 2014. Role of community service as a curriculum delivery tool in the outcome-based curriculum of the International Medical University, Malaysia. *International e-Journal of Science and Medical Education* 8(1): 24–31.

Nicholas, C. 2000. *The Orang Asli and the contest for resources: Indigenous politics, development and *identity in peninsular Malaysia*. Kuala Lumpur: Vinlin Press.

Nicholas, C., Engi, J., and Teh, Y. P. 2010. *The Orang Asli and the UNDRIP: From rhetoric to recognition*. Kuala Lumpur: Vinlin Press.

Payne, C. M. 1995. *I've got the light of freedom: The organizing tradition and the Mississippi freedom struggle*. Berkeley: University of California Press.

Toshihiro, N. 2009. *Living on the periphery: Development and Islamization of the Orang Asli in Malaysia*. Subang Jaya: Center for Orang Asli Concerns.

Lazord Academy in Cairo, Egypt:
Pedagogy for the Practice of Freedom

Nelly Corbel, Rana Gaber, and Amy Newcomb Rowe

It is spring 2012 and a new batch of Lazord fellows, freshly recruited, fill the room. They have stars in their eyes and dreams to change the world. We see this energy so often in new university students and fresh graduates—they are ready to take on the world. One new fellow stands out in the group. Her name is Reem. She is a short, quiet, young Egyptian woman. We soon learn she wants to work with street children. She doesn't know any street children, yet is aware of the dominant stereotype: they are dangerous to society. Yet few organizations in Cairo have the courage to work with children on the streets, and so Reem decides to work with a local NGO that works with children who have homes.

One week into the Lazord fellowship program, Reem disappears. That is, she no longer shows up for work at the NGO. Years of experience suggest we should not worry; she is no longer interested in our program. Suddenly, Reem shows up in our office. She is apologetic. Her body language points to a feeling of deep regret as well as determination. She wants to continue with her Lazord fellowship. But what should we do? Lazord aims to create purposeful leaders; her disappearance revealed a lack of commitment and damaged, to some extent, our relationship with a local NGO.

We decided not to give up on Reem. We responded to her request by inventing a new practice: the boot camp! In her case, as in others, the issue is one of ownership and a sense of responsibility. However, before we can take the risk of connecting her with another partner organization, we must be convinced she is ready to make the commitment. As luck would have it, a former U.S. president was soon arriving to campus to deliver a talk to an audience of more than a thousand people. What better way to test someone's dedication than have her take a lead role in organizing such an event in the midst of a revolution?

Reem works diligently for long hours, paying attention to details and never complaining. Day after day, her behavior illustrates her commitment as well as her leadership potential. At the end of the month, not a single doubt resides in us—Reem is ready to be placed.

She later opens up to us about her disappearance. Reem explains that she selected the "safer" placement when she realized the nightmares faced by street children. Once placed, however, she found *herself craving to work with street children. Her confusion and lack of self-confidence led her to drop out suddenly. Thanks to her honesty and humility, we were able to work with her, and she completed her fellowship. A few months later, during an ice-breaker requiring all to bring one personal object of importance, she brought a coloring set because making art with street children had become her life purpose. Reem was a renewed person, full of confidence, hope, and passion. Her work was so impressive that she was selected to represent the fellows at graduation. A couple of years later, she now has found ways to give purpose to others, specifically children, through art.*

Reem taught us that we should avoid making assumptions about why students disappear or drop out of the program. It is up to us to listen to them carefully without any judgment. We now prepare students for a month before placement. Also, she reinforced the importance of "tough love." Reem gained a lot by going through the boot camp, which later became a regular practice for dealing with tricky situations. Last, Reem reinforced the importance of the Lazord "journey"—leadership development requires time and patience. Being by the students' sides in these moments of growth, accompanying them through mentorship as they have their first working experience, their first pride, their first disappointment, is one of the most critical aspect to nurture purposeful leadership.

—Nelly Corbel, reflections on practice

Pedagogy for a Generation of Responsible Leaders

Education either functions as an instrument which is used to facilitate integration of the younger generation into the logic of the present system and bring about conformity or it becomes the practice of freedom, the means by which men and women deal critically and creatively with reality and discover how to participate in the transformation of their world.

—Paulo Freire, *Pedagogy of the Oppressed*

The Lazord Academy is housed at the American University in Cairo (AUC), a small, private liberal arts and professional education institution in Egypt. It is a shining example of teaching citizenship in the context of a larger struggle toward a citizen-driven society. Within a difficult context of polarization, marginalization, and curtailed human rights in Egypt, the Lazord Academy was created to integrate citizenship, ethics, and responsible leadership into professional development.

Though other universities in Egypt and the region have civic engagement at the core of their mission, they struggle to institutionalize university-based civic engagement programs for a number of contextual and logistical factors. American University in Cairo president Dr. Lisa Anderson envisions a future in which "teaching will increasingly be acknowledged as guided by learning-by-doing." For Anderson, the university's first female president, the cultivation of "creative problem-solvers, effective colleagues and collaborators, and responsible citizens in many domains is essential" in the Arab region and beyond (Anderson 2013; Hoyt and Newcomb Rowe 2015, 29).

The AUC mission statement includes goals such as "Social Responsibility":

We are committed to exploring the challenges that confront Egypt, the region, and the world and to using our intellectual and creative capabilities to address these challenges, serve our communities, and have a positive and sustainable impact on development, business, the environment, and society. In addition, the university also extends its civic mission to set "Outreach Enhancing Engagement and Access," where it is dedicating itself to serving communities in Egypt and around the world through extension and outreach programs that bring university expertise and insight to a wider public, that profit from the university's convening power, and that serve to inform and enlighten public discourse, enhance access to information and knowledge, and enrich artistic and intellectual life.

In 2010, Dr. David Arnold, at that time the president of AUC, received a proposal from a young social entrepreneur, Anna Irwin, to establish a graduate fellowship. President Arnold responded by creating a committee to support Anna's efforts in developing the new fellowship program that places recent graduates in local civil society organizations while offering them quality continuing education opportunities to advance their unique skill sets. The fellowship is a meaningful opportunity for graduates to prepare for employment and careers after university. Unemployment is a striking issue in Egyptian society: one-half of the Egyptian population is below the age of twenty-five, and already the "youth bulge" poses a high risk to Egyptian society's stability and economic growth (Assaad and Roudi-Fahimi 2010). The 2011 uprisings brought this demographic dynamic to light; it is a challenge that cannot be ignored, now more than ever.

Just after Lisa Anderson was appointed AUC's president in 2011, young Egyptians led the January 25 uprising that ended President Hosni Mubarak's thirty-year rule. Between 2011 and 2013, Cairo represented a tumultuous civil society characterized by continued demonstrations and violent struggles for political power. It is also a place where students have "a high level of energy" and need "the tools and vision" to move the country forward (Barker et al. 2013). Through its ever-changing, yet structured approach, the Lazord Academy provided the space, support, and guidance for students to take a timely journey.

Their Lazord journey begins "below the surface" with self-development and leads to the development of ethics, self-confidence, and active listening skills "above the surface" (Corbel 2014). The University is actively responding to the youth bulge. By using an "ecological" framework, the Lazord Academy discovers, cultivates, and liberates a new generation of civically responsible Arab leaders and professionals (Perkins, Hughey, and Speer 2002). University faculty and staff as well as community partners interactively design the program and revisit it year after year. They share their own understanding of what is happening locally as well as facilitate student reflection exercises, which are done by way of blog posts, diaries, pictures, and other methods. The program's flexibility is "what keeps learning meaningful to the students. We cannot pretend our students are not dying on the streets protesting, so we must acknowledge this real experience and assist students with the life and death questions"—and what could be more relevant than purpose in these discussions? (Corbel 2014; Hoyt and Newcomb Rowe 2015, 31).

Students and local leaders alike experienced intense moments of victory and loss during the months and years following the uprisings. Civil society organizations suffered various degrees of discrimination from the public and the government. There is skepticism surrounding the work of the civil society in Egypt. This skepticism can be traced to many factors, some of which can be attributed to the difficult conditions under which they operate; for example, 28 percent of Egyptians live at or below the poverty line (World Bank 2016), making it very difficult for organizations to have a major influence on economic well-being. Other reasons for public mistrust of NGOs can be attributed to the challenges different organizations face from starting up, social dynamics, and internal structure. Even so, civil society organizations remain the primary gatekeepers to engagement with local communities. Lazord aims to build long-standing partnerships with organizations so that the university-based program remains aware of and integrated with the many processes of engagement already happening. Lazord's approach seeks to develop the capacities of civil society in addition to giving students the valuable experience of engaging with local organizations and leaders. This builds and sustains trust across the board. "Much of the work involves building awareness of themselves [the students], the communities around them, and how they interact, communicate and meet challenges together" (Gaber 2014; Hoyt and Newcomb Rowe 2015, 34). Despite the highly restrictive laws governing local organizations in Egypt, many Lazord partners have been involved with the University for several years. Though the principles of university-community partnership articulated by Lazord are conventional, there are many noteworthy instances of equality, trust, honesty, and openness.

If 2011 is seen as a tipping point for civic engagement within the university context in Egypt, it reflects what had been an active participation prior to the revolution. Before 2011, the public sphere was not open and participation within this sphere was limited to a select few. Universities were no exception; the only means of civic engagement were the student activities that existed within the restrictions of the universities' administration. Private universities, however, were more open than public institutions when it came to promoting civic engagement. Within this restricted context, new spaces of engagement were slowly emerging in the public sphere where people advocated for more inclusion and participation. Volunteerism gained momentum as an early attempt to open the public sphere for engagement, though volunteerism was at first limited merely to charitable activities. At the turn of the twenty-first century, volunteerism gained a different understanding —one that emerged from the rise of organizations focusing on development rather than charity.

These organizations became platforms for youth to develop their skills while gaining a sense of responsibility for the country. They also found their way onto campuses of both public and private universities. Additionally, some of the on-campus student activities integrated themselves into the community by registering as nongovernmental organizations (e.g., Alashanek Ya Balady, from the American University campus, operating in one of the poor areas in Egypt, Ain Elseera).

This momentum built through the 2000s and gave way to the start of the revolution in January 2011. Young people have developed a strong sense of civic engagement in the wake of the first wave of the revolution. They are redefining their relation with the state, claiming different public spaces that were closed, and trying to find their way back from social exclusion and marginalization. Unlike the period preceding 2011, social responsibility and civic engagement have been redefined and are more appealing to young people. Political engagement (once restricted solely to "proregime" students) and social activism among university students started to increase (Corbel and Pollock 2012). Young people joined newly emerging political parties, social movements, and informal initiatives. Attention was directed toward civil society, revitalizing it and providing professional volunteers as resources for development. This wave of rising engagement in the public sphere began to recede with the instability that persisted within the political system. An indicator for this is the declining percentage of young people participating in elections, especially in the latest referendum on the constitution and the presidential elections in 2014. It is within this context that Lazord operates; engaged in a complex push-and-pull process for a peaceful and dynamic society.

The Lazord Journey

The word *lazord* is the Arabic name for lapis lazuli. This indigenous blue stone with gold flecks once embellished the most valuable jewelry of the royal courts in ancient Egypt and was considered the royal stone. Like the stone, Egyptian youth are precious gems worthy of attention who, with a little "polishing," can lead countries with vision, compassion, and skill. Lazord seeks to graduate a generation of civically responsible and skilled leaders that play an active and engaged role across all sectors of society.

In 2008, the John D. Gerhart Center for Philanthropy and Civic Engagement at AUC began fundraising for five scholarships. These scholars would undergo an experience inspired by Portland State University's Student Leaders for Service program, former recipients of the Talloires Network MacJannet Prize for student leadership. Soon, a systematized structure and staff were in place and the program began to gain momentum. In the first phase, student cohorts received training and mentorship. In conjunction with this development of skills and confidence, participants were required to create group projects. Although the students were eager to develop their projects, practical implementation became a challenging reality, one that has persisted year after year. A number of factors play into this challenge: workload, community obstacles, and staff capacity. As the fellowship grew successfully, the undergraduate track seemed to need some rethinking.

Based on student evaluations, the curriculum redesign limited the focus of projects to improving campus life and integrating civic engagement into the heart of university life, instead of allowing for a city or country-wide approach. It is important to allow students the autonomy to design projects because creative thinking and problem-solving are central skills the program seeks to develop. On the graduate fellowship front, the main challenge encountered was retention rate during academic year 2010–2011, the year of the Egyptian uprisings. Exit interviews with fellows leaving the program revealed two insights: (1) the euphoria of the public uprisings gave a feeling across the country that everything was possible and a simple fellowship was not enough, and (2) the need to strengthen the training and networking element for increased student ownership.

This academic year (2010–2011) could be described as an organized chaos. Often in program development, things get messy before finding shape. This start-up period is often full of setbacks punctuated by rays of hope for a smoother tomorrow. The doubling of the two programs (undergraduate and graduate) running in parallel at such an early developmental phase was trouble enough. Taking this on while maintaining the same staff time quickly became a challenge due to the central role of mentoring and curriculum development, two time-consuming efforts that require disproportionate staff attention. Students of the previous year were therefore engaged and encouraged to support both the development and the execution of the program.

Operating like a mind map coming to reality, the program developed several mostly independent "moving pieces" to be woven into one fabric. However, each piece first had to exist as an established entity before being able to connect meaningfully with the others. The Lazord Academy program required four key elements to evolve and survive in a peculiar context.

First, in order to better integrate students' projects and voices with the heart of the mission, the alumni were invited to come back to give life to their proposed project of the previous year: a team of student ambassadors on campus who would promote and support sustainable civic and community work. Three out of the five initial students rejoined the center and further developed the initiative to become Advocates for Civic Engagement, a position "which seeks to promote student civic engagement through volunteerism on AUC's campus." Based on the same model, this track would target primarily students not eligible for the scholarship, especially freshmen.

Second, the Lazord fellowship, then called the Lead On fellowship, was seeing its first year with three fellows. Though operating with the same methodology, the fellows were fresh AUC graduates who were to be placed in a civic organization. Their practical experience was therefore mostly contained in the internship. The need for a solid placement is a central issue for this "moving piece" (Underwood and Jabre 2010). Students are encouraged to identify an organization themselves to ensure it matches their interest. The eligibility of organizations is simply based on whether their missions are socially or civically oriented.

Third, the need to ensure growth and financial sustainability for the program to not only develop in depth, but also expand regionally, became a priority. Consequently, our supporting philanthropists engaged in an effort to build momentum for the program and eventually started a foundation.

Finally, we had to learn how to support and develop the student leaders for service in their project. For undergraduates to launch a community project can be both exciting and daunting at the same time, so ensuring that they have a strong support system behind them is crucial.

This academic year (2010–2011) witnessed the uprisings in Egypt; it was an energy-loaded moment of history that brought forth a set of dreams and difficult realities. From calls for more social justice to a more inclusive democratic society, aspirations for a better Egypt flourished. In such times of extreme emotions and confusion, information flows in an erratic way. Newly found freedoms of expression collide, leaving little space for strategizing and constructive dialogue.

Consequently, in September 2011, the Lazord Academy was launched to provide a clear institutional frame for a common methodology used across various projects. It improves the quality and streamlining processes of the different civic engagement programs at AUC. In 2012 a needs assessment was conducted that shaped the community partnerships. The program was replicated in Jordan. The years between 2013 and 2015 saw a strengthening of the curriculum with an added ecological approach, a refined recruitment processes, and the launch of a third chapter in Tunisia. This came at the cost of the student leaders for service component, which was converted to the Advocates for Civic Engagement initiative. The practical aspect for students was focused on clearly defined and achievable microprojects on campus, like supporting community-based learning projects, raising awareness, and leading campus conversations on a variety of topics involving faculty, staff, alumni, and students.

In the start-up years of Lazord, program founders envisioned that by providing youth with a space to explore how their passions can impact the common good, we would sow the seeds of a more dynamic and socially minded future (Nyerere 1967). The purpose is to foster generations of driven youth who leverage value-based change across sectors and who develop a more long-term sense of purpose than solely focusing on career aspirations. We can argue that university student learning coincides with the fifth stage of Kohlberg's model for moral development. According to his model, it is only in this stage of moral growth that an individual develops the ability to identify and integrate the ethical subtleties of the world. This internal development allows an individual to comprehend and accept a spectrum of societal behaviors, making constructive dialogue and exchange possible (Kohlberg 1985).

The program manager and team looked at means to solidify and deepen the curriculum in order to reach the objective of graduating value-driven young professionals. Upon reflection, it was decided to not only look at learning through skill building and knowledge transfers, but also by helping students attain various competencies (Easterling 2012). Though a seemingly irrelevant nuance for some, the difference between a competency and a skill is major and greatly impacts the curriculum methodology. While a skill allows one to know how to do something technically, a competency is founded on a holistic framework of learning including knowledge, skill, values, and attitudes. Ideal learning outcomes in the form of competencies were therefore defined in partnership with various stakeholders (staff, fellows, partners, and faculty).

The resulting Lazord Academy learning methodology is built on an ecological perspective; the curriculum is constructed around ecological systems surrounding the individual consisting of three layers: me, my community, and the world. The core, "me," being the discovery of personal potentials, is surrounded by a microsystem (the community), which is related back to the self and includes the job implementation practices. Then the macrosystem entails the national, regional, and international context. From here, the impact of political, social, and economic systems, and the means of influencing decision-making, are studied more closely. Each section includes training sessions that directly affect these ecological systems. Furthermore, the sessions follow a certain progression of four phases in each system. They start by exploring, then rationalizing, then planning, and finally end with action. Critical thinking is emphasized at the core of this journey of self-development and is well integrated in each system through the rationalization phase.

The learning journey is framed by two regional retreats that bring together fellows from each international chapter. This time allows students to engage in a safe environment and explore their opinions and values. In the opening retreat, we introduced five core pillars of civic education—values, knowledge, attitudes, skills, and practices. In an exercise, students are asked to place each pillar on an iceberg diagram. This activity allows for the students to visualize what Mahatma Gandhi expressed beautifully: "Your beliefs become your thoughts, your thoughts become your words, your words become your actions, your actions become your habits, your habits become your values, your values become your destiny."

The exercise begins by drawing an iceberg on a flip chart and asking participants to place the five pillars on it. As they place them from bottom to top (values, knowledge, skills, attitudes, and practices), an organic conversation ensues around the reasoning behind the placement of each pillar, and what implications it has on everyday life. Values act as their compass for aligning the other pillars above, allowing participants to reflect on whether this is already the case, or whether they may experience internal contradictions in their life. The example given is often one that is challenging to their cultural understanding, such as the issue of diversity and whether, and how, it should be protected and valued.

Iceberg Exercise

A vivid illustration of this last point would be a side discussion I had one day with a student regarding homosexuality. The student expressed diversity and equal rights as a central set of her values. I therefore asked if, according to her, everyone should have equal rights and their differences accepted by the larger society and legal system, as long as they do not call for hatred or violence. She agreed without conditions. Subsequently, I told her that I therefore assumed she was for same-sex marriage and she replied: Of course not! This is where reflection hits a nerve and becomes a true learning experience. We broke down her reaction and agreed that her attitude was in opposition to the value of diversity. As we further analyzed her feelings, we concluded that there were missing links between her stated values and her adopted attitudes. She did not know anyone openly homosexual and had limited exposure to this topic, mostly from opposing rhetoric. We consequently agreed that she had the right to be opposed, but her opinion had to be formulated on fact-based knowledge and exchange with the relevant community. We agreed that these conditions are required to formulate a solid argument as to why she is opposed to gay marriage, rather than merely perpetuating a cultural stigma. I believe it is critical as an educator to not formulate any opinion on behalf of students, but rather to give them the tools to formulate their own opinions based on evidence and critical thinking around personally held core values.

— *Nelly Corbel, reflections on practice*

Once the students lay the five pillars on the iceberg, they gain better self-awareness by realizing how their inner values inform their actions and opinions, and how they may or may not be in line with their dreams and aspirations. Realizing a higher level of self-awareness with a conceptual frame is usually all the students need to move forward with this work on values. The following session, they are asked to draft three key performance indicators for the year: one educational, one personal, and one professional. The mentors use these outputs throughout the year as part of a theme-based approach to student learning. By the end of the year retreat, the students have had a full experience of action, theory, and reflection along these themes and are ready to bring it all into a cohesive "life package." They can revise this document annually, providing themselves with a clearer sense of purpose and alignment with their dreams and true selves.

While Lazord's well-thought-out and ever-evolving approach provides a start and finish line, so to speak, the path is worn by walking side by side with other participants. Corbel points to "mentorship" as the key ingredient of the program's success, explaining, "When you establish friendships based on mutual respect and understanding, you open the soul of the learner and each of us learns better. Students trust us, which opens their learning beyond the classroom" (Corbel 2014; Hoyt and Newcomb Rowe 2015, 32).

Reflection is core to the mentorship so that students learn to link their experiences with theory. Creating these links helps teach students how critical reflection can affect their decision-making process for their life both on and off campus. This practice is central in order to ensure it becomes a lifelong habit.

The Role of Reflection

Reflection is learning that grows out of experience (Moffat and Decker 2000, 32). Through reflection participants analyze concepts, evaluate experiences, form opinions, and derive new meanings and new knowledge (Schön 1983). Written forms of reflection include journals, letters, editorials, personal web pages or blogs, essays, discussion boards, and reflective narratives. Oral forms include one-on-one discussions, directed and nondirected discussion, small groups, case studies, and quotes. Creative mediums include video making, painting, sculpture, music, dance, group skits, and theater.

In addition to being a critical learning tool, group reflection allows students to express feedback and take an active role in the creation of the program. This practice was applied with all students working at the center, including interns. In 2012–2013 the program hosted an intern, Hana Shahin, from the graduate Community Psychology Program. She designed her own assignments through the support of her academic supervisor and the reflection exercises. Hana's goal was to incorporate the Lazord experience with her field of community psychology. Together with the community partnership coordinator, Sherwet Ahmed, she began by running a needs assessment of local organizations for projects and capacity building. The assessment's results provided a chance to create a tailored set of joint trainings for both the community leaders and the fellows. This gave birth to the civic professional track, which plays a critical role in improving Lazord's relationship with community partners.

Hana's reflection did not end there. She had shown such dedication and ownership of the program that she was recruited as full-time staff to work in the university-based civic engagement unit at the center. Once exposed to the value-driven curriculum, Hana focused much of her energy and efforts to refining the methodologies used for reflection. Borrowing from the field of community psychology, Hana proposed the ecological approach. After some collaborative adjustment with the team, this framework became an integral part of the Lazord learning journey.

Lazord Academy Partners

Anna Irwin was a fresh Princeton graduate and finishing an internship in an international organization based in Cairo. She had a dream that was strikingly similar to Nelly Corbel's. Nelly was asked to chair the committee set up by David Arnold in 2010 and connected with Anna over their common goals. Anna and Nelly met at cafés in Cairo or on campus almost weekly for two months, visualizing how the program could unfold over the years, imagining different scenarios for growth. Should they increase the number of fellowships or expand regionally a smaller but well-rounded model? They opted for the second option to create a true leadership program. Once the fellowship launched in May 2010, the two programs started evolving in parallel on the same three pillars.

By the following academic year, Nelly was overseeing both programs while Anna was handling the external fundraising from the United States by setting up a foundation solely dedicated to the Lazord fellowship. As Anna and Nelly looked at these seed projects, they started to focus their work on the sustainability of the program and its development. The fellowship aspired to go international with another chapter. While Anna launched the Lazord Foundation to secure fundraising, Nelly diligently streamlined operations for the educational aspects of the programs. These efforts gave birth to the Lazord Foundation and the Lazord Academy, reflecting the two dimensions of the sustainability effort.

Community Partners

Defining the "community" was the first step for the Academy in its efforts to identify which partners to engage with the program. Accordingly, the Academy took a broader approach in its reflections on community, including any sort of organization that exists in and interacts with society. With this expansive definition, community partners could be identified both on and off campus. The long trust-building process between the Academy and the community has brought forth a partnership highly valued by everyone. The community partners are involved in setting up programmatic activities with the Academy. More importantly, their continual feedback is taken into consideration in the curriculum development and the training processes. The assessment established in 2012 to identify the professional development needs of community leaders and their staff also plays a big role in Lazord's process. The results of this research inform much of the civic professional track program supporting community partners' needs and assets. Since then, the fellows, along with selected professionals from the community, receive weekly trainings. This not only allows for skill building, but also community building among the partners and the fellows. This provides the essential support for all these individuals to increase their professional exposure, mobility, and capabilities—making the program an asset for young graduates establishing a foundation for their careers.

These stakeholder engagement strategies allowed for a buffer and sustainable tie during difficult and lean times. A good example is the long-standing partnership between the Academy and Egyptian Youth Federation (EYF). EYF is closely involved in the selection and training of the fellows prior to their community placements. The application process involves an interview between a prospective fellow and a panel composed of staff from community partners and the Academy. Though EYF and the Academy have had a strong partnership since 2012, no partnership is immune to problems. When two fellows failed to show up for their internships at EYF, the incident did not affect the positive involvement of EYF in both the training and recruitment of three generations of the Academy from 2012 until the present date. The two parties were able to discuss the issues and remain open to find other spaces for collaboration.

Beyond the example mentioned above, Lazord has always put community partnership at the center of its program development. Community engagement is seen as being at the core of civic engagement. Maintaining strong community ties has always been considered an organic need. Community, however, stretches beyond campus grounds; therefore, internal and external partnerships are critical. Internal partnerships on campus can be with other centers present on campus, other departments, or schools. An example of this is that one of the fellows in 2015 was hosted at the Social Research Centre on campus, instead of participating in an off-campus internship. This goes to show that the program always approaches partnerships not as a side thought with strict boundaries and responsibilities, but rather as a dynamic, integral part of the decision-making process and planning.

In 2011–2012, an in-depth needs assessment was conducted by the staff of the center to identify community staff and project needs. It was key for the Academy to act on the findings to improve the experience for the next cohort of fellows. In 2012–2013, the Lazord Academy provided free training for fellows and community-based staff of the host organizations. These trainings were organized in response to the needs assessment and were directed to developing the campsites of the host organizations. A yearly series of trainings was organized. The sessions ranged from project management, monitoring, and evaluation, to conflict resolution and communication, technical writing, and beyond. This allowed a community of practice to grow between the graduates starting their professional career and the staff of community organizations. With a meeting every week, this addition to the program was a perfect means for building solidarity within the community and providing opportunities for professional networking. In addition, the partnerships built around the fellowship allow the program to provide further professional and civic exposure to undergraduates on a formal and informal basis.

Learning from this process of building strong and sustainable partnerships, Lazord organically integrated the following values into its mission: equality, trust, transparency in communication, adaptability, and reciprocity. Equality in this context centers on the equal nature of the relationship between the two parties, where neither the Academy nor the community organization holds more power. In such a situation, the fellows are at the heart of the partnership. Trust means both partners feel confident in the capacities and intentions of the other; this value has been integrated into the program through a long-term trust-building process. It is fostered both formally through meetings and trainings and informally through casual meetings and conversations. Adaptability is also a crucial value since it shapes how the partners deal with each other in times of challenges. A high degree of adaptability to change is critical since the social situation in Egypt remains volatile, to say nothing of the inherent changes that organically take place in universities and nonprofit organizations. The last value is reciprocity, and this refers to the importance of achieving equal contributions to the program from both the Academy and its partners. This helps the partnership succeed and ensures that each partner benefits and that the learning journey of the fellows and students is at the heart of the partnership.

The Lazord Academy benefited from an enabling environment in a supportive ecosystem on the AUC campus. The first layer of this ecosystem was the Gerhart Research Center, which offered a perfect incubator for the program. Through the center, which operates at the crossroads of civic engagement and philanthropy, the Academy was able to use valuable expertise as a catalyst for forming new ideas about both program development and financial sustainability. The center's work created a perfect synergetic situation for improving both. Additionally, the center provides five practical benefits as the home for Lazord: (1) support from the university mission as "A Catalyst for change" (AUC mission statement); (2) a strategy to develop, incubate, and scale up methodologies to integrate community engagement into the heart of other Arab universities; (3) a platform for international exchange through the Ma'an Arab University Alliance, a regional subnetwork of the Talloires Network; (4) seed funding for the undergraduate track beginning with five start-up scholarships with support from an outside funder with ties to the center; and finally, (5) access to expertise in community-based and service-learning (Ibrahim and Hunt-Hendrix 2011).

The second layer of the ecosystem, the AUC new campus, also provides support to Lazord

Academy through an array of student support services. Three offices play a central role in supporting the program: The LEAD office, a merit-based full scholarship program for underprivileged students from all over Egypt; the Center for Learning and Teaching (CLT); and the Career and Placements Services (CAPS). LEAD helped to establish the structure for selecting applicants, evaluating them, and working with them on activities including the learning journey. CLT provides added value by assisting with curriculum development. Last but not least, CAPS is the perfect organization to provide support in selecting and maintaining community partnerships for internship placements. In addition, the latter offers insights on the type of skills employers are eager to find in our young graduates and improving the employability of our students.

Lazord Academy: Learning about Yourself, Becoming a Purposeful Leader

Built as a holistic experience, Lazord aims to provide students with a mindset that will allow them to move forward in their lives and careers with an open mind while having a clear focus and civic values. Student feedback during and after the program is therefore critical for Lazord's process of program evaluation. In the first year, a focus group was assembled to identify areas of strengths and needs. According to the students' feedback, though the three pillars offer them tangible support both at the personal and at the professional levels, the topics, projects, and mentorship needed to be further aligned.

Initial experiences with the professional mentorships revealed the need for more fine-tuned modifications in the matching process and to better prepare mentors for the task. Mentorships were primarily based on expertise matching; however, over time we have learned that matching personalities is just as critical to ensure a beneficial and long-lasting relationship. Placing students in mentorships with professionals who have very little or no background in student development (whether academic or cocurricular) has led to complications in communication with the student. It also results in a purely hierarchical relationship, hindering the reflective process central to experiential learning. Though supporting the students in their respective projects allows strong personal growth, the minimal role of group projects did not allow participants to develop meaningful experiences with teamwork, which is critical in helping to build a long-term network of alumni by creating a common sense of belonging and, therefore, identity.

Consequently, in the run-up to the following academic year, a number of modifications to the project were developed. They were implemented in order to (1) strengthen the reflective learning process through a more solid mentorship experience; (2) narrow down the subjects tackled in the workshops to provide more obvious links to the practice of the students; and (3) strengthen the sense of community among the students to lay the foundation for a network. In parallel to this development, a young philanthropist approached AUC to start a fellowship program inspired by young AUC graduates of the LEAD program she met. Jointly with other university departments and the support of leadership, the fellowship found a home at the Gerhart Center, following the same methodology used to launch Lazord.

As for the strengths of the program, students expressed that the program succeeded in empowering them to find their assets as leaders while enabling them to better define their purpose. A student recalled that the program helped students define what a civic leader was: "A Lazord civic leader is an intellectual person who is aware of all the issues in his/her community and has the ability/knowledge/skills to change it." Others reflected on how the program allowed them to be in touch with practice and realities on the ground: "This is [an] experience you won't get elsewhere. We are exposed to problems in real communities, and their roots. I wanted to personally make a decision [as] to whether I wanted to stay in this career path and now I know I do." Finally, as addressed earlier in the chapter, a main challenge Lazord has been tackling is the employability of youth, to address the youth bulge in the region. According to a student reflection: "[I] joined Lazord to increase my employability, other clubs do not provide actual knowledge, I do community work and I am a leader."

Fast forward to 2015; Lazord is now a regional program with three chapters led by a U.S.-based foundation. Multiple areas of needs have been addressed through a number of learning experiences. Each year, some fifty youths from across Jordan, Tunisia, and Egypt go on the Lazord journey. Graduates from Lazord go on to take jobs in civil society, international agencies, government, and corporate social responsibility or pursue further studies. To this day, across the various programs and countries, over 80 percent of graduates are either employed or pursuing studies. Reflecting on the journey, an Egyptian Lazord fellow summarized the key strength of the program: "Lazord is presenting a new way of civic engagement and leadership, and a new way of teaching civic education." This central asset of the program has allowed over three hundred youths to move forward with greater clarity regarding their life purpose and how to build a career around it.

Lazord graduates are spreading across the globe for work and studies. The number of success stories among them is inspiring and would require a true impact study to assess how big a role Lazord played in their experience. Heba Hesham, Lazord 2011–2012, recalls:

> My experience as a student associate at Lazord was the beginning of a very exciting journey that led me to my passion for Gender and Development. Little did I know when I first applied to join Lazord that it would be equipping me with the leadership skills that would encourage me to start my own student organization the same year. With the incredible support from our mentors and a network of passionate student leaders, I was able to co-found *Heya*, Egypt's first student-led women's rights organization. Throughout the whole process of growing Heya, from widening our network, to presenting at international conferences, to being endorsed by UN Women, the skills I learned from Lazord were indispensable, making me feel confident, prepared, and professional when I needed it most. My Lazord experience will always remain [at] the roots of my passion for development, and for that I will always be grateful.

As mentioned earlier, one of the region's main challenges is the youth bulge: millions of young people do not have a job or any prospects of getting one, nor the skills to create their own. Many live in precarious situations, inviting them to pursue more radical paths in search of a purpose, a raison d'être. Therefore, a critical outcome of the program is improving employability of students and fellows. According to Karim Aziz, Lazord Advocate for Civic Engagement (2013–2014):

> After joining the Ministry of Finance as an economist, it became clear how my time with Lazord made me see the world differently. When an unemployment rate of 15 percent is published, I see a father who feels he has failed his family. When I read that we have over 20 million people living in poverty, I see all

those who cannot afford their dinner tonight. Seeing the world through the lens of Lazord shows me the lives behind the numbers and provides an incentive to make things better. In short, Lazord has taught me to always seek to make a difference in people's lives.

The next key challenge Lazord is addressing is ensuring a scale-up that does not endanger quality. Three strategies are key to achieving this: using AUC as the pilot program for the curriculum, providing tested guidance to support new chapters; the Lazord Foundation focusing on mission alignment, quality control, alumni engagement, and financial sustainability, so individual chapters can focus on the actual program implementation; and scaling up horizontally by increasing the number of regional chapters rather than the number of students per country. This last point was discussed extensively as Lazord fellowships gained popularity in these countries, additional local organizations were eager to host fellows, and local chapters wanted to serve more organizations. However, one of the structural objectives was to have a regional program to offer a regional network of Lazordian alumni. Considering the extensive work put into the Lazord journey, a large number of students would automatically lead to a decrease in quality if staff was not increased as well. Therefore, for logistical, financial, and quality control purposes, it was decided to expand horizontally for the next few years until the program reaches five chapters. The issue will be brought back then, to be discussed by stakeholders.

Looking Back, Looking Ahead

During the summer of 2009, I was a senior coordinator for international student affairs and student life at the American University in Cairo. I was in charge of intercultural programs and orientation for degree-seeking students, working to develop a team of student leaders for over a year. As I worked with various departments and programs throughout the university, I met Barbara Ibrahim, then head of the John D. Gerhart Center for Philanthropy and Civic Engagement. She had received funding to award five undergraduate scholarships to students showing exceptional commitment to service on campus. She needed someone to set up a system for managing the awards and I jumped at the opportunity. From this moment, she supported my experiences, my trials and errors, and backed me. Her trusting leadership style allowed for the seed of a program to blossom into a recognized leadership program.

One morning during my first week on the job, I sat in the gardens of the university, wondering how to build a new program. How could I make it engaging for undergraduate students while building the values needed in an ethical leader? How could the program be of service to the community? These three distinctive criteria were born from a mix of the donor's requirements, the center's leadership, and my own aspirations.

I decided to start with what I do best: methodology. It struck me that mentorship was the missing link. Many programs have mentorship or training or activities, or two of the three. Lazord's foundation would rest on a strong relationship between all three of these interrelated elements.

Five colleagues played a critical role in helping to define the nuances which would eventually make Lazord a unique experience for the students and the coordinators. One is my office mate, Karim Shalaby, who was the philanthropy advisor of the center. His poised demeanor made him a trusted resource and advisor for many of us in the office. He helped me to visualize what a perfect civic leader looks like: s/he has a big heart, a big brain, eyes with far-away vision and big ears. Karim is a great example of a practical theorist, someone who strongly believes in practice and service to others. His many years of experience working in the nomadic cultures of Egyptian farmers brought a wealth of practical knowledge to our work.

Also, Amani Elshimi, the community-based learning director, radiated kindness and care while actively shaping Lazord. She taught me how to translate a philosophy into programmatic outputs. Her attention to detail was inspiring. When building a university-based program for civic engagement one should consider: (1) how the program benefits the university's mission of learning, teaching, and research; (2) how the students gain something of value; (3) how to ensure the community feels empowered; and (4) how the program appeals to the staff running it.

The third person who helped me shape Lazord was a community partner. We had endless discussions about the values and behaviors the next generation may find useful in the face of the daunting challenges of the twenty-first century. Perhaps most notable are the ongoing tensions in the region regardless of religion or affiliation. We often reflected on the universality of such values as tolerance and compassion. We came to the conclusion that Lazord needed to offer participants a true learning journey, a whole experience—one that would transform individuals while giving them solid skills to be able to carry forward their purpose.

The fourth person was Sulaf Taha, the associate director of the Lead Office at AUC who became my refuge when things were getting rough. Her office at the other end of campus became my thinking room for reinvigorating the dream and not losing the big picture. We spent hours looking at my mind maps, and she spent countless hours supporting me in coaching my team members on how to work with youth.

Last but not least, the most significant collaboration was with Anna Irwin. Despite her young age, by coming in with the same vision and a full dedication to see the program succeed, Anna quickly took a leading role by my side. Our visions became one almost instantaneously as she shared her proposal over a cup of coffee. Since 2010, she ensured the financial sustainability single-handedly, a feat which can never be understated. With her as a "partner in crime," we were able to bring Lazord into an independent foundation supporting the replication of the program around the region while keeping it contextualized.

—Nelly Corbel, reflections on practice

Conclusion

Youth around the world lead a challenge against the archetypal post–World War II vision of happiness (i.e., a job, a family, and a set of hobbies). They are looking for pointers, structures, and ways to give purpose to their lives. Lazord provides a yearlong journey to turn dreams into a purpose with a set of competencies, grounding participants in a solid understanding of their own version of happiness as an integral part of a cohesive society. Lazord has now graduated over sixty fellows regionally and supported the capacity development of over one hundred organizations. These value-driven, skilled, and purposeful young leaders are spreading their wings across borders. They carry with them the values of coexistence, humanitarianism, and responsibility, giving us hope in the face of terrorism, climate change, economic instability, and demographic challenges that we leave for future generations.

Lazord provides a model with a methodology that can easily be globalized, allowing for full or partial implementation in various contexts around the world. This gives the program an undeniable strength in promoting responsible and ethical leadership. It also promotes a sense of citizenship in a world that is becoming increasingly interconnected, where many youth attempt to create an identity as a global citizen (Astin and Astin 1996). Lazord does so by operating around key principles laid out in this chapter: institutionalize diversity, from planning to recruitment of partners and fellows; always accompany the learning with mentorship and coaching; leave room in the scheduling to integrate relevant current events (especially in unstable countries); use an ecological approach when developing the curriculum to allow the students to gradually connect themselves to the larger global society; and last but not least, include learning objectives for values, attitudes, skills, knowledge, and practice.

As the world braces itself to address challenges that transcend borders, humanity tries to define itself beyond the Westphalian understanding of a world with nation-states. Educating our youth to think beyond geographic, cultural, religious, or ethnic differences has become an urgent task. As educators, it is our duty to provide them with the tools to create this new world. Lazord philosophy and curriculum aims to humbly contribute to this process in a very practical way. Now established as a 501c(3) in Boston, operating in Europe and the Middle East North African region, the Lazord Foundation still shoots for the sun. It has aspirations to expand across the south Mediterranean and eventually in the northern part as well. More importantly, it seeks to integrate its methodology into mainstream education so that all students have the opportunity to become value-driven leaders and to achieve the change they want to see in the world.

REFERENCES

Anderson, L. 2013. Interview by Lorlene Hoyt, Boston, Massachusetts, May.

Assaad, R., and Roudi-Fahimi, F. 2010. Youth in the Middle East and North Africa: Demographic opportunity or challenge? *MENA Policy Brief.* Washington, DC: Population Reference Bureau.

Astin, H. S., and Astin, A. W. 1996. *A social change model of leadership development: Guidebook.* Version 3. Los Angeles: Higher Education Research Institute, University of California, Los Angeles.

Barker, D., Brace, E., Bravo, M. F. P., Catalano, J., Cirillo, M., Corbel, N., Diebel, A., Francis, J., Gaber, E. B., Hoyt, L., Ornelas Newcomb, A., Kabiti, H., Keegan, M., Koh, J., Layden, M., Martin, H., Naidoo, L., Putu, T., Wilson, M., and Zulkifar, P. 2013. Group meeting. December 16–20.

Corbel, N. 2014. Interview by Amy Newcomb Rowe, Boston, Massachusetts, January.

Corbel, N., and Pollock, J. 2012. *Citizens in the making: Civil society and civic education in Egypt.* Cairo: John D. Gerhart Center for Philanthropy and Civic Engagement.

Easterling, D. 2012. Scaling up civic leadership combining individual-level change and culture change. *National Civic Review* 101(4): 51–64.

Freire, P. 1998. *Pedagogy of freedom: Ethics, democracy, and civic courage.* Lanham, MD: Rowman and Littlefield.

Gaber, R. 2014. Interview by Amy Newcomb Rowe, Boston, Massachusetts, January.

Hoyt, L., and Newcomb Rowe, A. 2015. *Leaders in the civic engagement movement*. Http://talloiresnetwork.tufts.edu/wp-content/uploads/LCEM-Digital-Report-with-TOC-Feb-20151.pdf.

Kohlberg, L. 1985. Kohlberg's stages of moral development. In W. C. Crain, ed., *Theories of development*. Upper Saddle River, NJ: Prentice-Hall.

Ibrahim, B., and Hunt-Hendrix, L. 2011. Youth, service and pathways to democracy in Egypt. John D. Gerhart Center for Philanthropy and Civic Engagement Working Paper Series.

Moffat, J., and Decker, R. 2000. Service-learning reflection for engineering: A faculty guide. In E. Tsang, ed. *Projects that matter: Concepts and models for service-learning in engineering*. Sterling, Virginia: American Association for Higher Education.

Perkins, D. D., Hughey, J., and Speer, P. W. 2002. Community psychology perspectives on social capital theory and community development practice. *Journal of the Community Development Society* 33 (1): 33-52.

Nyerere, J. K. 1967. Education for self-reliance. *Ecumenical Review* 19(4): 382-403.

Schön, D. A. 1983. *The reflective practitioner: How professionals think in action*. New York: Basic Books.

Underwood, C., and Jabre, B. 2010. *Reflections on civic participation and emerging leadership in the Arab world*. Baltimore: Johns Hopkins University Press.

World Bank. 2016. Egypt Overview, Context. October 1. Http://www.worldbank.org/en/country/egypt/overview.

Living Democracy in Rural America: Engaging Students as Citizens

Mark Wilson and Marie Cirillo

The Clear Fork River leaves Kentucky and enters Tennessee at Claiborne County near the Pruden community. The river meanders southwest down through Valley Creek, behind Clairfield Elementary School, and alongside each of the many unincorporated towns that make up this historic valley—Fonde, Pruden, Valley Creek, Morley, Clairfield, Hamlin Town, Buffalo, Eagan, and others. Each community was once the site of a coal camp, and the population of the valley at its height was approximately thirty thousand. Highway 90 follows the route of the river, as does the railroad track, both of which continue to carry coal from the surface mines out of the mountains to some nearby city for processing. For the most part, the river and the road maintain a safe distance from one another; they are forced to interact in only a few places.

Y Hollow Road runs south into Log Mountain Road—which provides access to coal and timber through that section of the valley—but before it does so, it crosses the Clear Fork River by way of an unfortunate bridge. Built before state permits were required, the bridge is a series of steel corrugated pipes encased in concrete, so the bridge functions as a concrete dam with large holes through which water passes. The Tennessee Department of Transportation rates the bridge in "poor" condition, but only because the foundation of the bridge is being undercut by water, not because of the damage this type of bridge causes to everything near it during heavy rains.

For college students from around the nation who visit the Clearfork Community Institute (CCI)—a citizen-led initiative that transformed the abandoned Blue Diamond Coal Camp school into a center of educational and community activity—the bridge is part of an Appalachian classroom. This open learning environment does not separate the human experience into academic disciplines, but uses a curriculum built from the lived experiences of the people who have populated this valley for generations.[1] From an engineer's perspective, the bridge is not ideal but safe for passage. From a citizen's perspective, the bridge is a consistent emergency that arrives with every heavy rain. The culverts force violent volumes of water into the riverbank, permanently damaging property below the bridge and trapping residents below the river until the water recedes and debris is moved from the bridge. One local elderly couple rented a house and planted a garden, for example, only to find their produce washed away after a big rain. "When it flooded, it just washed everything out," Clarence Marlow told an Auburn University student who interviewed him in 2013. "It did that three times in the same summer and then I just quit" (Lamplugh 2013).

At first glance, the Y Hollow Bridge is a technical problem, one that requires an architect and engineer. But students learn that the bridge is a *political* problem, one that must be understood through history, culture, and the perspective of local individuals. Coal counties in Appalachia are replete with similar bridges, and the cost of replacement is more expensive than any one county—whose county seats are outside of the valley in more populated areas—can afford. There is no easy solution for the problem, but a concerned group of citizens is working to determine how state, federal, and county governments might work alongside citizens to build a new bridge. Civic commitment will build a new bridge where the regular mechanisms of institutionalized politics cannot.

The literature on civic engagement tends to reflect the work of universities in urban settings—the overwhelming majority of U.S. citizens (81 percent) live urban lives—but a focus on rural communities provides unique civic learning opportunities for college students. When President Lyndon Johnson declared a "war on poverty" in 1964, he had in mind the Appalachian communities where industry was extracting coal and timber resources at an alarming rate. Some parts of Appalachia have flourished over the last fifty years, but the scars from surface mining are a reminder that rural America is separated from its urban counterparts in ways that are difficult to comprehend, let alone overcome. Students who visit and study the region have a chance to study politics through the experiences of the generations of people who have called the mountains and hollows home.

When community developer Marie Cirillo moved to the Clear Fork Valley in 1967, the area was experiencing the trauma associated with out-migration, since nearly all the area's thirty-thousand residents moved north to find work. Marie was an unlikely newcomer. Born in 1929 in Brooklyn, New York, and reared by music teacher parents, Marie developed an affection for rural life through summer visits with grandparents in Kentucky. She joined the Glenmary Sisters of the Roman Catholic Church, an order that offered women the opportunity to serve as domestic missionaries. Eventually, when Marie and nearly fifty of the sisters found their service work stifled by the rules and regulations of the church, they left the order and created the Federation of Communities in Service. Forty-four sisters spread out in the region to live lives of friendship and service to people from and in Appalachia. (For a history of FOCIS see Lewis and Appleby 2003.)

In his award-winning book *Power and Powerlessness: Quiescence and Rebellion in an Appalachian Valley*, political scientist John Gaventa (1982) studied the Clear Fork Valley to understand the dynamics of power that exist in a place where stark inequities exist. Absentee companies own the overwhelming majority of the land in the valley; a *single* company owned 75 percent of the land the year his study was published. The valley is extraordinarily wealthy with respect to natural resources, but its residents are among the poorest in the nation in terms of family income. Traditional understandings of power are inadequate for understanding why people in the valley had not rebelled against a system of oppression, Gaventa argued, and he suggested that an insidious, invisible form of power is at work, one that is internalized by the oppressed and breeds a culture of silence. Small, local actions—the kind that generate a sense of self-worth and possibility—are the beginning points for a shift in consciousness and long-term success, he found. One active citizen had recently traded a nun's habit for a sturdy pair of shoes fit for mountains and hollers.

Upon her arrival in 1967, Cirillo began working with local people to organize themselves around issues that concerned them, while at the same time networking outside the community to develop pathways for sharing ideas, resources, and dreams. College students found their way to the valley with an interest in the social conditions of Appalachia. As early as 1971, Vanderbilt University students researched issues such as health care, land leases, and other legal matters; and thousands of students from across the United States since then have spent days and weeks alongside local residents who have had lasting impact on their understanding of life, community, and active citizenship.

In 2010, an inaugural group of eleven Auburn University students traveled to the Clearfork Community Institute for a week of living and learning as part of a newly created course called Practicum in Liberal Arts. The College of Liberal Arts had recently begun a minor in community and civic engagement, and the associate dean for educational affairs asked Mark Wilson to create a course that would include a spring break experience. He wanted to develop a course that would allow for a long-term, open-ended relationship organized around a place, not necessarily an issue. Auburn University is a land-grant university with 28,000 students in east-central Alabama. Though experiential courses and service experiences are not uncommon throughout Auburn University's colleges and schools, this practicum course was designed as a "living-learning" experience and not promoted as a service trip to Appalachia.

For the majority of Auburn University students who are native to the state, as well as perhaps the majority of American citizens, Appalachia is a region derided by stereotypes of poverty, backwardness, lawlessness, and primitive cultural and religious practices. Appalachia as a topic of study for a semester and place for a week of living-learning experience thus creates the potential for students to examine their own stereotypes of people and places. The relationship between Marie and the Institute began with a phone call from Wilson to Ashley Cochrane, service-learning coordinator at Berea College in Kentucky. Berea College continues a tradition of access for first-generation college students and commitment to the region. Ashley spoke highly of Marie, having coordinated many students to live and learn in Marie's community. Wilson reached out to her, and the relationship began. They first met in person in November 2009 before the spring course at a workshop for campus and community representatives, coordinated by Just Connections, a small organization founded with the purpose of creating and maintaining reciprocal relationships between universities and community organizations in the region. (For information on Just Connections see Ambler and Shiba 2007.)

Marie visited Auburn the month before the group traveled to her community for spring break, and she spoke at the College's community partner luncheon. In her public talk, she described the challenges of Appalachia, as well as the hopes, dreams, and progress of local people over decades in the community. Prior to her visit, journalism major Grace Henderson interviewed Marie for an article in the local weekly paper, and Marie discussed the reason why the Institute provides opportunities for college students to visit. "I would like to think that the students come here to do some work and to get to understand the community and why this work is important," she said. "It's just as important that they get connected to the people and understand how we think and how we're looking at our future" (Henderson n.d.). In a conversation over dinner with students who would be traveling to her community, Marie elaborated on this last point, describing the outcomes she hoped students would achieve—not necessarily a good feeling that they have accomplished a service activity in an impoverished community, but that they have a better understanding of hinterland, mountain communities from the people who live and work there. When students asked about projects they might help with, Marie named a few possibilities, but she reminded students that their understanding of time was different from her community's understanding of time. She noted that oftentimes projects arise out of what happens to be going on at the moment when students arrive. This open-ended, organic understanding of work would be a challenge for some.

When hosting groups, institute organizers begin each workday with visitors and local people in a circle, discussing a topic and making plans for the day. On the very first day of the experience, institute associate Carol Judy started the conversation with an important but surprising statement. "If you have come here to help us, you are wasting your time. The problems in this area didn't happen overnight, and they won't be solved overnight. But if you have come here to learn something with us—and if you are willing to share what you know from your schooling and lived experience, then we'll have a great week together." Service trips do not generally begin with a declaration that those coming to "serve" are wasting their time. As an instructor and course organizer interested in developing students as *citizens,* rather than servants, Carol delivered a statement that embodied all that we knew to be true about citizen-centered engagement and a philosophy of public work that acknowledges context, power, and human dignity.

Over the past five years, small student cohorts ranging in size from five to twelve have participated in the course. Each year a new group works with CCI volunteers on local projects. But the projects are simply the mechanism by which students examine their own stereotypes, trade constant technological communication for face-to-face interactions with their peers and new friends, and discover something important from the lives of people with whom they are democratically engaged throughout the week. The projects—which range from helping dig gardens for spring planting to home repair to cemetery clean-up and more—are meaningful, locally identified, and important because they advance the vision residents have of their community. But they are not as important as what seems to happen to the character of students, most clearly evidenced in the ones that find a way to return to the community—which is seven hours away from Auburn—for an additional experience coordinated mostly on their own with their new friends.

In nearly half of a century of community work in the hinterland of Appalachia, through scores of successes and an equal number of challenges, Marie has discovered lasting practices that undergird the kind of community development work where citizens are at the center. Auburn University students experience these practices in action as a result of the weeklong experience, preceded and followed by readings and discussions that provide historical and cultural context. Marie narrates the following practices.

Practice Number 1: Follow the lead of the people; listen for where they want to go

In September 1967 the postmaster of Clairfield, Tennessee, Louise Adams, was ready to introduce me along with the newly hired director of the Clairfield Center to the seven people in charge of funds allocated to their community from a new government program—the Office of Economic

Opportunity (OEO). Popularly spoken of as the "Poverty Program," the funds were for low-income communities to initiate their own programs.

This community wanted a doctor. Within a five-year period it not only got what it wanted but ended up with one doctor and four clinics throughout the Clear Fork Valley. Each clinic had its own local board of directors and built its own facility. Each had a full-time physician assistant with the one doctor making the rounds. My role was in helping them, and groups that came later, form their own nonprofit organization and pulling in any resources they might want to make use of. I found these mainly through government staff at the OEO office in Washington, DC, the Commission on Religion in Appalachia, the Tennessee Valley Authority, and a newly organized group following the lead of the OEO program and our regional women's network.

Local people clearly wanted some industry that would provide jobs. People did not want to keep seeing their children leave home the day after they graduated from high school. This sentiment found expression through a local effort that incorporated as Model Valley Development Corporation. It acquired a forty-acre parcel of land, five of which would be dedicated as an industrial site. In time, that became a for-profit group named Clairfield Pallet Factory. The front three acres became the Village Square, with the Clairfield Clinic group being the first to ask for a lot. Within a short time the Model Valley Development Corporation office was built, providing additional space for the newly formed Model Valley Craft group. Then there were negotiations with a family wanting land for a grocery store. Before long a new Clairfield post office, a library, and a telephone station, where private home phones replaced the eight party lines, became part of Village Square. In 1976, in celebration of the Bicentennial of the United States, the Presbyterian Hunger Fund gave the Development Corporation money to dig a well so that people whose water had been polluted or lost, some of which was due to mining, could bring jugs to fill and take home. The land behind the factory was surveyed for over twenty-five house sites, and soon after people built or bought their homes.

The community looked like a winner, so groups managed to get some good press coverage from Washington, DC, and Tennessee major newspapers as well as from church groups that were part of the Commission on Religion in Appalachia.

Adding to the community successes and sense of empowerment was the way Vanderbilt University students became part of our life. It started with a student from the Divinity School in 1969, who came to work with a few local women wanting a folk school. This student told friends in the medical school that the community wanted a doctor. While the medical students were here they realized our water was not safe, so they recruited a professor to test our water. The results of that research made it possible for three determined people to get permission to create a public water utility. By 1983 the community had that public water utility. Today it has thirty-six miles of water line serving over six hundred households. This same group of medical students also caught on to the land issue that a few people believed to be the root cause of Appalachia's extensive poverty. One summer we had law students, with an engineering student and a political science student. All of these students engaged local people in the specifics of their work. The people loved them! People were ready to house and feed the students every summer. The amazing grace is that now, even in their retirement, many of these former students stay in touch and from time to time are a major part of our continuing story.

We were, for sure, a threat to those who had held power all these years. The center opened in Clairfield in 1967 by the government's poverty program lasted about six years. The absentee land company, the American Association, headquartered in London, England, which owned almost 75 percent of the Clear Fork Valley, tore down the community center and replaced it with holding tanks for crude oil. They remain today as just one sign of the negative impacts wrought by an industrial culture whose science and technology, backed by big money, have gained control of these rich lands. The Clear Fork Valley residents, like many of those living in the hinterland communities of Appalachia, are known as "rich land—poor people."

During these years of active civic engagement by the local people it became clear to me that a major barrier to sustainable participatory democracy was the fact that people were often forced off the land. I understood the power of absentee land companies. I saw and felt the results of dedicating an entire region to mining, including local impacts in at least seven of the thirteen states and a total of 420 counties that are part of the federal office of the Appalachian Regional Commission. The states impacted by mining had lost three million people over a fifteen-year period (late 1940s into the early 1960s). At what price and whose loss was our nation building cities?

The following thirty years had me searching for ways people could live and speak to how ownership and governance were the more serious activities for civic engagement among rural people. This would have to be done through an engagement with city folks. Since about twenty-seven thousand of our original thirty thousand people who once lived in the Clear Fork Valley had migrated, we had them to call on when they came home for visits. College students have also provided that opportunity for the Clear Fork Valley. Having a professor like Mark Wilson from Auburn University engaged with the students as they enter the community through the Institute gives our students an opportunity to spend a week with the college students. Together they try to support local nonprofits and other engaged citizens or people with special needs. Here is a new generation ready to make the connections between natural materials taken from the land and industrial products made to fill the needs of all American citizens, most of whom now live in cities. This complex relationship also sheds some light on the unique place of rural life in American society. The globalization of the economy has added confusion to the chaos, as we struggle to find our rightful place in what appears to many to be a rapid deterioration of the American dream. We all struggle to understand millennium goals even as we get impatient about tomorrow's paycheck and basic human needs like clean water.

Practice Number 2: Recognize that a healthy economy is more than money-rich

I was in my twenties when I came across E. F. Schumacher, the economist from England, who wrote the book *Small Is Beautiful*. Years later, I read about a man who challenged him about his constant theme of small economies. I smiled and identified with Schumacher's response, that he probably would have written a book about "big is beautiful" if the world were too fixed on being small.

The lived experience of most people in the Clear Fork Valley is similar to most other small mining communities in Appalachia's rural hinterland. The conventional cash economy in these communities is part of a very sophisticated system of land, mining, and timber companies who lease lands to do their extractive works. By the early 1950s technology and science allowed machines rather than people to do most of the work of getting these raw materials from the earth. This led to a heavy investment in machines rather than human labor.

The industrialization of Appalachia began to change the population of hinterland areas in the mid-1880s. By the early 1940s the Clear Fork Valley had some thirty thousand inhabitants, with most living in coal camps. After the proliferation of automation in the 1960s, the area had about three thousand residents. Their kin scattered, for the most part, northward. Those who stayed in the valley lived surrounded by incredible earth-moving machines, mudslides, and loss of access to water.

Many of the remaining population stayed because they had a piece of land and a home. Many of these homes were built by the family, who cut and sawed lumber from the forest, dug their wells, or tapped a spring for household water. The family cleared the land and allocated sections for growing gardens, raising their animals, building a food cellar, a barn, and a toolshed, and making space for the children to play and a car to be parked. Their investment was not acquired with money but with another kind of an economic wealth. Like the big landholding companies, the people knew that a critical source of all wealth comes from natural resources. Those few who stayed and were there when I arrived in 1967 believed that Small Is Beautiful. Their small holdings meant the world to them.

The people I first met and began to work with were extremely creative about surviving and growing without a total dependency on cash. I remember how the clinic on Stinking Creek was built by the people. When they lost their first doctor they asked me to help them find a replacement. They assured me that even if they did not have the money to offer a good salary they could assure someone of a house to live in and enough food to put on the table. I looked for such a person and found it in a nurse. I quickly identified with the people's trust in the security that comes from a more diverse approach to a rural economy.

Given the fact that there are no jobs for the majority of the population, there is a push to make the best of things in other ways. Some make it with the food they grow and the fuel they get from picking up coal or cutting down a tree. They know how to hunt and sometimes enjoy the company of their sons or brothers coming home from Cincinnati, Detroit, or Chicago to spend this kind of time together with their family. Often, city kin send some money home to meet necessities like certain foods, the electricity bill, and keeping a car going. For some, the most lucrative way to generate the money needed was through an underground economy. I came to understand the extent to which brewing their own moonshine was hard work but lucrative. Most of the counties were "dry counties." There was no way to buy liquor at a store. One could, however, buy the mash and sugar and get water from the mountains. There were thousands of acres of company land in which to hide and make moonshine. Some of the moonshine was sold locally, and a lot of it was carried into the city neighborhoods where their kin had resettled. There are some wonderful tales that still linger about the interplay with the sheriff's department. It was a system as sophisticated as the drug business is today.

Over the years, as consumerism became integral to American life, younger people in rural areas felt the need for more money. They took less interest in engaging in building family and community wealth through their traditional ways of making it without a job. How, I keep wondering, can the skills going into an underground economy be transferred to something positive for the communities where we have more trees than people? Corporate corruption might show up on Wall Street, but where are the people who know the real source of that money? Very few people know that our nation's sources of wealth are being destroyed by machines that do what they have to do to keep money flowing for people who do not live on the land.

I understand how population growth calls for people to live in apartments so that land can be available to plant and harvest food, dig for fossil fuels, and minerals, fish in the sea, and hunt and gather in the wild. However, my dream would be for every college-age person from a city to have a year in the country and for every one that same age from some productive rural lands to have a year in the city. Part of the lesson would be making the best of both the cash and the noncash economies.

Several of our nonprofit groups have experimented with community investment certificates as a way to acknowledge how volunteer work and commitment to community development education have economic value. The certificates can be exchanged for things they need and our community can supply. We have had a few successful moments with this way of affirming how wealth is acquired and accumulated, but, for the most part, we are still exploring ways to enhance a theory and practice of an economy that is not limited to spending money. There have to be new words to better distinguish what community and economy mean within the framework of urban and rural settlements. Many urban settlements are not like New York. Many rural settlements are not like the hinterlands.

What college/community engagement contributes could be awesome. I greatly respect those who get their students out into the community, but I also see schools with professors and students working to get beyond the college city, town, suburb, or hinterland where they are located. Students from a college, university, or community living-learning center can begin to see how place-ism can be as dangerous as classism, racism, and sexism. Urban and rural places should not be places where people can pick and choose how to define the whole truth, the only truth, and nothing but the truth.

Practice Number 3: Remind each other that community is the union of all life, not just human life

When college students from Auburn, as well as Berea College in Kentucky, Carson Newman College in Tennessee, and Notre Dame University in Indiana, visit the Clear Fork Valley they have an opportunity to encounter local youth of their own age who are dependent on their family and community for what they are learning. Only in recent years has the Clearfork Institute focused on education for our working-age youth, most past high school age. We base the educational process on a continuation of learning from their lived experience of daily encounters within this place-based community. The suffering mountain communities have endured the corporate extraction of coal, gas, oil and timber and the suspicion that toxic waste once found its way to strip-mined pits in the dark of the night. However, once one gets past these abuses, there is an inner humility of mountain folk who also experience an awesome power of presence emanating from the majesty of the mountains that their lives are a part of. This capacity for growing with nature tends to minimize the role of its people. We have little need to outshine any aspect of such an all-embracing living environment. Deep down we know that nature is not there just for us.

All of nature is there to keep nature alive. Our task is to take this truth out of its hiding place.

We are trying to understand how to be present through who we are and what we love. We want to make a case for the wild so we don't do violence in the taming of it, or be too self-centered in the restoration of it. In our context we have something to offer our relatives living in the man-made cities where the visionaries, the developers, and the managers continue on a path that is wearing out, breaking up, and setting others, like us, out in search of new truths. What was once seemed beautiful and comfortable about city life is becoming revealed as ruthless and hardcore. Some city folks are minding people like us, and it is good to be together as we start making a different road to travel together.

From this sense of our place within the dominant American majority questions emerge from within our small institute where we are living and learning. We raise questions about the logic of urban settlements and the developments that make megasettlements possible. We question the degree to which the exportation and importation of humans has been motivated by people wanting more money and/or wanting more land and access to resources. We become interested in American history as we find answers to questions that emerge from serious problems and from sustainable, equitable, encompassing visions. Could there be anything wrong with wanting to invest our time in endowing our children to be more fully engaged and employed as restorers of mountain life and work?

We have been hurt. We have been damaged. We are the mountains. We cannot be separated. Given the chance, we can become whole again. We could, in nature's time, have much to contribute to America's great cities. The high price and long time necessary for healing the mountains would be one side of a trade-off that could be balanced by reducing the investment in wars that drive us to take from others what we no longer have.

A few of our people realize that we stand in defiance to most economic theories where investments have to be returned in a timely manner so we can keep pace with ever-accelerating worldwide industrial development. These few defiant residents also believe there could be a public education for jobs that would work in communities such as ours. But the timeline for returns on investments to restore the land, water, air, and all of nature that shares these resources, including us humans, has to come from the kind of research and perspectives that would be socially and systemically transformative. It would carry both rural and urban people who care about life beyond traditional ideologies and into another two hundred years of prosperity and interdependence with each other and nature.

There is a vision that is compatible with rural and urban lifestyles, different ways of living, a diversity of jobs and systems of employment, and a pluralistic approach to measuring time (with clocks or within seasons). We will move from rootlessness, confusion, and chaos to an understanding that creates a new type of indigenous peoples, ones who are rooted in every community from the largest city to the smallest rural hinterland settlement. Farming will become more dispersed and easier to identify. Other energies and systems from underground and above the ground will be understood in relation to human energy. Recognizing the dynamic connection between natural systems and humanity's place within nature will allow us to meet earth's needs. Over time, perhaps governance will emerge out of civic engagement with a kind of order that will allow for the institutional transformation of family and community to create their own living-learning centers. Everybody will honor and respect the role of rural economies in stabilizing institutions of government, education, and religion. Together people can lay a foundation around nature that will become a beacon of hope for a sustainable global economy.

Public education will someday enhance, rather than minimize, truths that so easily flow out of the family and their place-based community. We need today's young people from both city and country, from different classes, races, and religions, to start a new dialogue. They have the energy to build new relationships. Hopefully they will sustain some of those ties through life so that every generation can add values and visions until the new day will reveal itself.

Practice Number 4: Acknowledge and recognize those things people say and do that embody truth

I never knew Appalachia before coal was discovered, but I grew up in a house in Brooklyn where coal was delivered by a truck to a coal bin in our basement, where we also had a coal furnace. I also remember Dad's voice as he was reading the *New York Times* about a coal miners' strike. I was too young to make the connection between no production and no coal in our basement. However, in the late 1940s and during the 1950s I spent time in coal camps, meeting miners and their families who lived and worked surrounded by coal in their homes and coal being shipped to distant places. These were also the days when machines were replacing miners. Coal companies were dismantling the camps and families were moving to cities. Here, factories and other facilities were being heated by it. Since the coal is processed in ways so that no one sees it in its natural form, it is extremely difficult for people who have never lived in a place where coal is mined to grasp the significance of the damages done for hundreds of years wherever it is extracted and refined.

There is more to truth than what one sees, and having moved back to this mining community in Tennessee in 1967 I continue to be totally delighted when I recognize what community members hold as truth. In conversations, I can acknowledge truth-tellers and their experiences and move on to the question "What now?" There is another level of delight when visitors come to understand something from a perspective they had never thought about before. We feel rewarded by giving time to visitors who, in understanding something in a new way, realize that the experience changed their life.

It is moments like this that anger me about the school system and the fact that it teaches things that are not affirmed in this marginalized sector of American society. We are a people and a place that have been abused. This injustice was perpetrated over decades as we were being used to build and support the spectacular facade encasing this nation. If this had not been a region of such great abundance of natural life and beauty, the devastation might not have been so harmful. But in a region where there are more trees than people, as nature fell apart, so too did the people. Sometimes it is hard to control my rage with church groups who think the government does too much for the poor who, in their opinion, are lazy and without morals. They are falsely judged to be thieves and people who need to get out there and work like the rest of us. A crucial part of the living-learning experience is demonstrating the opportunities available to residents, and how those opportunities, or lack thereof, derive from a history of oppression and exploitation. This specific understanding of rural poverty in the valley can translate into a greater understanding of urban poverty and its origins for the visiting college students.

It is hard to know how to tame one's inner space in order to support local people in their living-learning space/place. Local youth are the best ones to walk with college students who enter into this relationship through the Institute. They best facilitate a mindful transition into the community. Together they inspire me. If we can just make this rural-urban connection a little bit more real, life would take care of itself. My role is to affirm what the local people know so much about, and envision what they could do if given wings. Our institute gives no college credits, but I believe that what is authentic will someday be formally recognized. Our day will come to offer something important to a nation gone urban at the cost of giving its productive lands to a global, corporate group of landowners.

Living so close to the Tennessee Valley Authority, once the largest purchaser of strip-mined coal, and the Oak Ridge National Laboratory, where uranium for the first nuclear bomb was made, I know that there are many people beyond Appalachia who know things that hurt deeply. I remember in the 1970s attending a church in Oak Ridge that was hosting a week of evening events as a retreat from work and into a reflection on themselves in their community. I lived sixty miles from Oak Ridge and was invited to give them something to think about—like the mining in our community that might be related to the nuclear plant in their community. I told the story and there were heads shaking as people lamented the neglect of government and corporations that inflict such misery on a place and its people. There were questions with answers from both the audience and me. Some thanked me, and I returned home believing I had a caring audience. It was a good feeling.

A few days later I returned to the group to listen to a presentation from one of the higher-up clergy from the denomination. I knew of this man and wanted to hear what he had to say about coal. He started on the nuclear plant in their community. He never mentioned coal but, of course, I knew. At any rate the responses to this presentation were different and, for me, surprising. First there was silence to the point of a bit of discomfort. The preacher was patient. Then a woman stood up, looked around at her friends, and said in a sort of pleading way to remember the day when her teenage son left them because he could not deal with his father contributing to the making of nuclear bombs. The silence oozed with familiar feelings and experiences. After a few minutes of silence another woman stood. She set a similar mood as she talked about the horrible death of her husband because of exposure to toxic materials while working at the Oak Ridge laboratory. Needless to say I was moved by the way this faith-based community exposed the costs of such high-ranking, well-paid professional occupations to family life. The lived experience of the people is never told to those who pass through this really nice-looking, prosperous town.

My favorite truth-telling story came from a next-door neighbor soon after a mining company owner made a plan for how his workers might get rid of me. I was one of a handful of leaders to mobilize Appalachian people to go to our federal government to make laws that would require mining companies to reclaim the lands they were tearing up to get to the coal. The men started threatening and attacking me and the other women in the house. It started with guns shooting into the house and cars. But, of course, the talk among the miners grew and the threats and harassments continued. One afternoon a neighboring man knocked on my door. He wanted to talk with me and he suggested a walk in the woods. It was a nice day and that sounded good. He was the man who once came to my rescue by getting a snake out of my living room. He also taught me how to put creek rock on the concrete block foundation of my house.

As we walked further in the woods I began to get a bit nervous. What were his intentions? But before my imagination got the best or the worst of me, we stopped and he told me what was on his mind. He shared his story of being married and having three sons. He refused to work as a strip miner. He knew in his gut that it was not right. He said a little about his first trip to a city in search of a job. Then he told me about coming home, looking once more for a job other than stripping the mountains of their vitality, with no luck. When he mustered enough money to get back to a city to find a job, he did so. But that was his last time to be disappointed. I don't know if it was his age, his health, or being without a formal education, but his last return home left him no option but to take a job at the mines. Then he said: "Marie, every time I pushed that bucket into the mountain I knew I was losing the future for my sons." To me, that was the truth I was waiting for. I really could not believe that the men working the mines felt good about what they were doing. It took that harassment from his coworkers to give him the courage to come and apologize for their behavior and then to give me the truth. I have lived to know his passing and see his prediction come true. His sons live a hard life, as do their sons, now his grandsons. I pass their house every time I leave my home. They are the truth that makes me strong.

I recognize his truth by often sharing this story with college groups. One never knows when one person's story might change the future of another generation's decision on how to make a living or when to change jobs.

Practice Number 5: Seek intergenerational interaction, which reveals the hidden truths that are essential for sustainable community development practice

It is true that because we have more trees than people, we sometimes have to travel longer distances than we choose to go to be with people our own age. And if you don't have a car, if it breaks down, or snow prohibits one from traveling in a car, you find yourself wanting to find anybody with whom you can talk. It was in such a situation that I realized how we depend on anyone at any age to talk, play, work, share meals with, and grow to become a unique kind of intergenerational living-learning community. When you stay for many generations, you become indigenous to the place. My own experiences have varied.

I was once confined to living without my car because of a three-week snowstorm. The only household I could see from my house and walk to was my next-door neighbors'—a mother with an eight-year-old son named Richard. The son and I played American checkers long enough for me to realize I could not win a game against this kid who was quick in ways that I was not. Maybe, someday, we would make a good team. When he graduated from Lincoln Memorial University, the local Community Land Trust hired him. This was at a time when we had no paid staff. At one moment in time, the older group of thirty-, forty-, and fifty-year-olds thought that with Richard we would try for some state funds to build seven houses through a training program for local people who were part Native Cherokee residents. The state officer said he would give us money under no condition. We brought with us, to our final meeting with this director at his Nashville office, two well-positioned developers from the city of Knoxville through whom Tennessee might channel funds. One directed the Community Designed Center, a nonprofit organization well known to the state director. The other was a department head from the Tennessee Valley Authority—a federal government program that helped make Tennessee what it is today. Both had provided support to the Community Land Trust over the years. What they did was convince the state official that the local young man from the community would be very capable of handling this program. We were given the funds and did a good job together facing challenging circumstances. Richard is now assistant to the head of Campbell County school finances.

A few years ago Mark Wilson had an idea about something his students could do while they were with us during their spring break. It worked for them and for the local youth involved, and I came out with two new experiences of intergenerational living-learning. The project was for schoolchildren to take pictures of one thing that, to them, was alive and beautiful. When the Auburn students arrived, they each worked with a student and his or her picture to put words to the picture that would be mounted and displayed at the Institute.

I do not know which of these photo-stories most impacted the teachers, the parents, the child, the college student, or anyone who tried to dig a little deeper into what it was saying to them. But, for me, the most compelling was a picture of a small and old house. I wondered how a child saw something alive and beautiful in the house. When I read the story, I realized that what he saw was his grandmother. This immediately touched something deep within me. It was the memory of homes that were made alive and beautiful for me as a child and through my years growing up. I saw clearly at that moment that it is the people living within a house who make sacred space for those who dwell therein and transform a house into a home that is beautiful and alive. As a community developer, I was pleased to know there was a child growing up in my community that was conscious of this kind of beauty in his life at such an early age.

As for the college students and the professor who designed this exercise, I do not know their intentions when they initiated this activity and how they planned to include the young participants at the Institute. Did this project mean enough that Mark Wilson would add it to his curriculum? Perhaps he had already done this in the Alabama communities where his students work. Were some inner truths revealed? We have not had the luxury of time to discuss this and begin to imagine how such topics as "alive and beautiful" reflect that which I call spirit culture. I can see how it could lead people into some related civic engagement. Will the water need protection for us and for the deer? And what about a house in need of repair? And so it is that the local participants, even with students staying just a week, were honored to display their spirit culture and with that boost will continue valuing the gift of life with all its beauty.

Living Democracy: An Adventure for Students and Citizens

These five practices, identified by Marie as part of our process for writing this chapter, have developed over the course of her nearly five decades of living and learning in Appalachia. The practices represent the values that undergird her work, and they are valuable for anyone—whether operating from a university base or community base—who seeks to bring diverse people together for the purpose of community development.

In the spring of 2010, around the time Auburn University students traveled for the first time to spend a week at the Clearfork Community Institute, a conversation began with the Kettering Foundation regarding a possible living-learning experiment for college students in Alabama communities.

The Kettering Foundation is an operating research foundation that studies what it takes to make democracy work for regular citizens. The Foundation focuses on relationships between citizens and citizens, citizens and communities, and citizens and institutions. David Mathews, president of the Foundation, employs the metaphor of "ships passing in the night" to describe what he sees as two separate "civic engagement" movements—one in communities and another in universities—that pass each other without much, if any, interaction or mutual productivity (Mathews 2014). Universities, particularly large research universities, tend to see themselves as being most helpful when they can develop solutions to problems. But the problems communities face defy easy solutions, so we wanted to experiment with a different way of relating to communities.

Our Auburn University team, including student Rachel Naftel, who participated in the spring break course and chose to return for a summer experience in Marie's community, traveled to Dayton, Ohio, to work with foundation collaborators to think through the possibilities. In particular, we discussed the possibility of a program that would focus on communities on their own terms, rather than as places with deficits in need of university expertise. We asked: could long-term, productive relationships be formed in a way that would allow students to move from a service mentality to one of active citizenship? Could students be a part of a process that would allow them to experience decision-making in a community context and live there long enough to experience the results and consequences of decisions?

As the team developed the experiment, the recent experience of students in Marie's community served as a guidepost for how we wanted to relate to Alabama communities. The practices espoused by Marie and CCI, although not explicitly stated or listed by Marie in a formal document, became a part of the fabric of the relationships and design of the program. Listening (rather than talking) to people would be key; we would start where people start. We wanted our students to learn about the interactions of daily life that were a part of an economy not easily seen or heard. We would emphasize the natural environment, not just the built environment. We would teach and remind students to seek and acknowledge all forms of truth, not just the kind found in university classrooms and textbooks. And we would describe the opportunity as one for intergenerational commitment and companionship.

As university professionals and a student meeting in Dayton, Ohio, we developed some assumptions that would guide the initiative:

- Politics is best understood as the work citizens do with each other and with governments to change their communities. Politics is a public activity, not just the election of leaders and the passage of legislation.
- The best student learning occurs when students take responsibility for their learning. Responsibility comes partly through choices, decisions, and consequences.
- Local communities desire relationships with a university that are ongoing, purposeful, just, and mutually beneficial.
- To understand democratic politics in a community, students need to live in a community for a period of time. There is no substitute for living in a community (Wilson and Fairley 2012).

Figure. Moving from Service to Engagement

SERVICE AND SERVICE LEARNING	POLITICAL ENGAGEMENT/LIVING DEMOCRACY
Organized	Calls for organizing
Requires time	Requires commitment
Meets a need	Meets people and their stories
Makes you feel good	Makes you feel dizzy
Followed by an exclamation point	Followed by a question mark

Source: Robinson 2011, 22.

We convened members of seven diverse Alabama communities, chosen based on existing professional relationships with individuals in each town. Diversity was key because we wanted the experiment to reflect our commitment to various communities, not just a particular profession or type of expertise. The group consisted of schoolteachers, a mayor, a pastor, city clerks, directors of nonprofit social service organizations and a community development corporation, a historical site director, and a chamber of commerce director. Rather than pose the question, "What does your community need?" we asked, "What could a student learn about democratic civic engagement while living in your community for ten weeks over the summer?" This allowed our conversation to focus on community relationships, an honest exchange of the hard realities of civic engagement and the possibilities that existed for students to enter into existing relationships, as well as create new ones as a result of their participation.

Many of our community collaborators are quite familiar with students as service participants, and they are often called upon to help fulfill school or club service requirements. Our goal would be to lead students beyond service. The experience would not be a "service-learning" experience, since it would not be volunteerism tied to course content. As we compared our understanding of service and service-learning, we developed a chart to help express what we see as the differences in concept and practice (see figure).

Seventeen students have participated in Living Democracy over the past three years, and most have traveled a particular curricular path. Students complete the weekly course Introduction to Community and Civic Engagement in the fall semester, which is an overview of context, issues, skills, and experiences of living in a democratic society. The course includes sessions on power analysis, systems theory, asset-based community development, issue framing, and moderator development for deliberative forums. In the spring, students take a course on community journalism, which develops their skills as community journalists who understand the mechanics of good interviews, reflection, and quality writing. Together these courses aim to educate students on important literature, concepts, and practices that will be of use during the summer experience.

Using language gained from experience with CCI and Marie Cirillo, we call the program a living-learning experience, rather than an internship, although the term *internship* is a more recognizable one for undergraduate students. Each student works in collaboration with a particular organization, but the purpose is not simply for a student to learn the ins and outs of an organization, which is typically the purpose of an internship. Instead, the purpose is for the students to learn the principles of democratic practice in a community. We describe internships as vertical relationships—students learning how an organization is structured, how it operates in relationship to its stakeholders, and what informs and shapes the professional culture. We describe living-learning experiences as horizontal in nature—how informal networks guide and shape a community, how people understand their relationships to institutions, and how citizens work together (or not) for the public good.

Students organize and execute a project in collaboration with their community partners, one that flows out of the goals, aims, and assets that the community has identified. Institutions, especially universities, tend to see the deficiencies in people and communities first and foremost, since the legitimacy of the institution rests on supplying resources and expertise. Our approach is informed by the work of John Kretzmann and John McKnight, who focus on the assets of a community, as opposed to needs, and see people and places as half full and not half empty (Kretzmann and McKnight 1993).

Projects have included art education classes for children, downtown redevelopment initiatives, youth development programs, computer literacy classes for adults, and more. But in order to arrive at a project that embodies the principles of democratic practice, we ask students and community members to work through five sets of topics and questions:

- HOPES: Every community has dreams, goals, and aspirations. What are citizens seeking to do to fulfill the community's potential? How will your project connect to citizen concerns and what people in the community consider valuable?
- A TABLE: Every community project has a table where thoughts are shared and plans are made. Are people in the community already at a table working on the problem or helping a community asset realize its full potential? Who, specifically, needs to be at the table for what you are hoping to organize citizens to do? Why will they want to be at the table? What might prevent them from being at the table?
- CONVERSATIONS AND CROSSROADS: Communication is key to productive human relationships and the work citizens seek to do together. And the communication we are talking about is different from publicity and advertising. How will you communicate regarding the project? How often? Where? Some of these conversations will result in decision-making. What decisions do you think will need to be made regarding the project? What decisions will be difficult but necessary? What will you do to make your conversations creative and productive?
- ACTIONS: What actions will need to take place to execute the project? When? Make a timeline for what needs to take place immediately, as well as over the next few months, as you prepare to live in the community.
- PUBLIC CELEBRATION/REFLECTION: We measure the success of our projects in terms of what we've learned and experienced. There is no such thing as failure, only failure to learn. And there's nothing more fun than a culminating event that documents, makes public, and celebrates the work of citizens. How will you document, celebrate, and lead a public reflection on your project? (Wilson and Fairley 2012, 41–42)

The communities in Alabama where Auburn students "live democracy" have unique qualities and characteristics. Citizens in these towns are working on both historic challenges and problems associated with a twenty-first-century economy. Collinsville, for example, in the northeast corner of the state, has a very high percentage of Hispanic immigrants, and in 2013, its high school soccer team became the state's first all-Hispanic team to win the state championship. Immigration over the past several decades contributed to the survival of the town, though not everyone in Collinsville or the larger region, of course, sees immigration that way. In the town of Elba, in the southeast corner of the state, residents remember two devastating floods in the 1990s, which decimated the town's infrastructure. They face an expanded highway in the near future, which will move traffic away from their town and affect the local economy. In Linden, on the other side of the state, citizens continue to suffer from the loss of manufacturing jobs, and, like many rural communities, they maintain two school systems—one public and one private—where local young people are divided mostly by race. Race relations in the city of Selma continue to dominate public discussion, while many local citizens work to overcome the stigma of the past in order to rebrand the city as a destination for tourism and business. Each community has its story, and students must understand the complexity of relationships long before they begin their living-learning experience, which leads to something deeper and more rooted than a typical service relationship.

In July 2012, as students in the first cohort were sweating through Alabama summer heat, the *Chronicle of Higher Education* published an article on the seven students who were living democracy. The writer titled her piece "Auburn Students Become Small-Town Citizens for the Summer," which represented the project well, and she accurately captured the unique experiences of students—like reading water meters with city employees for a day—that characterize the experience (Sander 2012). When the part-time mayor of Linden read the *Chronicle* article, she noted a quote that differentiated the experience from service-learning, since service-learning and other episodic community experiences can often leave students with more pity than respect for people. The mayor had taught freshmen service-learning courses at a nearby university for several semesters, and "the truth in that statement blew me away!" she said. "It opened my eyes to what Living Democracy was crafted to be and, in fact, IS because of that careful crafting . . . both Blake (their student) and Linden are changed in both ways perceptible and imperceptible . . . and everlasting!" This exchange reflects the kind of outcome Marie and others in the Clear Fork Valley strive for in their interactions between local people and those college students who visit their community—a relationship of mutual respect, solidarity, and friendship, as opposed to service, pity, and charity.

Student Jelani Moore discovered this in Elba during the 2014 summer. Jelani spent his high school years in north Alabama near Huntsville, and he applied for Living Democracy because of an interest in the issues that people face. "I hope to gain a better understanding of the social issues within the local community," he wrote in his application, "and a means of solving the problem here on a small scale in order to later apply the same formula to bigger, national or even global conflicts."[2] Jelani is a talented artist and media studies major with an interest in filmmaking. When he arrived in Elba, he discovered that a local business owner/artist had begun plans for a wall mural on her downtown business. Jelani had experience and interest in a wall mural, and he helped organize citizens for a weeklong Elba Renaissance Festival, which made the mural a reality. Other projects included creating a video entry for a successful matching grant for his partnering organization's newest project, a community garden, as well as designing the city a new flag. After the summer, Jelani stated that he learned that he has skills in organizing people around common interests and goals. That's living democracy.

Not all projects and plans succeed for students and citizens, but students seem to recognize that the process is where significant learning takes place. In September 2014, we convened the majority of the seventeen students who had participated over the past three summers for a reflection on what the experience has meant for their personal and professional development. One student said the experience shaped her career interest, while another mentioned that the "take home" message was that everyone in the community has a significant role and place.[3] "The bottom of the totem pole is what holds up the entire totem pole," she said. "This type of work matters," a student from the most recent cohort stated. Blake Evans, now a public administration graduate student who was in the middle of writing a book chapter for a service-learning anthology, stated that the experience shaped his understanding of "service." One student identified herself as an outlier of the group, since she felt most of the other Living Democracy students were seeking careers in some of public work, while she sees her future professional identity as primarily a schoolteacher. "But I am going to live in a community at some point," she said, and the experience taught her the dynamics of power and processes of change, which will give her a better opportunity for effectively participating in social change over the long term, wherever she ends up residing after graduation.

Reflection and writing is a central component of the Living Democracy experience, and students are required to write one article per week. Topics include a "wicked problem," a term borrowed from the community-planning literature to describe a persistent, complex problem; a city council meeting; a civic club meeting; a "third" space; a sacred place; a citizen "award"; an organization "award"; and a civic adventure. The assignments develop a habit of discovery for students, and the articles appear on the Living Democracy website. Twenty-six articles have appeared on the state's largest media outlet, al.com, most of which are pieces on community assets and individual citizens, and those articles provide deserved recognition and attention to the work of citizens in these communities.

On our best days, we believe we are acting in the educational tradition of pioneers Myles Horton, longtime director of the Highland Center in Tennessee, and Paulo Freire, Brazilian educator and author of *Pedagogy of the Oppressed* (Horton 1998; Freire 1970; Horton and Freire 1990). Education for social change cannot be "expert" driven, although we welcome experts into relationships where certain forms of knowledge are required. But the educational relationships we foster—between citizens in Clear Fork Valley of Tennessee, communities in Alabama, and students who come from places large and small—are built on principles and practices that are intended to build political autonomy and power among all participants. Institutions and programs will not create lasting change; local people—and students who will be members of a community following their formal education—are the agents of change.

Concluding Remarks

The Y-Hollow Bridge that spans the Clear Fork River in Marie's neighborhood is a lesson for understanding much in that community. From that bridge, visiting students are able to understand the practices through which Marie and her community interact with each other and with college students who want to understand the promise and challenges of modern-day Appalachia. Living Democracy students identify similar objects in Alabama communities—real and metaphorical. Through those complicated sets of circumstances that describe and explain hopes and realities, students learn about people living in a particular place at a particular time. Cirillo's practices—learned and developed over more than fifty years in the rural hinterland of the United States—are reflected in the design and program of Living Democracy. Some Living Democracy students half-jokingly refer to the experience as "surviving democracy," since what they encounter in these real-life relationships is fraught with challenges and a mix of disappointments and exhilaration. But to survive is to live, and to embody the practices and principles inherent in the work is to live fully human, ebbing and flowing like the Clear Fork River as it winds its way from the mountains, to the valleys, and ultimately into the sea.

NOTES

1. In 1997, the Woodland Community Land Trust purchased a twelve-acre parcel of land that contained the old Eagan School for the purpose of developing an educational center. In 2006, the land trust transferred the building over to a small group of citizens with a vision of the school as a place for public discourse, education, and celebration of the land and each other. The Clearfork Community Institute organizes college students from around the country and visitors from around the world for meaningful visits and collaborate projects with local citizens.
2. Jelani Moore application for Living Democracy, Mark Wilson's file.
3. Interview of students, Mark Wilson's file.

REFERENCES

Ambler, S., and Shiba, K. 2007. Separate paths lead to just connections. *Appalachian Journal* 34 (Spring-Summer): 389–394.

Freire, P. 1970. *Pedagogy of the oppressed.* New York: Herder and Herder.

Gaventa, J. 1982. *Power and powerlessness: Quiescence and rebellion in an Appalachian valley.* Urbana: University of Illinois Press.

Henderson, G. N.d. Marie Cirillo: Nurturer of community. Author's files.

Horton, M., with Kohl, J., and Kohl, H. 1998. *The long haul: An autobiography.* New York: Teachers College Press.

Horton, M., and Freire, P. 1990. *We make the road by walking: Conversations on education and social change.* Ed. B. Bell, J. Gaventa, and J. Peters. Philadelphia: Temple University Press.

Kretzmann, J. P., and McKnight, J. L. 1993. *Building communities from the inside out: A path toward finding and mobilizing a community's assets.* Evanston. IL: Institute for Policy Research.

Lamplugh, G. 2013. Clarence's story. The Y Hollow Bridge problem. Http://yhollowbridge.wordpress.com/clarence.

Lewis, H. M., and Appleby, M. 2003. *Mountain sisters: From convent to community in Appalachia.* Lexington: University of Kentucky Press.

Mathews, D. 2014. *Ships passing in the night?* Dayton, OH: Kettering Foundation Press.

Robinson, A. 2011. Living democracy: From service learning to political engagement. *Connections* (Kettering Foundation), 20-23.

Sander, L. 2012. Auburn students become small-town citizens for the summer. *Chronicle of Higher Education*, July 9.

Wilson, M., and Fairley, N. 2012. Living democracy: A project for students and citizens. *Higher Education Exchange*, 35-47.

Contributors

Derek W. M. Barker is a program officer at the Kettering Foundation. Derek brings a background in political theory to research concerning the democratic role of higher education institutions, philanthropy, and the nonprofit sector. He also works closely with the Foundation's team of graduate fellows and research assistants. Before coming to Kettering, Derek received a PhD in political science at Rutgers University and taught at Pitzer College. Derek has recently published articles on Aristotle's concept of oligarchy, populist themes in the work of political theorist Wilson C. McWilliams, and the role of the virtues in deliberative democracy.

Ernesto Benavides Ornelas has been the director of Social and Citizenship Education of Tecnológico de Monterrey since 1999. He currently leads a program that incorporates service-learning pedagogy and citizenship across the curriculum. He is a PhD candidate in social anthropology at the Universidad de Salamanca, in Spain, where he also obtained the advanced studies diploma in social anthropology. Ernesto graduated from the Program for the Strengthening of Social Leadership by the Academic and Professional Programs for the Americas, affiliated with Harvard University. He is certified as an agronomist by the Universidad Autónoma Agraria Antonio Narro, and holds a master's in agricultural productivity sciences and administration with specialization in human resources.

Eric Brace is the Executive Educational Advisor for the Australian Literacy and Numeracy Foundation, where he coordinates the Refugee Action Support and Community Action Support programs. Eric has been involved in the education sector since he began teaching in 1998 in the alternative education system of San Diego, California. He worked for the Foundation for Young Australia, where he was in charge of the organization's Youth Participation and Engagement Strategies. Additionally, he has worked as a literacy and learning support teacher for a diverse range of students, including young people with significant learning difficulties as well as ESL students, and remote indigenous communities. His research interests include the social construction of literacy, particularly in how social interactions influence literacy engagement and perception.

Brianda Hernandez Cavalcanti joined the Talloires Network in October 2013 as the Spanish Language University liaison and then as the University Volunteers Program coordinator in May 2014, becoming Program Administrator for the Network in July 2015. She holds a master's degree in Urban and Environmental Policy and Planning from Tufts University and a B.A. from California State University Northridge in Urban Studies and Planning. Prior to joining the Network, Brianda worked in the areas of advocacy, community based-urban design, and urban greening projects. She was born in Mexico and is a firm believer in education and the power of diversity.

Koh (James) Kwee Choy is associate professor and head of the Department of Medicine at the International Medical University, where he has been a faculty member since 2000. He also serves as the Infectious Diseases Consultant at the Hospital Tuanku Ja'afar in Seremban, Malaysia. James completed his subspecialty training in infectious diseases at the Peter MacCallum Cancer Centre and the Royal Melbourne Hospital in Australia. His research interests lie in the area of HIV medicine, infectious diseases, advocacy, marginalized communities, and the use of information technology in the practice of medicine. James has served on many conference and workshop program committees in delivering updates on HIV medicine and infectious diseases and the training of medical officers aspiring to be physicians. He has served in an advisory role for a number of NGOs that cater to the needs of marginalized communities in Malaysia. Koh was the leader of the team that pioneered the adoption of an aboriginal village as an avenue for providing teaching-learning experiences for IMU students. This initiative received the MacJannet Prize for Global Citizenship in 2013.

Marie Cirillo is a community developer in Clear Fork Valley, Tennessee, and a lead community partner to Auburn University. At age nineteen she moved to Appalachia, where she eventually followed Appalachian migrants to Chicago. There she received a degree in sociology from Loyola University. Upon returning to the mountains in 1967, she organized community action programs for thirty years, and worked with two mountain women to turn the last of the old coal camp schools into a living-learning center for young adults. Marie remains active even in her eighth decade, convinced by the possibilities of a healthy rural society and better connectivity between rural and urban America. Auburn students, in collaboration with Mark Wilson, have become welcome additions to the life and work of her community.

Nelly Corbel is founding executive director of Global Civic Consulting and co-founder of the Lazord Foundation. She previously served as the associate director of the Gerhart Center for Philanthropy and Civic Engagement at the American University in Cairo where she established the university engagement unit. She has over twelve years of experience in university student development and program management. Franco-Egyptian, Nelly Corbel is an alumna of the Harvard Kennedy School, the American University of Paris, and the Institut Catholique de Paris. She dreams of a citizen driven world where solidarity rhymes with growth.

Joseph Francis is a development practitioner and academic who holds a PhD in integrated crop-livestock systems from the University of Zimbabwe. Currently, he is associate professor as well as director of the Institute for Rural Development at the University of Venda in South Africa. Prior to this appointment, he was senior lecturer in the Institute for Youth Studies at UNIVEN, postdoctoral research fellow at University of Pretoria's Postgraduate School of Agriculture and Rural Development, and lecturer at the Zimbabwe Open University. He has worked extensively with grassroots communities in southern Africa, including Botswana, Lesotho, Mozambique, South Africa, Swaziland, and Zimbabwe. Particularly noteworthy is his leadership of the ongoing Amplifying Community Voices program, which won a silver award in the Impumelelo Innovation Trust competition in 2008 and third place in the MacJannet Prize for Global Citizenship in June 2011. He has authored academic books and more than forty peer-reviewed journal articles.

Margaret Fraser has worked in the housing and community service sectors for the past twenty-five years. She is currently Regeneration Manager of ng homes, the largest community-based housing association in Glasgow. Margaret's primary role is within social regeneration; she works within an asset-based community development model to bring the skills, life experiences, and knowledge of the local community and partners together to create a more resilient community. She is a graduate of Glasgow University with postgraduate experience in housing studies and a BA in community development. Over the past ten years she has been working in partnership with Glasgow University in the delivery of the Activate course. This program has been instrumental in supporting and inspiring community activists and has led to high numbers of people progressing to higher education and into the field of community work.

Rana Gaber is the director of programs in the Egyptian Youth Federation and a leading figure in the field of youth development NGOs in Egypt. She is also a cofounder of Majal for Consultancy and Training, a social enterprise acting as a network of youth initiatives working in the field of nonviolent communication, conflict resolution, dialogue, and citizenship. In addition to being a volunteer in an NGO working in one of the poorest villages in Egypt, she is an active member in a number of youth initiatives and projects. Among them is the Ambassadors for Dialogue, where she was able to build a national team of facilitators in different universities acting as a hub for spreading the culture of dialogue. Throughout the past two years Rana has participated in numerous international conferences to provide expertise on Egyptian youth. She is a graduate of the Faculty of Economic and Political Science at Cairo University and holds a diploma in international relations from the American University in Cairo.

Wong Chin Hoong is a lecturer at the International Medical University in Malaysia, with the Department of Family Medicine. He has served at the International Medical University since September 2012. Chin Hoong was previously a general practitioner in the United Kingdom before returning to Malaysia. He is currently a member of the Royal College of General Practitioners in the United Kingdom. His research interests lie in the areas of ethics and professionalism in community service, and he is also pursuing a master's in counseling. Chin Hoong is presently the coordinator of the Kampung Sebir IMU Cares project, the extension to the Kampung Tekir project. He is passionate about serving the community, and in his spare time volunteers with his local church.

Lorlene Hoyt is interim executive director of the Talloires Network and associate research professor in the Department of Urban and Environmental Policy and Planning at Tufts University. Lorlene was associate professor of Urban Planning at the Massachusetts Institute of Technology, where she founded MIT@Lawrence, an award-winning city-campus partnership with the city of Lawrence, Massachusetts. She holds a PhD in city and regional planning from the University of Pennsylvania, a master's in landscape architecture from the State University of New York, and a bachelor of science in landscape architecture from the Pennsylvania State University.

Hlekani Muchazotida Kabiti holds a bachelor's degree in agribusiness management and a master's degree in agricultural economics from the University of Venda, where she is currently completing her doctorate in rural development. Since 2010, Kabiti has been an integral participant in the Amplifying Community Voices program, which promotes engaged scholarship in rural community development. She was one of the pioneering leaders and served as the chairperson of the Amplifying Community Voices Students Association (ACVoSA) in 2013. ACVoSA leads efforts to develop students' capacity to contribute to community-engaged scholarship for rural development. In 2012 Kabiti participated in the Eastern/Southern African and Virginia Networks and Association Study Abroad Program run by the University of Virginia as well as the 2013 Intensive Inter-session Program.

Helen Martin teaches community development at the University of Glasgow and is the Program Coordinator for Activate, the university's community-based introduction to community development practice for activists and volunteers. She has a strong background in community activism after spending many years campaigning in her local community. She returned to the University as an adult student and gained her BA in community development and subsequent qualifications at the University of Glasgow. She has held the posts of Service Manager for a third-sector community development organization and Development Officer for a national antipoverty agency. She is currently a panel member of the Standards Council for Scotland for Community Learning and Development as well as the Active Learning Centre, Glasgow.

Loshini Naidoo is a senior lecturer in social justice education at Western Sydney University, Australia. Her research interests include social and cultural diversity and difference and transnationalism. Her current research is related to refugee and indigenous issues. She is particularly focused on levels of literacy among newly arrived refugees in Greater Western Sydney secondary schools, and the literacy needs of Aboriginal students in the Northern Territory, Australia. She was the recipient of a teaching excellence award from the Australian Teaching Learning Council for her outstanding contribution to student learning in 2011. In 2012 she won the outstanding individual educator award from the International Centre for Service-Learning in Teacher Education at Duke University. She has also been awarded a federal government research grant to support pathways for the transition of refugee students from high schools into tertiary education.

María Fernanda Pacheco Bravo earned an undergraduate degree in communication at Instituto Tecnológico y de Estudios Superiores de Monterrey Campus Querétaro. As an undergraduate, María was student vice president and obtained both the Student Achievement and Social Service awards. She spent five years as a Brigadista volunteer with A Roof for My Country, an international NGO that works to overcome poverty in slums through training and community action. There she conducted public relations and coordinated volunteers and support from government and business. She obtained a master's degree in humanistic studies with a concentration in ethics.

Amy Newcomb Rowe is program manager for the Youth Economic Participation Initiative with the Talloires Network at Tufts University. She worked as program manager of the Gerhart Center for Philanthropy and Civic Engagement at the American University in Cairo in 2010-2012. Amy holds a master's in the Anthropology of Development from University of London's School of Oriental and African Studies.

Mark Wilson is the Director of Civic Learning Initiatives in the College of Liberal Arts at Auburn University. Originally from Saraland, Alabama, he holds degrees from the University of Mobile (BA), McAfee School of Theology at Mercer University (MDiv), and Auburn University (PhD). He currently teaches the Introduction to Community and Civic Engagement course and a practicum that includes a living-learning experience in an Appalachian community. He is an Appalachian teaching fellow with the Appalachian Regional Commission. He coordinates research and action projects with partners including the Kettering Foundation, David Mathews Center for Civic Life, Appalachian Regional Commission, and communities around the state. He is the author of several articles and the book *William Owen Carver's Controversies in the Baptist South*. Wilson serves as the secretary of the Alabama Historical Association.

Index

A

Activate Program, 4, 37-55
American University in Cairo, 5, 7, 128, 143
Amplifying Community Voices, 4, 10, 14, 57-79
Apartheid, 1, 4, 16, 59-60, 78-79
Appalachia, 6, 19, 145-151, 154-155, 157, 163
Arab Spring, xiii, 5, 16, 129
asset based community development, 39, 53-55, 70, 138, 159
Auburn University, 6, 147-152, 157-158, 161
Australia, 4, 81-102
Australian Literacy and Numeracy Foundation, 4, 82-87, 94

B

Bantustans, 60
Boyte, Harry, 88, 90, 93, 122
Brace, Eric, 4, 86
Brigadas Comunitarias, ix, 3, 15, 21-35
Campus Querétaro, ix, 3, 15, 19, 21-35
Cirillo, Marie, 6, 146-147, 159, 163

C

civic capacities: and courage, xx, 11, 13, 39, 123, 127, 142, 156; development of, xiv, xv, 27, 53-55, 69, 91, 130; and empathy, xx, 11, 15, 119-120; and humility, xix, xx, 11, 128, 152
civic engagement, 1, 9-11, 18, 20, 24, 32-35, 59-60, 107, 120, 128-132, 139-143, 146-159; approaches to, 61; challenges of, 130; commitment to, 50; and community engagement, 89; concept of, xiv; and governance, 150; movement, xiii, xviii, 26, 158
civic life, xi, xviii, 3, 9, 11, 32, 50
City of Glasgow, 4, 8, 11, 37-46, 50-55
Community Brigades. *See* Brigadas Comunitarias
consciousness, xiv, 6-7, 16, 90, 121, 146
Corbel, Nelly, 5, 12, 134-135
corporate social responsibility, 104, 139

D

democracy, xv-xix, 2-8, 14-16, 24-33, 41, 59, 75,78, 89-90, 99-101, 142, 145, 158-164; and Apartheid, 60; and civic engagement, xiv, definition of, 18; emergence of, 1; and learning by doing, 9; problems of, xiii
demonstrations, 2, 29. *See also* protests; uprisings
Dewey, John, 88

E

Egypt, 5, 12, 17, 19, 128-142
Egyptian Youth Federation, 136

engaged universities, xix, 1–3, 7–9, 14–19
engagement. *See* university civic engagement programs
epistemology, 2, 20
equity, 83–87–90, 98
extension, xix, 2, 129

F

faculty, 6, 11–14, 33–34, 51, 64, 68–78, 87, 103–106, 121–122, 129, 132–133; engaged in community, 4, 63, 70, 76, 88, 112–116; and incentives, 7
Francis, Joseph, 11
Fraser, Margaret, 8, 42,
Freire, Paulo, 4, 9, 39, 47, 49–50, 60, 90–91,

G

Gaventa, John, 146
Gandhi, Mahatma, 133

H

Habib, Adam, 1, 16–17
higher education institutions: future of, xii–xv, xx, 20, 77; generative utility of, xx, 16–18; growth in the number of, 17; and knowledge generation, 7, 24–26; and social movements, 17, 60, 75; as spaces for debate, 17, 19
Hoyt, Lorlene, 50

I

International Medical University, 5, 103–122
internships, 5, 118, 132, 135–138, 159, 160
ivory tower, 1, 2, 16, 19, 38, 40, 42, 43–46, 53, 55

K

Kampung Tekir project, ix, 5, 14, 20, 103–125
Kettering Foundation, xiii, xiv, xvii, 14, 50, 157–158
knowing, ways of, xvii, 7, 9, 20
knowledge: local, 11, 29–30, 69, 85, 93, 121; multidirectional flows of, xix, 2, 3, 6–9, 11; reciprocal, 88, 98; relevant, 8, 39; and scholarship, xix, 2, 7, 19, 20, 121; and technical rationality, 2

Koh, Kwee Choy, 5, 105–123

L

Lazord Academy, 5, 127–143
leadership, 9–10, 54, 76–78, 83, 93–95, 105, 112–127; in crisis, 116; institutional, 2, 122; student, 14, 26, 63–68, 118–119, 128–140; transformative, 58–59, 69, 75
learning by doing: and civic capacities, 11–16, 27–31, 87–88; and power, 9–11; reflections on, 46–48, 73, 89–92, 96–97, 118–121, 138–139, 157–161, regional perspectives on, xviii; stories of, 3–6; types of, xix
Living Democracy, ix, xix, 6, 10, 14–15, 145–164

M

Ma'an Arab University Alliance, 137
MacJannet Prize for Global Citizenship, 75, 118, 123, 131
Mafatshe, Itumeleng, 13
Malaysia, ix, xv, xix, 2–5, 14–20, 103–126
Mathews, David, 42, 158
mentorship, 5, 12, 38, 64, 81, 84, 94–98, 112, 128, 131–142
Mexico, ix, xix, 2–3, 8, 15–19, 21–35
MIT@Lawrence, xvii

N

Naidoo, Loshini, 4
Nyerere, Julius, 20, 132, 143

P

partnerships, identifying stakeholders for, 23, 45, 63, 107, 135–137; making, 6, 12, 22–24, 41–45, 60–61, 85–87, 106–108; sustaining, 9, 92–95, 117, 159–160
poverty: changing perceptions of, 49, 139, 149; fighting, 59–60, 139, 149–150; notion of, 10, 21, 27, 154
power: building inclusive systems of, xix, 3, 6, 7, 9–11; and corporate corruption, 16, 151; and a culture of silence, 65, 146; imbalances, 11, 64; and oppression, 146, 154
problems of civic life, 3, 9, 17, 113, 119

INDEX

protests, 4, 12, 16, 60, 74, 129. *See also* demonstrations; uprisings

R

racism, 5, 85, 152. *See also* xenophobia

rationality, 2

reflection: circles, 11, 62–68, 70–72, 78; in groups, 33, 135, 155, 162; methods of, xx, 11, 12, 62–68, 70–72, 78, 129, 134, 159, 162; on practice, 7, 9, 26, 49, 90, 96

Refugee Action Support Program, 4, 81–98

relationships, 121. *See also* solidarity

resilience, 81; development of, 85, 97–98, 100

S

Scotland, ix, xix, 3–4, 8, 17, 20, 37–56, 168

service-learning, viii, xiv, xix, 2–3, 50, 97–100, 121, 159–164

social capital, 32, 39, 45, 52, 93, 143

social movements, 17, 130, 158

societal polarization, 128

solidarity, xix, xx, 7, 16, 29, 32, 137, 161

South Africa, ix, xiv, xvii, xix, 1–4, 9–10, 13–20, 57–79

South African Higher Education Community Engagement Forum, 78

T

Talloires Network, xiv, xvii–xviii, 14, 17, 56, 118, 123, 131, 137, 143

technical rationality, 2

Tecnológico de Monterrey University, ix, xix, 3, 16, 19, 21–35

Temuan, 5, 107–109, 123–124

tutors, 15, 23–24, 38–39, 46–50, 53, 81–98

U

unemployment, 3, 5, 6, 8, 35, 40–41, 46, 52, 92, 129, 139

United States, xix, 8, 10, 15, 17, 23, 72, 73, 135, 145–164

university civic engagement movement, xviii, 1, 26, 158

university civic engagement programs: frameworks for, 39–40, 61–62, 107–108; funding of, 44, 47, 76, 85–87, 94, 98, 107–109, 114, 131, 135, 137, 149; histories of, 22, 38, 44–45, 82–87; impetus for, 59–60, 105, 128–130; implementation of, 24–26, 94–95, 105–107; institutional barriers to developing, 50–52, 75–76, 97; institutional support for developing, 24–26, 52–53, 75, 92–93; and legitimacy in the community, 22–23, 110–112, 117, 135–138; outcomes of, 27–31, 95–97, 118–120, 138–140; recruiting faculty for, 69–70, 77, 106, 112–113, 121; recruiting students for, 26, 45–46, 68–69, 112–113

University of Glasgow, ix, xix, 4, 8, 11, 37–56

University of Venda, xix, 4, 10, 14, 19, 57–79

University of Witwatersrand, xix, 1, 18

uprisings, 5, 129–132. *See also* demonstrations; protests

V

Vhembe District, 4, 10, 57, 59, 74

village adoption, xix, 5, 103–125

volunteerism, xiii, xix, 2, 8, 14, 21–22, 33, 39, 41–52, 61, 74, 119, 130–131, 148, 152, 159; and recruitment, 12, 23, 120, 132; and service-learning, xiv

W

Western Sydney University, 4, 81–102

wicked problems: awareness of, 10; causes of, 59; engagement with, 13, 15, 54; measuring impact of, 6; types of, 2, 8, 17, 46

Wilson, Mark, 147, 157

Wong, Chin Hoong, 5, 118

X

xenophobia, 2, 5

Y

youth bulge, 5, 129, 139